*THE GREAT
AMERICAN CRIME
MYTH*

Recent Titles in Contributions in Criminology and Penology

THE GREAT AMERICAN CRIME MYTH

Kevin N. Wright

CONTRIBUTIONS IN CRIMINOLOGY AND
PENOLOGY, NUMBER 9

GREENWOOD PRESS
WESTPORT, CONNECTICUT • LONDON, ENGLAND

Library of Congress Cataloging in Publication Data

Wright, Kevin N.
  The great American crime myth.

  (Contributions in criminology and penology,
ISSN 0732–4464 ; no. 9)
  Bibliography: p.
  Includes index.
  1. Crime and criminals—United States. 2. Criminal
justice, Administration of—United States. I. Title.
II. Series.
HV6789.W75   1985   364′.973   85–5420
ISBN 0–313–24792–7 (lib. bdg.)

Library of Congress Catalog Card Number: 85–5420
ISBN: 0–313–24792–7
ISSN: 0732–4464

First published in 1985

Greenwood Press
A division of Congressional Information Service, Inc.
88 Post Road West
Westport, Connecticut 06881

Printed in the United States of America

10 9 8 7 6 5 4 3 2 1

To Karen

Contents

Part Three: Dealing with Crime

Preface

Crime is a social phenomenon of some consequence. Each year millions of people are injured and billions of dollars are lost, yet the significance of crime goes far beyond the physical pain and economic loss. Crime has become such a focal point in our lives that it is often a basis for interpreting the events around us. If you see a group of teenage boys moving toward you, you worry that they may be muggers. If you are awakened during the night, your first thought is that someone is breaking into your home. Fear of crime appears to be gnawing away at the very fabric of our culture.

Crime is a common topic of public debate and is often an important issue of public policy. Elected officials have gained office by promising to do something about it. But the significance of crime does not stop there. Americans are mass consumers of the sensationalism of crime. We watch television and movie crime dramas, read report after report in our newspapers of violent crimes, and view in our homes during the six o'clock news the victims and the perpetrators of crime.

During the three years it has taken me to write this book, violent and predatory street crimes have declined in the United States. Most experts attribute these changes to reductions in the absolute number of people in the high-crime-prone age-group of fifteen- to twenty-five-year-olds. But during these same years the American public has grown more fearful and less tolerant of criminal offenders. The vast majority now favor capital punishment and believe the courts should give harsher sentences. Many Americans applauded a New York City man who gunned down four would-be robbers.

So how does one begin to sort out the myths about crime from the realities, the facts from the rhetoric? How serious is the crime problem? How threatened are we? What can we realistically expect government to do about the problem?

This book presents a perspective on crime that is different from that held by most Americans. It is based on facts, but it has been subjected to my interpretations of those facts, so I cannot claim that the viewpoint is unbiased. My perspective on and interpretation of crime lead to a different set of conclusions about how serious the problem is and what can realistically be done about it. Wars on crime appear as policy priorities with cyclical regularity, yet they are never won. Present punitive policy trends are no more likely to be successful than anything else. Not all readers will agree with me, but I hope this book will challenge your opinions and encourage you to reevaluate the beliefs you hold about crime.

I would like to thank my friends and colleagues who have read and commented on earlier drafts of the manuscript—David Cingranelli, Rick Hofferbert, Harold Pepinsky, William Chambliss, and Elmer Johnson. Never could an author have had such a diverse group of critics who were so helpful. I also want to thank April and Will for being understanding of my occasional physical and often mental absence from their lives. This book is dedicated to Karen, my critic, editor, typist, friend, and always the one who forces me to be realistic. Finally, I would like to thank the staff at Greenwood Press for being such a pleasure to work with.

PART ONE

Crime Problem

1

Testing the Myths of Crime in the 1980s

Most Americans believe that crime is worse today than in the past. Many can recall times when the doors of homes could be left unlocked. They remember when city streets, parks, and other public places were safe for walking, even alone and at night. The past represents a time when violence was not only less prevalent but also less senseless. Now, all too often, we hear of vicious thugs who attack for no discernible reason. Crime appears to be more violent, more irrational, and more widespread than ever. Two recent cases typify this trend:

Sarah Ribicoff, age twenty-three, an editorial writer for the *Los Angeles Herald-Examiner* and niece of retiring Connecticut Senator Abraham Ribicoff, was leaving a Venice, California, restaurant with a male friend when two robbers appeared and demanded money. The friend quickly handed over his wallet, but the robbers opened fire anyway. The friend miraculously was unhurt. Ribicoff was shot dead.[1]

Suzanne Marie Rossetti, age twenty-six, a technician at a burn treatment center in Phoenix, had attended a performance of *Dancin'* at Arizona State University. On her way home, she drove into a grocery store parking lot, and mistakenly locked her car with the keys inside. Two young white men helpfully unlocked the door, asked for a short lift— then forced her to drive to her apartment, where they beat and raped

her for several hours... the men then drove 50 miles to an isolated
desert area and hurled Suzanne off a cliff. They heard her moaning
and climbed down to her side. She pleaded with them to leave her
alone because she said, "I'm dying anyway." The response was swift.
"Damn right you are," one man said, and picked up a large rock and
crushed her head to still her sounds.[2]

Such acts of savagery are beyond understanding. Their violence
is excessive and without focus, reason, or meaning.

Beyond the increasing viciousness of crime, Americans also
appear to face greater risks of criminal victimization. A government study recently reported that the chance of becoming the
victim of violent crime is greater than that of being affected by
divorce.[3] Neighborhoods and social classes in which crime seldom surfaced now experience violence and theft regularly. Once
virtually isolated members of the middle class—residents of suburbia and rural America, the "respectable" and "comfortable"—
now hide behind locked doors.

Noted social anthropologist Marvin Harris expresses a common sentiment about crime when he says, "It's not the same
old America." Like others before and since, Harris describes the
situation as one of "terror in the streets" where a "unique, per-
manent racial underclass consisting of millions of blacks and
Hispanics" continues to produce growing numbers of frustrated
and angry individuals, lacking social responsibility and all too
willing to take advantage of others.[4]

We never know what to expect from the next person who
walks into the convenience store where we are shopping. Young
people on the street corner threaten our sense of security. A
squeak in a floorboard at home may suggest an intruder. Faced
with these fears, we never feel secure. As *Newsweek* magazine
puts it, "In the public mind, violent crime has come to have a
special meaning: not the murders erupting from domestic fights,
not the violence of a ghetto Saturday night, not white-collar nor
even organized crime, but the specter of random assault or robbery by vicious strangers."[5]

FEAR OF CRIME AND CHANGING PUBLIC POLICY

As a result of the perceived threat of crime, Americans are
becoming more and more fearful. On a personal level, fear eats

away at feelings of safety and security, elements so important to our sense of well-being. On a social level, it destroys patterns of interpersonal relations, particularly among strangers, thus constricting the social environment of many people and reducing the variety of life for them. Charles Silberman explains: "Crime does more than expose the weakness in social relations; it undermines the social order itself. . . . To live with fear—to be suspicious of every sound and every person—converts the most elementary and routine aspects of life into an exercise in terror."[6] As Americans are convinced they will be attacked, robbed, raped, and murdered, they change their lifestyles, restricting the places they go and the things they do.

THE PERVASIVENESS OF FEAR

Public opinion surveys report a steady pattern of growth in the fear of crime. Early in the 1980s the proportion of Americans afraid to walk alone at night in their own neighborhoods topped the 50 percent mark, up 11 percent from 1978 alone.[7] One person in every seven is afraid in his own home.[8] The bad news does not stop there. Not only are people concerned about criminal victimization, but most believe the problem is growing worse. When asked if crime had increased, decreased, or remained the same, the majority interviewed in 1981 stated that there definitely is *more* crime. They also view crime as becoming qualitatively worse. Criminals are considered to be more violent and irrational then ever before.[9] So people believe not only that their chances of criminal victimization are increasing but also that they are more likely to be seriously injured or even killed if attacked.

With the spread of fear, the importance of crime as an issue of public policy has steadily increased. When the U.S. Department of Housing and Urban Development sought in 1978 to identify what people perceived to be the most pressing problem in their own city, more people identified crime than anything else, over such other problems as unemployment, air pollution, housing, and things to do.[10] In a similar public opinion survey, which asked what would improve the quality of life, crime control was suggested by more people than anything else, outranking such goals as achieving quality education, curbing water pollution, protecting privacy, and making products safer.[11] In

1980 citizens of New York City, for the first time in over a decade, recognized crime as the most pressing problem their city faced. Despite other weighty issues in the city, including a budget crisis, housing and transit problems, unemployment and inflation, as well as minority issues,[12] crime had come to the forefront of public concern.

Throughout the United States many signs and symbols of changes to prevent victimization are observable. People try to protect themselves. Heavy metal window bars and gates adorn many homes today. Even in neighborhoods where doors never used to be locked, an entryway without a second dead-bolt lock is seldom observed. Such preventive devices are found not only in high-crime neighborhoods but also in areas once isolated from such worries: suburbia and rural communities.

Other symbolic but nonetheless real manifestations of concern and the desire for protection can be seen in human behavior. Body language of people in public places is an excellent example. When police officers appear on a subway platform, the crowd gravitates toward them. Fewer people wear jewelry in public places, instead concealing it beneath clothing for fear it will be snatched. To isolate themselves psychologically, people avoid making eye contact with one another in crowded public places.[13] Apparently, fear seldom leaves the conscious mind of many people. They are wary and, much like wild animals, constantly check and evaluate the environment for potential predators. Such steps are perceived to be the only way to survive.

People are also adopting more aggressive and violent means of self-protection. Many enroll in self-defense classes. Others arm themselves, with Mace, knives, handguns, and other weapons.[14] One person in three informed *Newsweek* survey takers that they now own a gun or other weapon to protect themselves against the criminal.[15] To prevent property loss, people keep guard dogs and install burglar alarms and security systems.

But you do not need to be told that fear of crime is changing American life. You know it from personal experience. Crime is a real concern. You worry about your own safety as well as your family's. Because you are afraid, you take precautions to protect yourself, both from violent crime and from property loss. This may involve an action as simple as locking your car doors when in the past you did not bother. When you go away for the weekend, you hide valuables and ask a neighbor to pick up your mail and keep an eye on things. If you own porch furniture, a barbecue grill, or a bicycle, you keep them chained and locked so no one can walk away with them. You try to escape being mugged or attacked by avoiding situations and locations known to be dangerous. When these are unavoidable—late at night as you walk through a deserted parking garage to your car—you are poised and ready, watching for signs of danger. You grasp your keys with one protruding between your fingers as a weapon, just in case. You walk streetside rather than next to the building, for fear someone is lurking in a doorway. Yes, each of us has reacted to the threat we believe to be present. We are more cautious and through instinct and training try to acquire "street smarts" to survive in the dangerous environments in which we live. Despite these precautions, that nagging fear—of strangers, unfamiliar places, and general uncertainty—remains. Perhaps more than once you have walked through your home late at night because you thought you heard an intruder. Fear of crime is so woven into the fabric of our lives that it is a basis for interpreting the unexpected or the unusual. When startled or caught off guard, your first thought is that an unknown assailant is about to attack you.

The growing fear of crime has led to a steadily decreasing tolerance for criminal offenders and a desire for greater punishments as fear grows. Americans have never been particularly happy with the severity shown criminals by the courts. In the early 1970s, two out of three people thought the courts did not deal harshly enough with criminals. By 1978 the proportion jumped to 85 percent,[16] indicating that practically every American believes the criminal-justice system should be more punitive. Attitudes toward the death penalty changed in a similar way. During the 1960s, less than half the population favored execution, but the proportion started to drift upward in the 1970s, and today two out of every three citizens favor capital punishment.[17]

As crime has risen as an issue of public concern, politicians and public officials have attempted to respond to the problem. In recent years the direction of these efforts has been toward "getting tough" on criminals. Comments by U.S. Supreme Court Chief Justice of the United States Warren Burger in a speech to the American Bar Association reflect this mood. He asked, "Are we not hostages within the borders of our own self-styled, enlightened, civilized country?" and "Why do we show indignation over alien terrorists and such tolerance for the domestic variety?" The Chief Justice concluded that *crime control* is "as much a part of our national defense as the budget of the Pentagon." Greater stress on the deterrent effect was singled out as the key to a "damage-control program." We need more prosecutors, defenders, and judges to see swift arrests, prompt trials, and certainty of punishment. Burger spoke against "massive safeguards for accused persons" built up over the past few decades, arguing for limited judicial review and stringent standards for bail.[18]

Following Burger's lead, state and federal courts have reversed earlier decisions that allowed offenders to go free because of procedural technicalities. Many states have passed new legislation that has tightened sentences, reduced judicial and correctional discretion, and restricted probation and parole in order to strengthen punitive efforts. The law enforcement establishment has undertaken new programs aimed at detecting career criminals. Each of these efforts is intended to increase the chances of detection and the severity of sanctions, so offenders will reconsider the profits of crime, and to remove from the community those offenders who are most dangerous.

RECONSIDERING CRIME MYTHS

Fear of crime and the motivation to do something about it are based on two commonly held beliefs. The first is that we are engulfed in a historically unprecedented wave of violent and predatory crime. This implies that the situation today is different from that in the past. Furthermore, there is a belief not only that there is more crime but also that criminals are more dangerous. The problem is therefore seen as qualitatively worse, more violent and less rational than in the past. The second belief is that responsive government should and can respond to the problem. Implicit in this assumption is the conviction that crime is a solvable problem, that action can be taken to reduce crime and return the nation to the safety and harmony known in the past. It is surprising that these ideas are seldom questioned in a public forum. Few people—the media, politicians, or agency officials—ever investigate their validity, ever ask whether crime is as bad as most people believe or whether public action can reduce the incidence of crime.

In this book, eleven myths about crime, which are considered to be "truths" about human life and human nature by much of the American public, are identified. These myths serve as the basis for what government is doing to control crime, but they may or may not be valid, and they can be subjected to rigorous analysis. That is the purpose of this book. The eleven myths are:

Crime Myth 1: Crime is becoming quantitatively and qualitatively worse.

Crime Myth 2: The chances of victimization by either a violent criminal or a property criminal are extremely high.

Crime Myth 3: People who are the most vulnerable—particularly the elderly and adult women—are the favorite victims of criminals.

Crime Myth 4: People who are most vulnerable to crime have the greatest fear.

Crime Myth 5: Fear of crime is reducing social cohesiveness and deteriorating the modern urban community.

Crime Myth 6: Criminal-justice officials understand the causes of crime and are motivated solely by a desire to attack those problems to reduce crime.

Crime Myth 7: A no-nonsense approach to crime control where violent and predatory criminals are made to pay for their offenses will reduce crime.

Crime Myth 8: In using the "exclusionary rule" to dismiss cases when evidence is obtained illegally, the courts protect criminals and reduce the deterrent effect of sanctions.

Crime Myth 9: American prisons are humane alternatives to barbaric physical punishment, and settings for rescuing criminals from a life of social and personal wickedness.

Crime Myth 10: The crime control strategy of the criminal-justice system is correct in assuming that personal gain is the primary motivation for crime and that eliminating the "profit" will reduce criminality.

Crime Myth 11: Because crime control efforts have not been effective, additional resources must be allocated to ensure a fuller implementation of the strategy, and the administration of deterrent sanctions must be made more certain and more severe.

None of these eleven myths about crime will be validated by our analysis. Some will be found to be false, others will turn out to be significantly more complicated than the simple relationship implied by the statement. By examining each crime myth, we can gain a better understanding of the problem. But more important, we will discover the source of these myths and learn the purposes they serve for the people who shape public opinion about crime and its control. We will also gain a better understanding of how and why Americans react to crime as they do.

The remaining chapters in Part One will explore Crime Myths 1 through 5 to determine how serious the crime problem in the United States actually is and some of the reasons fear is at such a high level. Part Two of this book will look at Myths 6 through 10 to determine the extent to which the criminal-justice system can reduce crime, particularly through more punitive policies. The causes of crime in relation to control of crime, as stated in Myth 11, will be considered in Part Three, where we come to some conclusions about what the criminal-justice system in the United States is achieving and can expect to achieve.

NOTES

1. John Leo, "The Menace of Any Shadow—Americans Are Worried and Frightened as Violent Crime Increases Sharply," *Time*, December 22, 1980, p. 30.

2. Ed Magnuson, "The Curse of Violent Crime—A Persuasive Fear of Robbery and Mayhem Threatens the Way America Lives," *Time*, March 23, 1981, pp. 16–30.

3. Leslie Maitland Werner, "Risk of Crime Said to Exceed That of Divorce," *New York Times*, December 11, 1983, p. 41.

4. Marvin Harris, "Why It's Not the Same Old America," *Psychology Today*, 15 (August 22, 1981): 22.

5. Jeff B. Copeland et al., "The Plague of Violent Crime," *Newsweek*, March 23, 1981, p. 48.

6. Charles Silberman, *Criminal Violence, Criminal Justice* (New York: Vintage Books, 1980), pp. 16, 18.

7. Aric Press et al., "The Plague of Violent Crime," *Newsweek*, March 23, 1981, p. 47.

8. George H. Gallup, *The Gallup Opinion Index*, no. 154 (May 1978): 30, reprinted in Michael J. Hindelang, Michael R. Gottfredson, and Timothy J. Flanagan, eds., *Sourcebook of Criminal Justice Statistics—1980*, U.S. Department of Justice, Bureau of Justice Statistics (Washington, D.C.: Government Printing Office, 1981), p. 172.

9. Press, "The Plague of Violent Crime."

10. U.S. Department of Housing and Urban Development, Office of Policy Development and Research, *The 1978 HUD Survey on the Quality of Community Life* (Washington, D.C.: Department of Housing and Urban Development, 1978), p. 217, reprinted in Hindelang et al., eds., *Sourcebook 1980*, p. 176.

11. Louis Harris, "The Harris Survey," *Chicago Tribune*, July 3, 1978, p. 2, reprinted in Hindelang et al., eds., *Sourcebook 1980*, p. 178.

12. Richard Levine and Carlyle C. Douglas, "Crime Is Chiefly on Their Mind in New York," *New York Times*, December 27, 1981, p. 6E.

13. Richard J. Meislin, "Fear of Crime Is Now Woven Into the Fabric of City Lives," *New York Times*, January 31, 1982, p. A1.

14. Ibid.

15. Press, "The Plague of Violent Crime."

16. Hindelang et al., eds., *Sourcebook 1980*, pp. 196–197.

17. Ibid., pp. 200–201.

18. Warren Burger, Address to the National Convention of the American Bar Association, New Orleans, February 8, 1981.

2

The Overdramatization of Crime in America

To begin unraveling the mystery of crime in the United States, we should consider how public opinion is shaped. Who is responsible for producing information about crime? Some people form their opinions based on actual experiences. They have been attacked, or some possession has been stolen. Yet surveys indicate that fewer than 10 percent of the population report criminal offenses of any kind against them.[1] Americans for the most part draw on secondary sources of information to know how bad crime really is.

The press—in newspapers, television, and magazines—keeps us apprised of the seriousness of the crime problem. A big-city daily newspaper rarely publishes an issue without at least one article about some violent crime committed the previous evening. Syndicated news services, such as the Associated Press (AP) and the United Press International (UPI), allow newspapers to carry not only local stories but also reports of violence throughout the nation.

The broadcasting industry also engages in vigorous crime reporting. During the evening news, viewers are often taken to the scene of a violent crime. Remote capabilities allow us to see a victim being loaded into an ambulance or the police outline on the pavement. Reporters interview investigators, witnesses, and even victims. By bringing violence right into American homes, such dramatic portrayals make crime seem less remote.

Beyond the continuing barrage of reports of violent crimes, what may shape public opinion most are the editorials and review articles in which the press informs the public that crime and senseless violence are nearly out of hand. These reports often claim that the dangers on streets and in our homes are greater now than ever before. For example, *Time*'s "The Curse of Violent Crime" appeared behind a cover that depicted a surrealistic violent face.[2] And a *Newsweek* cover that had viewers staring into a barrel of a handgun contained an article that said 1981 was the "year that mainstream America rediscovered violent crime," that "people feel it [crime] as an epidemic come to crisis point," that "crime rates have replaced mortgage rates as the favored topic of concern," and that "life now seems pitifully cheap."[3] Even special-topic magazines, which traditionally give no space to crime, now carry stories about the problem. The fashion and glamour magazine *Mademoiselle* published an article entitled "Crime in America: Living Scared."[4] *Glamour*[5] and *McCall's*[6] had similar pieces. The message in these articles rings clear: Violent crime in America has risen to a crisis point. There is no adequate explanation for what is happening, and few pragmatic solutions to the problem exist.

In analyzing the crime problem, the media often call on law enforcement officials to affirm the seriousness of violent and predatory crime:

Former New York City Police Commissioner Robert McGuire claims, "The random, senseless violence has shocked me more than anything. It's like the torturing of butterflies and pussycats, only it's human beings that are being tortured."[7]

Los Angeles District Attorney John Van de Kamp states, "Violent crime has been a very significant problem for a long time, particularly in the black community. Now, because of the trespass of really horrible, senseless violence into places that were relatively sacrosanct, the white community realized that no one is immune."[8]

Former Houston Police Chief B. K. Johnson observes, "The fear of crime is slowly paralyzing American society. We have allowed ourselves to degenerate to the point where we're living like animals. We live behind burglar bars and throw a collection of door locks at night and set an alarm and lay down with a loaded shotgun beside the bed and then try to get some rest. It's ridiculous."[9]

Atlanta Police Chief George Napper states, "There are a lot of young guys who just don't care, who go out and blow people away just for the hell of it."[10]

Chicago Gang Crimes Commander Edward C. Pleines suggests, "The attitude seems to be, 'what's the use of having a gun if you're not going to use it.' "[11]

Compounding the terror of escalating violence is an attitude among law enforcement officials that the system is unable to inhibit such trends. "Many criminals have no respect for or fear of the crime-prevention system," says Judge William Callow of the Wisconsin Supreme Court.[12] Former Police Commissioner McGuire adds, "The criminal justice system almost creates incentives for street criminals."[13] Throughout the system a pervasive sense of frustration lingers. Faced with budget cuts, growing caseloads, and a system which bears little resemblance to a coherent, smoothly running organization, the chances of bringing violent offenders to justice appear to be hopelessly mired. To improve the likelihood of arrest and punishment and make justice procedures more efficient, additional resources are essential.

CRIME BOOMS

If these reports leave you with the impression that the nation is on the brink of catastrophe, you should realize it is not the first time that message has been delivered to the American public. The United States has been through supposedly major crime waves every twenty years or so, and more than once Americans have been told that the social order hangs in trembling peril. Speeches by politicians and officials, and the news articles, of the 1920s, the latter part of the 1940s, and the mid-1960s, are identical to those of today. Contemporary news magazines need not employ reporters to write about the present crime wave. They can simply reprint stories written in the 1920s. The titles alone bear striking similarity to those of today:

"Accounting for the Crime Wave" (*Literary Digest*, August 21, 1921)

"The Carnival of Crime in the United States" (*Current History*, a monthly magazine of the *New York Times*, February 1922)

"Cities Helpless in the Grip of Crime" (*Literary Digest*, April 22, 1922)

"What Shall We Do to Stop Crime?" (*Current History*, September 1922)

"The Rising Tide of Crime" (*Literary Digest*, August 15, 1925)

Even the cartoons are similar. One shows Uncle Sam facing a hoodlum labeled "Crime"; the caption states simply "Day After Day."[14] In another, a choking Uncle Sam holds a poison bottle labeled "Crime Record"; the caption reads "Quick, somebody, an antidote!!"[15] But best of all is a cartoon captioned "A New Yorker Starts to Business" in which a wife and daughter, each packing a revolver, bid the well-dressed but heavily armed father good-bye as he leaves for the office.[16]

More revealing and significant than the news stories or the cartoons are people's perceptions and opinions about crime during the 1920s. A growing concern about the problem led the American Bar Association (ABA) at its 1920 convention to appoint a special committee to investigate violence and law enforcement. After a year of study the committee reported: "Since 1890 there has been, and continues, a widening, deepening tide of lawlessness in this country, sometimes momentarily receding, to swell again into greater depth and intensity. At intervals this tide billows into waves that rise and break, but only for a time attracting public attention."[17] One reporter pointed to the "astounding statistics showing the rapid increase of murders and robberies," observing that "encouragement of criminality is becoming a national cult."[18] The *St. Paul Pioneer Press* stated, "The truth is that the United States is approaching a condition somewhat resembling anarchy, and that unless something practical is done pretty soon it may be too late."[19]

Chicago, with its gangsters and corrupt law enforcement, and New York, suffering a rash of robberies and general lawlessness, were centers of criminal activity. Most large cities—including Indianapolis, Detroit, and Boston—had serious crime problems.[20] One description of life in New York City sounds remarkably similar to what one might read today:

Never before has there existed in this city such a situation as exists today. Never before has the average person, in his place of business, in his home or on the streets, had cause to feel less secure. Never before has a continuous wave of crime given rise to so general a wave of fear.

New York is becoming a community of gun-toters because everybody knows that the police administration has completely broken down, and because the record of crimes of violence is fast growing longer, and murder and robberies are rapidly increasing.

Instead of being a safe city New York is now the most unsafe of all the great capitals, so far as the protection of life and property is concerned. . . . Crime in New York has become a public scandal and a public reproach to the richest city in the world. It is a confession of governmental impotence which has no parallel among the great municipalities of the world. All the quantities that civilized government is supposed to provide are suspended. The security of life and the security of property are equally a gamble. If the citizen is lucky he may not be robbed, if he remains lucky he may not be murdered, but it is all a matter of chance.[21]

A frequent complaint of the period was the lack of adequate statistics on the seriousness of the problem, but there was enough information to lead many to conclude that the situation in the United States was the worst in the world. Crimes of violence as well as the number of criminals incarcerated in this nation far exceeded those in France, Germany, England, and Wales. Comparing the crime situation in Chicago with the crime situation in all of Canada, which had a population three times greater, the ABA's Special Commission on Law Enforcement found that Chicago experienced twice as many burglaries and four times as many robberies.[22]

Not only are the descriptions of the 1920s situation similar to those of today, but the reasons given for the rise in crime and the proposed solutions to the problem resemble contemporary ideas. Among the factors identified as contributing to the growing criminality of the 1920s were the lessening of respect for law and property, greater opportunity for dishonesty, veterans returned callous and more reckless, unemployment and low wages for some contrasted to the wealth enjoyed by others, prohibition and corrupt law enforcement.[23] The most often stated explanation for the problem was the laxity of law enforcement and punishment. Abuses of probation and parole were cited. Exaggerated delays in criminal trials were seen to benefit the criminal at the expense of public safety. Abuses of bail and the right to appeal were viewed as signs of laxity. The proposed solution was to "get tough" on the criminal and to eliminate the abuses and corruption of the system. The *Boston Post* stated that attitude succinctly: "Let citizens, juries, and judges do their duty fearlessly and strictly. Put criminals where they belong. Stop this nonsense of coddling lawbreakers. Get back to sane justice. That's the only medicine for the disease." People believed that the criminal-justice system stressed rehabilitation at the expense of punishment. The *Post* went on to observe, "The only way to stop crime is to punish the guilty and do it quickly, firmly and severely. The trouble at present is that we are spending millions of dollars and valuable time in providing ways to 'reform' criminals and make it easier for persons who ought to be in jail to escape the law."[24] One judge summarized public attitudes: "It is time for well-meaning reformers who have wasted a good deal of sympathy and given too much consideration to hardened criminals to step aside and permit honest citizens to have the protection the courts want to give them."[25]

After the 1920s, the scourge of the Great Depression and the weight of World War II temporarily diverted attention from the crime problem. But as veterans returned and Americans tried to reestablish their lives, crime resurfaced as a major urban problem. The 12.4 percent increase in crime in 1945[26] was the largest in history, yet it paled beside the increase of almost twice that in 1946.[27] The situation was described by reporters as the "worst ever" and the "blackest picture." J. Edgar Hoover, then director of the Federal Bureau of Investigation (FBI), stated: "America is in the grip of a rising wave of crime. Thus far, there is no indication of a decrease, and the record of the past holds little hope for early improvement unless something positive is done."[28] Yet the utter despair and terror of the times may have been best described by a reporter who argued:

[The American] finds today [1949] that the streets of his city have become a no-man's-land where his children must risk the psychopathic killer; his wife must risk the molester, the purse snatcher and the rapist;

and he himself has taken to treading the center of the roadway for fear
of the marauder in the bushes, the mugger, the slugger, the knifer—
the hoodlum who will kill for whatever is in a wallet, be it only a dollar
bill![29]

Just as the aftershock of World War I was considered to be an
important factor in the crime wave of the 1920s, so were the
effects of World War II. One reporter stated: "The postwar crime
wave is a delayed reaction to war. . . . The dislocation of families,
the easy money for young workers and the general demorali-
zation of war boosted crime rates relatively little in wartime."
Yet the effect of these factors dissipated after the war, and crime
soon began to soar.[30]

A pervasive laxity of enforcement and punishment was singled out once again as a primary factor in the crime wave. J.
Edgar Hoover, throughout his career with the FBI, was quick to
point to this problem:

I know of nothing which would help choke off the growing crime wave
more effectively than a general tightening of our attitude toward the
criminal who has established the fact that he is completely untrust-
worthy. We have become soft in such matters. We have listened too
much to the wails of the sob sisters.

Law enforcement is aware that it faces a crucial test in the current
wave of crime. But we are willing to accept the challenge despite the
handicaps of manpower shortages and the failure of the public to attack
contributing factors which might be eliminated.[31]

Hoover's underlying message about the necessity for greater
funding of law enforcement endeavors if the rise of crime was
to be curtailed was not camouflaged. He believed law enforcement could handle the problem if given the necessary freedom,
support, and resources.

As Americans settled into the routine of the 1950s, they became accustomed to the postwar levels of crime. Threats from
foreign sources overshadowed any worry about domestic public
safety. Not until the early 1960s did Americans discover again
that they faced a significant crime problem. Crime surged into
public consciousness as never before:

"By every measure, America is on the brink of a major crisis in crime."
(*U.S. News & World Report*, August 26, 1963)

"Crime shows more and more signs of being out of hand in this
country." (*U.S. News & World Report*, September 9, 1963)

"Across the U.S., in one city after another, a spiraling crime rate stirs
alarm." (*U.S. News & World Report*, April 20, 1964)

"Lawlessness is in a steep and steady rise, especially in city streets."
(*U.S. News & World Report*, August 3, 1964)

"Crime running wild . . . city streets turned into jungles . . . murders,
rapists, muggers, robbers on the loose in cities and suburbs." (*U.S.
News & World Report*, March 22, 1964)

"City streets now are more unsafe than ever." (*U.S. News & World
Report*, August 9, 1965)

These statements suggest a stronger and more pessimistic reaction to crime than in earlier times. Implied, if not directly
stated, was a belief that social life and the political structure
were on the verge of total destruction. Not only did the individual face a high probability of being attacked or robbed, but
widespread lawlessness threatened the very fabric of the American way of life.

Official statistics showed that crime increases far outstripped
population growth. Between 1958 and 1962 the U.S. population
increased by 7 percent, yet crime soared by 27 percent—an increase four times that of the population.[32] An additional increase
of 13 percent in 1963[33] and 11 percent in 1964 pushed the spiral
of crime to six times the population increase.[34] This staggering
surge was the largest recorded increase in American history.

Observers noted that crime was taking on new features in the
1960s. For the first time it was no longer confined to slums and
deprived areas; it had invaded the suburbs.[35] Traditionally protected middle and upper classes faced a danger that had formerly
been a disturbing but distant phenomenon. And public parks
and transportation systems were no longer safe.[36] In addition to
the spread of crime across geographic and class boundaries, the
1960s saw the rise of irrational crime. *U.S. News & World Report*
cited a substantial jump in "senseless" violence in 1963, noting
that seven brutal, random, and unexplainable murders had oc-

curred across the nation in a space of a few days after the FBI released its annual report on crime.[37]

These new characteristics of the crime problem led many to believe the "new" wave was different in intensity and nature from "crime waves" of the past. Crime during the 1920s and 1940s could be attributed to the aftereffects of war and the social chaos of ensuing years, but crime in the 1960s did not follow a major world war, falling between the Korean conflict and the Vietnam action. Other forms of social upheaval and unrest which accompanied the apparent crime wave were viewed by some to be criminal in themselves. Many Americans feared total social disorganization. Charles E. Whittaker, associate justice of the U.S. Supreme Court, foresaw the danger of a complete breakdown of law and order resulting from the spread of crime and violence. He warned that people were taking the law into their own hands, revolting against authority, and concluded that the survival of the nation was at stake.[38] Other criminal-justice officials argued that if crime growth was not checked, anarchy might result, precipitating a police state.[39]

Within its historical context, the current crime problem does not appear to be so new or so frightening. So we see that Crime Myth 1, "Crime is becoming quantitatively and qualitatively worse," is not valid. Others in the past have been quick to predict the imminent destruction of American culture resulting from crime and lawlessness. Given this tendency, we must reevaluate the situation today. Is the crime problem as bad as we think? The United States appears to have gallantly survived other periods when crime supposedly ran wild, public streets became jungles, and violence was rampant. Given this history, one might be justified in suggesting that the mass media are overdramatizing the crime situation.

HOW THE MEDIA DISTORT CRIME INFORMATION

One need not closely scrutinize media reports to find numerous examples of distortions and exaggerations in crime reporting. Newspaper and magazine articles, as well as the evening news, offer illustration after illustration. A few examples will make it clear that overdramatization is the norm rather than the exception in modern crime reporting.

The media distorts its presentation of crime patterns by selecting particular incidents to report. Unusual, bizarre, violent, and macabre incidents receive more media attention. A recent review of research about patterns of crime reporting found that "without exception, violent individual crimes—particularly murders—are represented disproportionately in news media presentations." This was true in Minneapolis; St. Louis; Houston; Chicago; Oslo, Norway; Ontario, Canada; England; and the Netherlands. Typical of these findings is an analysis of the 1976 crime news appearing in the *Chicago Tribune*: "Murder accounted for 26 percent of the specific crimes mentioned; robbery, assault, and rape together accounted for another 20 percent. In contrast, common property crimes (burglary and larceny/theft) accounted for less than 6 percent of the crimes mentioned. Tax cheating, embezzlement, and drunken driving accounted for only 3 percent." These percentages bear no relationship to the percentage of the total number of crimes each actually represents.[40]

Television's prime-time dramatic programming also distorts its image of crime. Between 1958 and 1977, shows featuring crime and law enforcement claimed one-fourth to one-third of prime-time television programming. Other programs, not primarily crime dramas, often portrayed such events. Murder, assault, and armed robberies accounted for 60 percent of the offenses depicted.[41]

The effects of these distorted portrayals on public perceptions and opinions are not clear. Research has shown that, for most Americans, the media serve as the primary source of information about crime, yet perceptions of the relative frequency of various crimes are determined more by official counts than by media emphasis.[42] Unfortunately, when the media report official statistics, crime seems worse than it actually is. An article by Ted Gest in *U.S. News & World Report* exemplifies how this is done:

Figures released by the Federal Bureau of Investigation give only a hint of the problem. They show violent crime rising 11 percent in 1980 over 1979. For a true perspective, it is necessary to look back further.

Since 1960, the number of violent crimes in America has more than quadrupled.

In 1980, 23,000 people died at the hands of murderers, up from 9,000 from two decades earlier.

The same year, 82,000 women were raped, up from 17,000 reported in 1960; more than half a million people were robbed, up from 108,000 and 165,000 plus were assaulted, up from 154,000.

During the same 10 years, crimes against property—burglary, larceny and car theft—tripled, causing billions of dollars in losses.[43]

This presentation either reflects a serious misunderstanding of crime statistics or it reflects an attempt to distort information. The use of absolute numbers rather than rates conveys a more pessimistic message about the magnitude of crime. To read that 23,000 murders were committed in 1980 is far more frightening than being told that one person in 10,000 was murdered. Because it reflects population size, a rate is a better indicator of the chances of victimization, yet the author of the article chose to use absolute numbers. He also failed to adjust his statistics for population increases. Even if the rate of victimization remained unchanged because the population grew 25 percent since 1960, the absolute number of crimes would increase by the same proportion. These differences can be of some magnitude. The figures in the article make it appear that murders increased by two and a half times, but in fact the proportion of the population murdered only doubled.[44] Such growth is not comforting, but the article's failure to account for population increases did little to still fears.

Several other issues make the comparison of 1960 figures and 1980 figures difficult. Gest is citing official statistics generated by the FBI each year and reported annually in the Uniform Crime Reports (UCR). Since 1933 the agency has compiled information about criminal offenses reported to local, county, and state law enforcement agencies. Records are maintained for eight primary serious crimes often referred to as Index crimes: murder and non-negligent manslaughter, forcible rape, robbery, aggravated assault, burglary, larceny-theft, motor vehicle theft, and arson. According to the FBI, the figures include all reported crimes "received from the victims, officers who discovered the infraction and other sources" and reflect "actual offenses known regardless of whether anyone was arrested for the crime, the stolen property is recovered, or prosecution is undertaken." When complaints are determined to be unfounded or false, they are deleted from the total count. Monthly reports from local agencies are scrutinized for accuracy and the quality of the data.[45]

During the early 1960s, several articles critical of the FBI were published.[46] Variation in the methods used by different law enforcement agencies across the nation to gather and compile data was found. The data were found to be incomplete. The Uniform Crime Reporting Program responded by improving its reporting methods, thereby producing a more complete set of statistics. The effect was significant. In New York City from 1965 to 1966, the rate of offenses known to the police jumped by 72 percent, but the true increase was estimated to be 6.5 percent.[47] Experts argue that an actual increase in crime occurred during the late 1960s and early 1970s, but they attribute much of the fluctuation in the UCR data to improvements in crime measurement technology. Therefore, when 1960 data and 1980 data are compared, some of the observed growth does reflect an actual increase, but improved reporting accounts for a significant proportion of the increase. Ted Gest did not make his readers aware of this.

Changes in willingness to report crimes also contributed to an increase that was more apparent than real. Efforts to integrate the poor, particularly blacks and other minorities, into mainstream society during the past two decades encouraged a group of citizens who in the past did not report crime to do so. Sociologist Albert Biderman described the phenomenon: "As people who once felt they were outside of the society feel more and more that they are a part of it, and as our law enforcement officials come to judge them by the same standards and give them the same protection as the middle class, we shall go through a period of decreasing crime but of increasing crime statistics. There will not be new crimes, but more recorded crime."[48] Any increase in willingness to mobilize the police to enforce community conduct will be reflected in the FBI data because the UCR records *reported* crime. Ted Gest also failed to make note of this facet of crime data.

The interpretations added to stories also distort the image of crime. *Senseless* violence will be reported as increasing, yet there is no official statistical category for "senseless violence." This kind of media interpretation is usually supported by graphic descriptions of gruesome murders for which no motives seem to exist. Such presentations encourage the conclusion that such crimes are a recent development and suggest that criminals are becoming less rational and more ruthless.

There is no basis for such arguments. History is replete with violent atrocities. The book *Bloodletters and Badmen* by Jay Nash documents this unfortunate aspect of our history. From Burton Abbott, the mild-mannered man executed for the murder of a fourteen-year-old girl, to Abwar Zwillmen, syndicated gangster, Nash recounts a national legacy of "outlaws, thieves, brothel keepers, gangsters, arsonists, rapists, kidnappers, murderers, forgers, embezzlers, bombers, assassins, bank robbers, and hijackers" who have punctuated American history with mayhem since colonial times. Our violent tradition was initiated by John Billington, who became America's first murderer when he ambushed a fellow pilgrim with whom he was feuding. The atrocities today are no worse than the deeds of ax murderess Winnie Ruth Judd in the early 1930s; or Edward Gein, who retained various anatomical parts as trophies of his numerous murders and engaged in cannibalism during the late 1940s and 1950s; or Herman Webster Mudgett, who became America's most prolific murderer by taking the lives of more than two hundred victims in the late nineteenth century.[49]

So senseless violence is not new. Americans have a lengthy history with such bloody acts. In fact, careful inspection of UCR statistics reveals that senseless violence may be decreasing. Stranger-to-stranger murders reported in 1976 accounted for 18.4 percent of the total murders, but by 1981 the percentage had dropped to 15.5 percent. This change suggests that random acts of savagery in which an unknown victim's life is taken are declining.[50]

The mass media tend to impose a negative image of the situation on the public, as sociologist Michael Fisherman documents. The process begins with a series of similar news stories, for instance, a rash of bank robberies or offenses against the elderly. If these incidents are selected for reporting, a pattern may appear. The events need not be unique or indicate an actual change in incidence rates. The key factor is their selection for reporting. Once the stories have appeared, the media need only suggest that there may be a crime wave. At this point, the response of politicians and law enforcement officials becomes important in establishing the trend. Authorities may "augment, modify, or deny a burgeoning crime wave" by their public statements. Since journalists rely on police accounts of crime, officials actually control the raw material of the crime wave. By selectively releasing information, they have the power to make news. The interplay between law enforcement officials and the news media is the key in producing a crime wave.[51]

The publication of the FBI's Uniform Crime Reports each year provides an excellent example of this process. The statistics, which are gathered, analyzed, and presented by the law enforcement establishment, provide the statistical basis on which assertions may be made. The media take this information, interpret it, and may even distort it to suggest that there is a crime wave. Then the media turn to the elite members of the law enforcement establishment to substantiate their claims. Big-city police chiefs, nationally recognized judges, and prosecutors are interviewed to confirm the trends. In this way, the media extend to law enforcement officials the opportunity to legitimize the trends established by the crime statistics they produce. As we will see in the next chapter, law enforcement agencies, like the national news media, distort crime data to fit their particular needs. The information from the UCR is used to show that crime is increasing or decreasing, depending on current political demands. To date, neither the law enforcement establishment nor the media questions the validity or accuracy of the other's use of crime information, thereby promoting a symbiotic if not collusive relationship between the two.

NOTES

1. William J. Chambliss, "The Crime Menace in the Hands of Politics" (Working paper, Department of Sociology, University of Delaware, 1983), p. 6.

2. Ed Magnuson, "The Curse of Violent Crime—A Persuasive Fear of Robbery and Mayhem Threatens the Way America Lives," *Time*, March 23, 1981, pp. 16–30.

3. Aric Press et al., "The Plague of Violent Crime," *Newsweek*, March 23, 1981, pp. 46, 47, 48.

4. "Crime in America—Living Scared," *Mademoiselle*, August 1981, p. 34.

5. Hugh C. McDonald, "Violent Crime: How to Save Your Own Life," *Glamour*, January 1982.

6. "How Fear Is Changing Our Lives," *McCall's*, March 1981, pp. 43–44.

7. In John Leo, "The Menace of Any Shadow—Americans Are Worried and Frightened as Violent Crime Increases Sharply," *Time*, December 22, 1980, p. 30.

8. Press, "The Plague of Violent Crime," p. 46.

9. Magnuson, "The Curse of Violent Crime," p. 16.

10. Ibid., p. 20.

11. Press, "The Plague of Violent Crime," p. 48.

12. Ted Gest, "Our Losing Battle Against Crime," *U.S. News & World Report*, October 12, 1981, p. 39.

13. John Leo, "Why the Justice System Fails," *Time*, March 23, 1981, p. 22.

14. "The Rising Tide of Crime," *Literary Digest* 86 (August 15, 1925): 5. Cartoon by Kirby, first appearing in the *New York World*.

15. Ibid., p. 7. Cartoon by Sykes, first appearing in the *Philadelphia Public Ledger*.

16. "Cities Helpless in the Grip of Crime," *Literary Digest* 73 (April 22, 1922): 10. Cartoon by Kirby, first appearing in the *New York World*.

17. Report of the Special Commission on Law Enforcement presented at the meeting of the American Bar Association in San Francisco, August 10, 1922, reprinted in William B. Swaney, "What Shall We Do to Stop Crime?" *New York Times Current History* 16 (September 1922): 924.

18. Charles Frederick Carter, "The Carnival of Crime in the United States," *New York Times Current History* 15 (February 1922): 753.

19. Quoted in "The Rising Tide of Crime," p. 5.

20. "Cities Helpless in the Grip of Crime," pp. 10–11.

21. Ibid., p. 11. Quotation from the *New York World*.

22. Report of the Special Commission on Law Enforcement, p. 923.

23. "Accounting for the Crime Wave," *Literary Digest* 70 (August 27, 1921): 30.

24. The *Boston Post*, quoted in "The Rising Tide of Crime," p. 6.

25. Judge Otts A. Rosalsky of the New York Court of General Sessions, quoted in Carter, "The Carnival of Crime in the United States," p. 761.

26. "Crime: Every 20 Seconds," *Newsweek*, April 1, 1946, pp. 24–25; and "Crime Goes Booming Along," *Collier's*, May 18, 1946, p. 98.

27. "Rise in Crime in U.S.," *U.S. News & World Report*, May 17, 1946, pp. 30–31.

28. J. Edgar Hoover, "The Crime Wave We Now Face," *New York Times Magazine*, April 21, 1941, p. 36.

29. Howard Whitman, "Stop Terror in the Streets," *Collier's*, July 16, 1949, p. 22.

30. "Rise in Crime in U.S.," p. 30.

31. Hoover, "The Crime Wave," p. 37.

32. "Crime in U.S.—Is It Getting Out of Hand?" *U.S. News & World Report*, August 26, 1963, pp. 38–43.

33. "Is Crime in U.S. Out of Hand?" *U.S. News & World Report*, March 22, 1964, p. 38.

34. "Crime Runs Wild—Will It Be Halted?" *U.S. News & World Report*, August 9, 1965, pp. 64–67.

35. "Crime Goes on and Gets Worse," *U.S. News & World Report*, September 9, 1963, p. 76.

36. "Crime Runs Wild," p. 64.

37. "Crime Goes On," p. 76.

38. "Lawlessness in U.S.—Warning from a Top Jurist," *U.S. News & World Report*, July 5, 1965, pp. 60–63.

39. "How Much Crime Can America Take?" *U.S. News & World Report*, April 20, 1964, pp. 66–72.

40. James Garofalo, "Crime and the Mass Media: A Selective Review of Research," *Journal of Research in Crime and Delinquency* 18 (July 1981): 319–350.

41. Ibid.

42. Ibid.

43. Ted Gest, "Our Losing Battle Against Crime," *U.S. News & World Report*, October 12, 1981, p. 39.

44. Federal Bureau of Investigation, *Crime in the United States—Uniform Crime Reports, 1980* (Washington, D.C.: Government Printing Office, 1981), pp. 7–13.

45. Ibid., p. 2.

46. For example, see Thorsten Sellin, "Crime in the United States," *Life* 48 (September 9, 1957): 48.

47. Harold E. Pepinsky, "The Growth of Crime in the United States," *Annals of the American Academy of Political and Social Service* 423 (January 1976): 27.

48. Albert D. Biderman, "Social Indicators and Goals," in Raymond A. Bauer, ed., *Social Indicators 1966* (Cambridge, Mass.: MIT Press, 1966), p. 125.

49. Jay Robert Nash, *Bloodletters and Badmen* (New York: M. Evans & Co., 1973).

50. Federal Bureau of Investigation, *Crime in the United States—Uniform Crime Reports, 1976 and 1980* (Washington, D.C.: Government Printing Office).

51. Michael Fisherman, "Crime Waves as Ideology," *Social Problems* 25 (June 1978): 531–543.

3

Confusing Crime Statistics

In Chapter 2 we saw that the primary source of information about crime for most people is the media. Stories about criminal incidents account for a considerable proportion of media coverage, and because the volume of crime is too great, not all crime can be reported, so only stories that will grab the public's attention are selected. These incidents tend to be the more violent, bizarre, and unusual acts, which probably contributes to a distorted image of crime. Yet these reports alone fail to indicate whether crime is actually increasing. Official statistics are used to show how crime rates vary over time. The FBI produces these figures from local reports of criminal activity. When an increase is indicated, the media report it. They then turn to politicians and law enforcement officials to confirm the trends, which allows those responsible for producing the statistics an opportunity to verify them.

In this chapter we will evaluate the accuracy of those official statistics. We have already seen that the way statistics are gathered changes over time, making comparisons of present with past statistics meaningless and inappropriate. Are there other problems that make it difficult to understand the crime problem using this set of indicators? Do public and law enforcement officials misuse the statistics, as the media do, to convey a particular image of crime to the public?

THE ACCURACY OF THE UNIFORM CRIME REPORTS

The first statistical presentation in each annual volume of the Uniform Crime Reports is an example of how crime information is distorted. The well-known Crime Clock, shown below as it appeared in the 1980 volume,[1] fosters the impression that crime is pervasive. It is terrifying to think that someone is murdered every half hour in this country. (See Figure 1). But this form of data presentation is misleading. It gives the impression that crime is a frequent occurrence, but it gives no information about a person's actual chances of being victimized. The reason for this is that the Crime Clock does not control for population size. This problem can be easily illustrated with actual data. In 1933 the FBI reported 12,124 murders in the United States. If the total number of minutes in a year (525,600) is divided by that number, we find that a murder occurred every forty-three minutes in 1933.[2] By comparison, 23,044 murders occurred in 1980,[3] and when this figure is divided into the number of minutes in one year, we find as indicated by the Crime Clock that a murder occurred every twenty-three minutes. When one looks at this, it appears that the murder rate is much worse today than in the past. It even appears that the chances of being murdered have doubled. Based on this information, one could conclude that the United States is more violent today and long for the safer days of the 1930s.

But the population of the United States in 1933 was about half what it is today (125 million, compared with 225 million in 1980). When the number of murders is divided into the population, we find that approximately 1 person in 10,000 was murdered in 1933. When we do the same for 1980, we find that approximately 1 person in 10,000 was murdered. The rates are the same. A person's chances of being murdered are no higher today than they were in 1933.

The Crime Clock serves only to make people believe crime is a frequent occurrence, yet frequency not adjusted for population

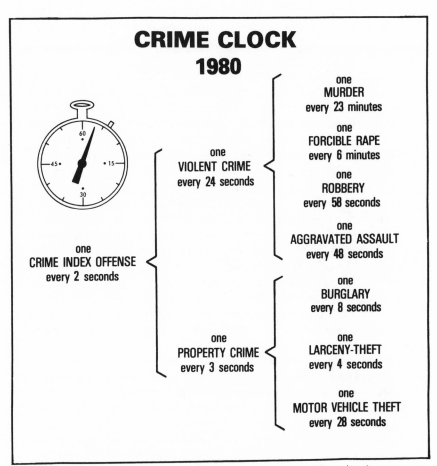

CRIME CLOCK
1980

one
MURDER
every 23 minutes

one
FORCIBLE RAPE
every 6 minutes

one
VIOLENT CRIME
every 24 seconds

one
ROBBERY
every 58 seconds

one
CRIME INDEX OFFENSE
every 2 seconds

one
AGGRAVATED ASSAULT
every 48 seconds

one
BURGLARY
every 8 seconds

one
PROPERTY CRIME
every 3 seconds

one
LARCENY-THEFT
every 4 seconds

one
MOTOR VEHICLE THEFT
every 28 seconds

The crime clock should be viewed with care. Being the most aggregate representation of UCR data, it is designed to convey the annual reported crime experience by showing the relative frequency of occurrence of the Index Offenses. This mode of display should not be taken to imply a regularity in the commission of the Part I Offenses; rather, it represents the annual ratio of crime to fixed time intervals.

Figure 1

size is misleading. Absolutely nothing is indicated about the chances of becoming a victim, but the figure is used for that purpose. Current periodicals often reprint the FBI's clock to suggest that crime is pervasive.

Noted English economist Josiah Stamp (1880–1941) questioned the validity of public statistics when he stated: "The government are very keen on amassing statistics. They collect them, raise them to the nth power, take the cube root and prepare wonderful diagrams. But you must never forget that every one of these figures comes in the first instance from the village watchman, who just puts down what he damn pleases."[4] Stamp's warning captures a fundamental problem with the Uniform Crime Reports: data are gathered at the local level and simply compiled at the federal level. While the statisticians at the federal level may be conscientious, there are numerous opportunities for manipulation at the local level. To the extent that invalid data are forwarded to the UCR program, the national statistics are distorted. A study recently completed by the Police Foundation, a Washington-based law enforcement research center, confirmed this, finding that local arrest statistics are highly inaccurate. Evidence suggested that the data are often manipulated for political reasons.[5]

There are four ways a police department can knowingly or unconsciously manipulate crime data. These arise primarily out of the discretion individual police officers exercise in recording reported crimes. Most complaints that a crime has been committed come from citizens rather than from the police. Officers on patrol only rarely stumble on a crime in progress. Most crimes are reported by a citizen, who notifies the police dispatcher, who then sends a patrol car to investigate. The responding officer decides whether a crime has been committed and whether it is serious enough to be officially recognized. Research shows that experienced police officers do not report all alleged crimes and even ignore certain citizen complaints.[6] Chronic complainers—like the wife who frequently asks to have her husband arrested for beating her but refuses to cooperate in his prosecution—may be ignored. The complaints of certain categories of people, including the elderly and some racial or ethnic groups, may also be dismissed as unreliable.[7]

A change in official policy regarding such discretion can have a direct and often dramatic effect on the incidence rate. For example, when Orlando Wilson was appointed Chicago police superintendent in 1959 in the wake of a scandal, he encouraged more accurate crime reporting as one way of improving agency integrity. Within the next two years, reported robberies and burglaries more than doubled in Chicago, while similar cities that had not undergone administrative changes experienced only marginal gains.[8] It has been said, "A change in the incentive system of a department which had been hiding crime can raise a city's official rates, more even than an invasion from the Mafia."[9]

The discretion involved in deciding whether a particular act is a crime also affects the officially recognized magnitude of incidence. For example, a death that results from a fight may be regarded either as accidental or as criminal. The decision is made by the police, the coroner, and the prosecutor. When the police investigate suspicious circumstances vigorously and report doubtful cases as offenses, reported rates of crime increase. A broken window and a tripped burglar alarm may either be ignored or be considered a case of breaking and entry or burglary. Whether certain kinds of conflicts are labeled as crimes greatly influences the amount of reported violence. When a fight breaks out between family members or acquaintances in a local tavern, the police decide whether to make an arrest and to charge participants with assault. Such decisions determine the number of recorded acts of violence in a particular jurisdiction.[10]

Some decisions regarding whether certain acts are interpreted as crimes are left to individual discretion, others are dictated by departmental policy. Most often they are made as matters of convenience and moral interpretation. Harold Pepinsky provides an example of a decision that involves a covert attempt to distort the public image of crime: "A friend of mine was on a large East Coast urban police force. For the sake of good appearance in a burglary prevention project, he had been instructed by his sergeant not to report burglaries with minor losses."[11]

Police departments vary not only in the diligence with which they respond to complaints but also in the conscientiousness exercised in correcting official statistics when cases are determined to be unfounded. Most urban police departments require officers to write and file reports for every complaint they respond to and for each official action taken. The department tallies these reports to produce its statistical records. According to the FBI, "Whenever complaints of crime are determined through investigation to be unfounded or false, they are eliminated from an agency's count,"[12] but how carefully different departments follow up varies considerably. Tying a subsequent finding to an earlier complaint is often difficult and requires time and manpower. The more professional police departments with adequate fiscal resources can respond to this need, but the quality of data collection and compilation suffers during fiscal retrenchment, which many departments are undergoing.

The most significant way local crime statistics are manipulated involves the least serious but most frequent crime for which statistics are maintained—larceny/theft, which is the most frequent criminal offense reported to the police and accounts for over 50 percent of the total amount of serious crimes reported. Larceny is the most difficult crime to define; a great amount of discretion is required in deciding whether a crime has been committed. The FBI uses the following definition of the offense:

Larceny-theft is the unlawful taking, carrying, leading, or riding away of property from the possession or constructive possession of another. It includes crimes such as shoplifting, pocket-picking, purse-snatching, thefts from motor vehicles, thefts of motor vehicle parts and accessories, bicycle thefts, etc., in which no use of force, violence, or fraud occurs. In the Uniform Crime Reporting Program, this crime category does not include embezzlement, "con" games, forgery, and worthless checks. Motor vehicle theft is also excluded from this category for crime reporting purposes in as much as it is a separate crime index offense.[13]

In the discussion that follows, we will see that this definition has been totally inadequate to prevent unconscious and intentional manipulation of local crime statistics.

In order to understand the problems involved in measuring larceny, a review of the recent history of data collection concerning this offense is necessary. Until 1973 the definition of larceny/theft used in the UCR program stipulated that the value of property stolen must be $50 or more, to differentiate less serious offenses generally referred to as petty larcenies from more serious crimes known as grand larcenies. But this attribute created a built-in accelerator to the crime rate. Between 1962 and 1973 the incidence of larceny/theft steadily rose in the United States, yet, as suggested by David Seidman and Michael Couzens, this increase in large part resulted from inflation, which drove the value of frequently stolen articles above the $50 limit. Grand larcenies accounted for increasingly larger proportions of all thefts as inflation effected a shift from petty larceny to grand larceny.[14] Substantial variations in the amount of reported larceny also resulted from methods law enforcement agencies used to value stolen property. Whether the replacement costs or depreciated values were used, and whether the victim or the officer determined the value, were important in the final dollar specification and ultimately in whether a *serious* crime had been committed.

The ambiguity associated with the definition of larceny provided an opportunity for law enforcement agencies to manipulate their statistics. In the early 1970s the District of Columbia Police Department did exactly that, for political reasons.[15] When Richard Nixon campaigned for president in 1968 he pledged to crack down on violent crime, arguing—like numerous other politicians, past and present—that criminal justice had become too soft and overly concerned with the rights of the criminal. Nixon proposed that the nation's capital be used as a test site, "a national laboratory," for his anticrime program. Shortly after the inauguration, he implemented an extensive program to fulfill this campaign promise. His administration pushed for enactment of an omnibus crime bill for the District of Columbia that provided "no knock" entry for the police and "preventive detention" of arrested but not yet convicted criminals. It became law in July 1970. A 70 percent increase in the police force gave the District of Columbia the highest police-to-citizen ratio in the nation. The department acquired a new and highly refined computer that provided instant information about arrest subjects and stolen merchandise. High-intensity streetlights were installed throughout the city as a crime prevention measure, and a program to deal with drug offenders was initiated. Most significant of all the measures taken to control crime was the installation of Jerry V. Wilson as chief of police. Wilson took a strong stand, threatening to replace police commanders who were unable to reduce crime in their jurisdictions. According to Nixon, these initiatives would make Washington a "model city as far as law enforcement goes."[16]

Shortly after the anticrime program began, Nixon's prediction appeared to have been correct. For the first time in many years, reported crime declined. A 5 percent drop in Index Crimes occurred in 1970, followed by an impressive 20 percent decline in 1971. For some, these figures indicated that "getting tough" worked. Yet the validity of these statistics was soon questioned. Patrick Collins, a reporter for the *Washington Daily News*, who thought that decreases of this magnitude were extraordinary, compared police records with insurance claims, where he found gross discrepancies. The police consistently valued property at roughly $49, while insurance claims and payments were several times higher. Collins suggested that the department had created an artificial decline in the total amount of crime by undervaluing stolen property, thus downgrading serious larcenies.[17] Since larceny is the most frequently occurring Index Crime, decreasing its incidence reduced the total index.

By comparing the percentage of all larcenies of $50 or more in the District of Columbia to national figures, Seidman and Couzens confirmed Collins' claim. Until Wilson was installed as police chief in 1969, the percentages in the District of Columbia paralleled those across the nation. Then, while the percentage of grand larcenies continued to climb in the United States, they plummeted in Washington, D.C. Large thefts became much less common.

The resulting political hullabaloo led to an audit of the city's crime statistics by a private accounting firm. The findings showed that "one-sixth of the police valuations were erroneous and that most of these errors (87 percent) were underestimates of the value of the goods in question. Consequently, in the critical zone between $35 and $65 where the police discretion can be decisive, the proportion of grand larcenies to all larcenies dropped from 59 percent in 1970 to 40 percent in 1971 and 36 percent in 1972."[18] The audit confirmed Collins' conclusion: the decline in crime could be attributed to downgrading of larcenies. Chief Wilson's comment during the political controversy is revealing: "I never had any doubt that my function in this city was to reduce crime and that if crime was not reduced I would probably be replaced as chief of police."[19]

This example of improbity in the production of crime statistics is significant for several reasons. First, it is but one example of how statistics are manipulated for political purposes. Seidman and Couzens also report that "manipulation of crime statistics is an old tradition in Baltimore" and that "numerous conversations with professionals and academics concerned with crime statistics lead us to believe that the Philadelphia statistics are a standing joke in the field."[20] They also report finding dubious figures in Atlanta, Chicago, Cleveland, Oakland, and Seattle.[21] The Washington, D.C., incident simply provides a clear illustration of the political utility of official crime statistics.

The problems associated with classifying acts of larcenies also render any analysis of UCR statistics over time inappropriate. The comparison of 1960 and 1980 figures by Ted Gest discussed in Chapter 2 is a case in point. Up until 1973, inflation by expanding the definition produced annual increases in grand larcenies that were more apparent than real. Since larcenies account for more than half of all serious crime, variations in their numbers affects the overall crime rate.

Recognizing this problem, the FBI announced in 1973 that $50 would no longer be used to distinguish types of larceny. All thefts, regardless of property value, would now be included. Unfortunately, this new policy also encumbers longitudinal analyses. After 1973, what was considered a serious crime changed. Acts previously not counted are now included. The effect is clearly reflected by the percentage increase in crime from 1973 to 1975. Larceny increased by a whopping 35 percent, while murders increased by only 2 percent, rapes by 7 percent, robberies by 19 percent, assaults by 13 percent, and burglaries by 25 percent. A significant proportion of the quadrupling of crime since 1960 is attributable to these two factors: inflation before 1973 and the inclusion of all larcenies after that year.

The modification of the definition of larceny raises a third issue regarding the validity of UCR statistics: Did it remove the opportunity to manipulate data? The answer to this question is mixed. The change did eliminate the incentive to misvalue property and remove one *technique* for manipulating statistics. However, if I call my local police department and report that a gum wrapper has been stolen from my front porch, the incident may be recorded as a larceny and regarded as a serious offense. The FBI Crime Index now includes very minor thefts of property on par with murder.[22]

A complex cognitive and interactive process involving the complainant and the investigating officer actually determines whether an act is a crime. The victim initiates the process by deciding to report an offense. Unless my gum wrapper was of particular sentimental value, I probably would not report its theft. The investigating officer must also decide whether the incident merits formal recognition. One study found "that police do not file written reports on almost 40 percent of citizen calls about major crime."[23] It appears that these decisions are not random but are affected by the circumstances surrounding the incident. Neither the characteristics of the victim nor those of the officer seem to be important determining factors, but the completion and the seriousness of the act are important.[24]

WHAT CRIME STATISTICS ACTUALLY INDICATE

Because crime is a politically charged issue, its measurement is significant in determining public attitudes, opinions, and ultimately government policy. If crime appears to be increasing, people become fearful and demand action to bring it under control. If it is perceived to be declining, a positive evaluation of crime control strategies and agencies will be forthcoming. Since public interest in what the statistics suggest varies and even conflicts, the process of measurement is subject to political pressures. Awareness of how measurements are taken and what they mean is crucial to interpretation of crime statistics, understanding their benefits, and sensitivity to the potential for deception.

No completely accurate source of crime statistics exists. As Levine, Musheno, and Palumbo so wittily describe:

If an omniscient God exists, only he (or she) can render a full and complete accounting of all crimes that are committed. Any earthly measure that we employ will miss some crimes and include some non-crimes; there is no perfectly reliable and valid way of counting crime. . . . Even the all-knowing Lord might have trouble producing an accurate enumeration of crime because a crime is a socially defined act rather than a physical event.[25]

These statements summarize conclusions about complex statistical issues regarding the measurement of crime and identify two important interrelated issues in enumeration. The conceptual problem of deciding whether a crime has been committed is the first. The person making this decision and the criteria used will affect the events classified as crimes and ultimately determine the volume and nature of officially recognized crime. The second issue involves development of an accurate data-gathering process for detecting, communicating, classifying, and recording offenses. How effectively the system filters out incidents that are not illegal but records all serious crimes that take place determines the accuracy of the statistics. Ideally, we would like a system that identifies all "true" crimes but ignores all noncrimes.

The Uniform Crime Reports do have desirable properties. Their most important attribute is that the person deciding whether a crime was committed, the investigating officer, is usually knowledgeable about criminal law and can accurately decide whether an act violates a particular statute. Studies have found that the average citizen knows relatively little about what constitutes a crime. The public generally considers any personal injury or property damage as criminal. Police investigations clarify citizens' misconceptions and add independent corroboration to some complaints while eliminating others.[26]

The usefulness of the UCR statistics as a social indicator of crime is negated to a large extent by its reliance on *reported* infractions. Victims often do not report crimes to the police "because the crime was trivial, because they think nothing can be done or will be done, because they are too embarrassed (e.g., in the case of rape), out of fear of retaliation from the criminal (e.g., in wife-beatings), or simply to avoid the inconvenience." For many people, suffering the crime is bad enough without facing official and impersonal investigations and time-consuming legal processing.[27] Unreported crime (referred to as the "dark figure" of crime) includes all incidents that are technically criminal but never become part of the official record. While some of these incidents may be less serious, two-thirds of all *violent* crimes never come to the attention of the police.

In response to this problem, the National Crime Survey was begun in 1973 to estimate the total amount of crime. The problem of unreported crime is avoided by interviewing citizens to find out if they have been victims of serious crime. Since interviewing everyone would be prohibitively expensive and time-consuming, a proportion of the population (approximately 130,000 people from 58,000 households, each year) is interviewed and the total amount of crime is estimated from the information obtained.[28]

Crime surveys are conducted annually under the highest standards of survey research by the U.S. Census Bureau for the Bureau of Justice Statistics. Great care is taken to assure a high degree of reliability and validity. Interviewers are highly trained, and their performance is carefully monitored to make sure the information recorded is accurate. To determine whether the interview subject is really the victim of a crime or has simply suffered some noncriminal injury, a series of probing and detailed questions are asked about the experience. This information results in more accurate classifications without relying solely on the victim's inadequate knowledge of the criminal law.[29]

The National Crime Survey is produced under highly professional conditions and represents the state of the art in survey research. Still, a certain amount of response error arises. Those interviewed may be dishonest or inaccurate in reporting victimizations. People forget what happened or may exaggerate it. The direction of bias tends to be undetermined; some response error causes overestimation of crime, while other errors produce an underestimation.[30]

Survey statistics provide a perspective on crime and violence that is drastically different from that the FBI figures provide. Victimization data indicate that crime, if changed at all, decreased from the mid-1970s to the mid-1980s, a period in which FBI figures indicated significant gains. It is perplexing that the FBI, an agency of the Department of Justice, tells us that crime is increasing while the Bureau of Justice Statistics, which coordinates and analyzes the National Crime Survey and is also located in the Department of Justice, claims that crime has decreased. Such conflicting reports makes us inclined to agree with Mark Twain's conclusion that there are three kinds of lies: "lies, damned lies and statistics."[31]

Yet we need to understand crime, and in order to do that we must understand what crime statistics indicate. Let us first compare two sets of data and examine their trends over the past two decades. As noted earlier, reported crime according to the Uniform Crime Reports literally and substantially increased from 1960 to 1980. In 1981, reported crime stabilized and then in the following two years declined.

In contrast, the FBI statistics, crime figures produced from the National Crime Survey, showed slow but steady declines in crime throughout the 1970s and into the 1980s. In the 1970s the overall declines were attributable to decreases in the number of larcenies, burglaries, and auto thefts. Crimes of violence showed considerable stability until 1983, when all forms—rape, robbery, and assault—dropped substantially.[32] Thus, while FBI statistics were climbing in the 1970s, survey statistics indicated stability and decline in crime. Both data sources picked up declines in the early 1980s.

There is an important difference in the two sets of information. The Uniform Crime Reports indicate that just under 13 million serious crimes occurred in 1982 (including murder and nonnegligent manslaughter).[33] The National Crime Survey estimated that almost 40 million serious crimes occurred in the same year.[34] According to the second source, almost three times more crimes occur than are known to the police. So while you might be comforted to know that crime is not increasing, it might be disturbing to realize that three times as many crimes occur as you originally were told.

Research shows that a large portion of the "dark figure" of crime (crimes not reported to the police and therefore not part of the UCR data) tapped by the National Crime Survey involve less serious offenses. Completion of the act is an important element in determining whether people bother reporting the incident. An increase in reported crime during a period when victimization rates remain stable might indicate that crimes, while not increasing in absolute number, are becoming more serious. Completion may be becoming more common. This proposition has not been tested empirically, yet it does not seem right that seriousness would increase while incidence would not.

On the other hand, there appears to be an increasing willing-ness on the part of the public to report criminal victimization, as suggested by Charles Kindermann, acting director of the Sta-tistics Division of the Bureau of Justice Statistics.[35] To the extent that the social programs of the 1960s and 1970s were successful in bringing minorities and the poor into dominant, mainstream society, a growing number of the newly integrated should utilize and depend on police services. Reliance on formal institutions also appears to be increasing. Many incidents that in the past were resolved within the family or the neighborhood are now reported to the police. Illegal acts have always occurred; it is only now that they are being formally defined. As society moves in this direction, the change produces yet another stimulus for the increase in reported crime.

Expert evaluations consistently regard the National Crime Sur-vey as the superior source of crime information.[36] As criminol-ogists Levine, Musheno, and Palumbo state: "Unquestionably, survey data give a fuller accounting of the dimensions of the crime problem."[37] Or, as Kindermann stated before the House Subcommittee on Crime:

The ability of the National Crime Survey to collect information on crime victimization, regardless of whether incidents have been reported to police, provides us with a data base that is more representative of the dynamics of personal and property crime in the country as a whole than a data base utilizing only crimes that come to the attention of the police. Further, the survey allows us to estimate the proportion of crimes not reported to the police as it asks a respondent whether an incident was reported to the police, and the reasons why it was or was not reported.[38]

NOTES

1. Federal Bureau of Investigation, *Crime in the United States—Uni-form Crime Reports, 1980* (Washington, D.C.: Government Printing Of-fice, 1981), p. 6.

2. William Lerner, *Historical Statistics of the United States* (Washington, D.C.: Bureau of the Census, U.S. Department of Commerce, 1975), p. 414.

3. FBI, *Crime in the United States—1980*, pp. 7–13.

4. Josiah Stamp, quoted in Gwynn Nettler, *Exploring Crime*, 2nd ed. (New York: McGraw-Hill Book Co., 1978), p. 57.

5. "F.B.I. Arrest Data Found Inaccurate," *New York Times*, July 29, 1984, p. 17.

6. D. Gamble, "In Search of Linkage—Citizen Evaluation, Police System Activity, and Unreported Crime," *Criminology* 17 (February 1980): 471–476; and Harold Pepinsky, "Police Offense-Reporting Behavior," *Journal of Research in Crime and Delinquency* 13 (January 1976): 33–47.

7. Albert J. Reiss, Jr., *The Police and Their Many Publics* (New Haven: Yale University Press, 1971); Pepinsky, "Police Offense-Reporting Behavior"; and Harold Pepinsky, *Crime Control Strategies* (New York: Oxford University Press, 1980), pp. 94–95.

8. James P. Levine, Michael C. Musheno, and Dennis J. Palumbo, *Criminal Justice—A Public Policy Approach* (New York: Harcourt Brace Jovanovich, 1980), p. 506.

9. Dorothy Guyot, "What Productivity? What Bargain?" *Public Administration Review* 36 (May–June, 1976): 341, as quoted in Levine et al., *Criminal Justice*, p. 506.

10. See Pepinsky, *Crime Control Strategies*, pp. 95, 101.

11. Ibid., pp. 100–101.

12. FBI, *Crime in the United States—1980*, p. 2.

13. Ibid., p. 27.

14. David Seidman and Michael Couzens, "Getting the Crime Rate Down: Political Pressure and Crime Reporting," *Law and Society Review* 8 (Spring 1974): 469.

15. The following description is based on reports by Seidman and Couzens, in ibid., pp. 457–493; and Levine et al., *Criminal Justice*, pp. 492–495.

16. Quoted in Seidman and Couzens, "Getting the Crime Rate Down," p. 457.

17. Patrick Collins, "Are District Police Falsifying Reports to Reduce Crime Rate?" *Washington Daily News*, August 25, 1971; and "D.C. Crime Dip! (Really?)," *Washington Daily News*, September 30, 1971.

18. Levine et al., *Criminal Justice*, p. 494.

19. Quoted in Seidman and Couzens, "Getting the Crime Rate Down," p. 488.

20. Ibid., pp. 480, 482.

21. Ibid., pp. 483–484.

22. Ibid., p. 488.

23. Paul W. Valentine, "No Reports Filed on 40% of Crime Calls," *Washington Post*, September 17, 1972, pp. A1, A3.

24. R. Block and C. R. Block, "Decisions and Data: The Transformation of Robbery Incidents into Official Robbery Statistics," *Journal of Criminal Law and Criminology* 71 (Winter 1980): 622.

25. Levine et al., *Criminal Justice*, pp. 501, 502.

26. Ibid., p. 504.

27. Ibid.

28. Ibid., p. 506.

29. Ibid., pp. 506–507.

30. James P. Levine, "The Potential for Overreporting in Criminal Victimization Surveys," *Criminology* 14 (November 1976): 307–330.

31. Mark Twain, *Autobiography*, vol. 1 (New York: Harper and Row, 1959), p. 246.

32. Adolfo L. Paez, "Criminal Victimization, 1983," Bureau of Justice Statistics Bulletin, U.S. Department of Justice, June 1984.

33. Federal Bureau of Investigation, *Crime in the United States—1982* (Washington, D.C.: Government Printing Office, 1983), p. 40.

34. Paez, "Criminal Victimization, 1983."

35. Charles R. Kindermann, "Crime Statistics" (Speech before the Subcommittee on Crime, Committee on the Judiciary, U.S. House of Representatives, June 10, 1981).

36. See, for example, R. M. O'Brien et al., "Empirical Comparison of the Validity of U.C.R. and N.C.S. Crime Rates," *Sociological Quarterly* 21 (Summer 1980): 311–401.

37. Levine et al., *Criminal Justice*, p. 510.

38. Kindermann, "Crime Statistics."

4

How Serious Is the "Crime Problem"?

Are you safe in your home at night, on the streets of large cities? What are the chances your life will be snatched away by some unknown, armed assailant? How wary of the passing stranger should you be? Is the terror you feel after being awakened by a creaking floorboard justified? Must you fear the loss of some valuable or sentimental possession to some unfeeling thug? These questions are important in determining the quality of everyday life. The answers to them will suggest whether you must live in fear and terror or can rest comfortably in our civilized society.

In the previous chapters, we found that the first myth, that crime is worse today than in the past, is false. This still leaves the question of how serious the problem really is. Is Crime Myth 2, "the chances of victimization by either a violent criminal or a property criminal are extremely high," valid or not? Even though the incidence of crime has not climbed, crime is still a problem to be reckoned with. The rate of victimization must be considered and analyzed to give meaning within the context of everyday life to the myths and realities associated with criminal victimization. Unlike many injurious events, the selection of crime victims is not random. Within a particular geographic area, a tornado is indiscreet in what it destroys. Similarly, within age-groups, victims of illnesses are selected with little attention to personal characteristics. But this is not true for criminal victimization, and for this reason any attempt to suggest some probability that a person will become a victim must be qualified according to that person's social position.

We will begin by examining incidence rates for various types of crimes. These rates do not provide an exact estimation of a person's odds of becoming a victim, but they do furnish an approximation. The logic behind using rates to suggest the probability of victimization is that if an average of 100 people per year are victimized over several years, it is reasonable to expect that 100 people will be victimized the following year. If these 100 are members of a group of 1,000 people, then 1 in 10 would be expected to become a victim. However, each individual will not have precisely a 1-in-10 chance, since occurrence varies according to personal characteristics. For this reason, after considering victimization rates, we will examine various demographic factors related to criminal victimization. With both sets of information you can begin to assess your chances of becoming a victim of crime.

In evaluating rates and probabilities of victimization, the use of numbers, figures and statistics cannot be avoided, but to minimize the pain and boredom of an actuarial analysis, complexity and detail will be kept to a minimum. To facilitate exploration of the facts, the author has asked questions on the reader's behalf and answered them.

MYTHS AND REALITIES ABOUT CRIME

In terms of actual numbers, isn't there a tremendous amount of crime in the United States? And isn't most crime of a violent type?

Over 35 million criminal victimizations occur each year. This figure is based on the National Crime Survey and is about four times as large as the number of offenses known to the police as indicated by the Uniform Crime Reports. To get some sense of its magnitude, we note that this figure is smaller than the number of accident injuries (estimated to be just over 69 million)[2] but significantly larger than the number of automobile accidents each year (estimated to be just over 24 million in 1980).[3] This rate of occurrence suggests that crime, as an event that carries with it some social and human costs, is important in our everyday lives, but a single figure specifying the number of incidents is limited in what it tells about the problem. It fails to specify the basic human costs of crime. What are the dollar losses, how many lives are taken, and how many days of work are missed?

To begin to evaluate human costs, one might consider what proportion of the population these 35 million incidents actually affect. This is not as easy to determine because a ratio of the number of victimizations to the total population cannot be computed. If each of the 35 million victimizations involved a different person, the number of victims would exceed the combined population of New York, New Jersey, and Pennsylvania,[4] but because some poeple are victims more than once, the number of victimizations exceeds the number of victims. When the home of a family of four is burglarized one incident has taken place, but there are four victims. A number of crimes, including burglary, auto theft, and household larceny, suffer from this accounting problem. To overcome this, the Bureau of Justice Statistics created a new indicator of criminal victimization which measures the prevalence of crime among households. For 1983 at least one member of more than 23 million households—about *one out of every five*—fell victim to some type of serious crime.[5]

This figure is staggering. As you look down the street of your neighborhood or down the hallway of your apartment building, someone behind every fifth door will have personally experienced crime during the past twelve months. From this perspective alone, no wonder Americans are fearful. Crime is so pervasive that it touches almost everyone. In fact, at this rate some member of your household should be the victim of a crime once every five years. But before you head for the pawn shop to purchase a handgun, or for the hardware store to buy locks and burglar bars, further assessment should be made.

As noted above, depending on your age, sex, socioeconomic status, and other factors, you may be much less likely to be victimized than these figures indicate. In addition, these statistics include many relatively minor offenses that are not personally threatening and in which the victim plays a significant role.

For example, when you leave your sweater lying on a park bench and someone walks off with it, that may become an official crime—theft. Larceny (personal and household thefts with no force involved) accounted for two-thirds of the 35 million victimizations, and quite often the value of the stolen property was small.[6]

Because only 5 percent of the households across the nation experience *violent* crime each year,[7] and many of these incidents are unsuccessful attempts that do not involve serious injury, specific types of crime must be considered. We begin with the most threatening, violent personal crime. In 1982, 21,012 murders came to the attention of the police, slightly more than the previous year.[8] This number represents a rate in which only 1 American in 10,000 will die at the hands of a murderer each year. Compared with other forms of fatal mishap, this rate of occurrence is relatively infrequent. More people take their own lives than have their lives taken.[9] More people die each year from excessive alcohol consumption resulting in cirrhosis of the liver. A drunken driver is more likely to kill you than a murderer. Your chances of being murdered are less than your chances of dying in an accident in or around your home. And finally, you are much more likely to be killed in an automobile accident than to be murdered.[10] But when was the last time a local politician ran on a platform to get tough on home accidents, or citizens formed a group to see that their neighbors wore seat belts? We fear the unknown assailant, stalking us and mercilessly taking our lives, but most murders are not committed by strangers. Over half of all known murders are committed by family members, friends, and acquaintances. In only 17 percent of the murders is the assailant a stranger.[11]

Considering that only 3,000 or so Americans (1 in 100,000 people) are murdered by strangers, you would be well advised to stop worrying about the bumps in the night and the seedy-looking man standing at the street corner. Your life is safe from victimization by the unknown assailant. You are more likely to die as a result of a motor vehicle crash (sixteen times), a fall (four times), drowning (two times), or a fire or burn (two times). Almost as many people kill themselves accidentally with fire-arms (2,000 each year) as are killed by unknown assailants

(3,000);[12] (with these statistics, I am skeptical that purchasing a "little" gun for protection bespeaks sound judgment).

But murder is not the only violent crime, and certainly not the most frequent. Many more rapes, assaults, and robberies occur than murders. A recent report by the Bureau of Justice Statistics indicates that just under 6 million of these crimes are committed each year. Rape is the least frequent of the four non-fatal violent crimes, while simple assault (not involving a weapon or serious injury) is the most frequent. Robberies and aggravated assaults occur with similar frequency and fall between rape and simple assault in the number of offenses that occur each year.[13]

Unlike murder, strangers commit most—about 3 out of 5—nonfatal violent crimes. The rate of violent crimes by strangers averages about 20 victimizations per 1,000 people and has remained stable since the early 1970s. In contrast, the less frequent nonstranger victimization rate for violent offenses (12 per 1,000 people) increased somewhat since that time, about 10 percent. For violent crimes in general these minor fluctuations between stranger and nonstranger victimizations average out, and a pattern of great stability has been established, with a yearly average of 32 victimizations per 1,000 people.[14]

From studying types of violent crimes individually, an interesting pattern emerges. Rape and robbery are extremely rare. Only 2 women out of 1,000 over the age of twelve are raped each year. Of these, only about 1 act in 3 is completed. In all, only 5 women in 10,000 suffer the completed act of rape each year. Of these, 2 will know their assailant and 3 will not. With only 7 victimizations per 1,000 people, robbery also is a relatively rare event. Most robberies, 5 out of 7, involve only the threat of violence and the victim suffers no physical injury. Less than 2 people in 1,000 will be robbed by a stranger and seriously injured.[15]

Assault is a different case. Americans have a high propensity for attacking one another. Almost 3 percent of the population over age twelve is physically assaulted each year.[16] Several reasons are given for this—most often that violence is an integral aspect of our culture. One author suggests that it is as "American as Jesse James."[17] Violence is reinforced by violent sports, television, movies, and even Saturday morning cartoons. Social and cultural values of individuality, autonomy, machismo, and a keen sense of moral indignation also contribute to the high levels of assault.

Even so, the magnitude of the problem is apparently exaggerated. Only about one-third of all assaults result in any injury.[18] In 1980 more than 5 million people were injured in automobile accidents, yet only 600,000 Americans were injured in aggravated assaults.[19] Some 24 million people were injured in accidents at home, and more than 3 million of them suffered disabling injuries.[20] Only 6 percent of the assault victims incurred any medical expenses in the treatment of sustained injuries.[21] These figures indicate that Americans may be quick to attack but are rarely vicious. Attacks are more likely to be simple assaults without a weapon than aggravated assaults with a weapon. No injury is more likely than some, and if injury does occur a minor wound is more likely.

These are interesting statistics, but taken as a whole, what threat does violent crime hold for me as an individual?

Once again, you must realize that the figures given are aggregate statistics and that your actual chances of being victimized depend on your particular social circumstances. It can be said, however, that violent crime is not as threatening to safety as people think. In considering this proposition, four points should be reviewed.

First, violent crimes—rape, robbery, and assault—make up only about 16 percent of all crime.[22] Property crime is far more frequent (chances are greater you will be injured in an accident at home, on the job, or in an automobile than that you will be the victim of a violent criminal act).[23]

Second, if you are unlucky enough to be attacked, it is more likely that your assailant will not have a weapon. In only 35 percent of crimes of violence is the criminal armed. This varies from crime to crime, with 23 percent of the rapists, 32 percent of the assaulters, and 46 percent of the robbers being armed.[24] It is interesting that victims are more likely to sustain an injury if the weapon used is not lethal. The likelihood of injury is greatest when the weapon is something other than a firearm or a knife—a club, bottle, or wrench, for example. The use of a knife instead of a firearm is also associated with a higher rate of injury. Perhaps the victim is more willing to resist an assailant using a less lethal weapon and consequently more likely to be injured. (It should be noted that statistics are for violent crimes that do not result in death. It is unlikely that the relationship between the lethalness of the weapon and the injury will hold in the case of murder.)[25]

The third important point is that victims of violent crimes are seldom injured. In only 1 out of every 12 violent personal crimes is hospital treatment required. Of those who must go to the hospital, the vast majority are treated in the emergency room and released. Only 1 victim out of every 100 requires inpatient care. So even if you have the misfortune of being the victim of a violent crime, it is not likely that you will be seriously hurt.

What we fear most—suffering serious physical injury at the hands of an unknown violent offender—is exceedingly uncommon. Since less than 2 percent of violent victimizations by strangers result in inpatient hospital care, only 3 people in every 10,000 suffer this most feared event each year.[26] Compared with murder, 4 people are seriously injured by an unknown assailant for every 1 murdered; still, this remains an extremely rare event, compared with other forms of accidental injury.

A final point worth noting about the threat of violent crime is that the chances of being seriously injured are greater if you *know* your assailant. Robbery and assault victims are more likely to require hospital care if they know the assailant. This is particularly true for the crime of aggravated assault and is more pronounced for women than for men. Furthermore, people attacked by someone they know are likely to be more seriously injured than those attacked by strangers.[27] So, violence does occur, and innocent people are seriously injured, but such incidents are relatively infrequent, and cases in which actual injury is sustained are even rarer. Most crimes are not violent, and most victims suffer no physical injury.

Because the FBI likes to use units of time to illustrate the frequency of crime (i.e., 1 serious crime is committed somewhere in the nation every 2 seconds, and 1 aggravated assault is committed every 48 seconds), it is interesting to examine the chances of violent criminal victimization with time as the unit of analysis. Since 1 person in 10,000 is murdered each year, you should expect to be murdered once every 10,000 years. Similarly, since 3 people in 10,000 are seriously injured by a violent criminal the victim does not know, you should expect to be seriously injured under such circumstances about once every 3,333 years. Women over the age of twelve should expect to be raped about once every 2,000 years. You should expect to be robbed approximately every 150 years. Your chances of being assaulted are considerably higher, and you should expect to be the victim of an assault every 40 years, yet you will be the victim of an assault involving a physical injury every 125 years. Perhaps Americans can live with these probabilities and feel safer than in the past.

All right, violent crime may not be as serious as I thought, but what about theft and burglary? Isn't the incidence and dollar loss of property crime exceedingly high?

The answer to this question is an unqualified yes. We are a nation of light-fingered pilferers. We steal from stores, from neighbor's yards, and from the places where we work. We steal in residential buildings, in the streets, in parks and on playgrounds, and in parking lots. Some 31 million of the 37 million crimes commited each year involve property theft of one sort or another.[28] Of these, just over 14 million are perpetrated against individuals, while the remaining more than 17 million offenses are crimes against households.[29] The offenses consist of purse-stealing and pocket-picking and other forms of personal larceny that do not involve contact of the victim with the offender, including burglary, household larceny, and motor vehicle theft. Because robbery is both a violent personal crime and a property crime, it will be considered again in this section.

You and your family should expect to fall victim to the thief. In 1980 some form of property crime touched approximately 1 family in 4. One home out of every 15 was burglarized, or about 1 house on every four-sided suburban block and 1 apartment on each floor or two of every high rise. A motor vehicle was stolen from every 70th family across the nation.[30] In focusing on individuals, we find that 1 out of every 12 people fell victim to personal theft.[31] In contrast to the infrequency of violent crime, property crime is a common event that will be experienced several times during an individual's lifetime. The family automobile will be stolen about once every 50 years, the home burglarized every 15 years, and personal property stolen every 11 years. Because property crime is so frequent, most readers of this book should be able to relate at least one personal experience of this sort.

The cost of property crime is extremely high. Using 1980 FBI statistics, the Insurance Information Institute estimates that 550,000 known robberies involve a yearly property loss of $333 million, that the 3.8 million reported burglaries represent a $3.3 billion loss, that the 7 million reported larceny/thefts produced $2.2 billion in losses, and that the 1 million motor vehicles stolen cost $3.3 billion. Totaled, crime costs $9 billion each year,[32] an amount that represents 0.34 percent of the gross national product.[33] This figure is larger than the combined yearly income of the three largest corporations in the world: General Motors, Exxon, and Royal Dutch/Shell Group.[34] It exceeds the individual revenues of all but ten states. Since the median family income in the United States is about $20,000, crime costs approximately the same as the combined income of 450,000 families.[35] The $9 billion figure is twice the total yearly outlay of the federal government for criminal justice.[36] Such an economic burden must place a substantial drag on the economy and create hardships for many businesses, families, and individuals.

Furthermore, the $9 billion loss is substantially underestimated. Researchers base it on reported crime, which as we have already learned ignores the vast "dark figure" of crimes never reported. Three-quarters of all thefts, half of the burglaries and robberies, and one-third of the motor vehicle thefts are never reported to the police.[37] Unreported crimes tend to be less serious, but some monetary loss is often involved. A conservative estimate would project the total cost of property crime to be at least half again, if not double, the $9 billion estimate.

In spite of the extremely high incidence rate and dollar costs, property crime may not be as serious as one might think. To explore this idea, five points need to be examined. First, because people most fear crimes where there is direct contact with the criminal, property crimes with confrontation should be regarded as the most serious. The two property crimes that involve contact between the victim and the offender but do not contain the element of violence are pocket-picking and purse-snatching. These crimes are the rarest forms of theft; only 3 people out of every 1,000 (1 percent of American households)[38] are so victimized each year. Only murder and rape occur less frequently. Most larcenies are without contact: a purse is stolen from an office desk, a child's skates are carried off from the playground, a package is removed from an automobile. These crimes irritate us, but they are less threatening than face-to-face victimizations. The reaction of victims reflects this; larcenies—both personal without contact and household—are the crimes least often reported. Only about 1 in 4 are brought to the attention of local authorities.[39]

A second reason that property theft may be less serious than generally believed is that monetary losses are seldom great. For most offenses the value of the property does not exceed $50. Only 44 percent of the larcenies and half the burglaries and robberies are known to involve losses greater than $50. Not all property losses are low. When an automobile is stolen the loss is usually substantial. In 20 percent of all robberies and 33 percent of all burglaries, the value of the goods stolen exceeds $250. Still, as a general rule, the economic losses are not great.[40]

Third, the seriousness of property crime is also minimized because many events officially recorded and counted as crimes are attempted rather than completed acts. Specifically, 1 in 3 motor vehicle thefts, 1 in 4 burglaries, and 1 in 20 household larcenies are unsuccessful attempts in which the owner retains possession of the property.[41]

The public's distorted view of the act of burglary is a fourth important point. Burglars are perceived as one of two types: the burly man who breaks down a door or pries open a window to gain entry into a residence, or an agile and cunning cat burglar who will gain entry to a well-secured home. In both cases, the criminal forces his way into the premise. In most burglaries (6 out of every 10) the perpetrator enters through unlocked doors or windows or by using keys.[42] The burglar does not have to be a brute or particularly cunning, but simply someone who walks off the street through an unlocked front door.

You should also consider that while the costs of property crime are high, they pall beside other forms of loss. Motor vehicle accidents are estimated to cost $57 billion each year, while the annual monetary loss from work-related accidents is estimated to be $28 billion.[43] Other crimes that elicit far less concern than that associated with common street crimes involve far greater dollar losses. Embezzlement alone is estimated to cost in excess of $3 billion and cause one-third of all business failures. The costs of consumer fraud are estimated to run as high as $20 billion each year. Some claim that white-collar and corporate crime cost $100 billion each year.[44] Other forms of disaster, such as fires and violent natural catastrophes, including earthquakes, hurricanes, and tornadoes, come close to costing as much as crimes in the damage they cause—$5 billion and $1 billion respectively.[45] So even though the cost of ordinary property crime may be high, other social evils are comparable, and some far exceed it.

Just as the tragic aspect of lives lost and injuries sustained from violent criminal acts cannot be ignored, an unfortunate element of property crime cannot be overlooked. For most crimes, the victim never recovers stolen property, either by return, restitution made by the offender, or insurance payments. In 3 out of 4 burglaries and robberies and 4 out of 5 thefts, the loss is never recovered.[46] When the item stolen belongs to a poor or elderly person and is necessary for economic survival (a stolen social security check, for example), the social as well as economic impact may be devastating. This element of property crime exposes the way our system of justice ignores the plight of the victim. Americans spend billions of dollars unsuccessfully chasing criminals while virtually ignoring the real social harm. This practice does not achieve justice. The system fails to ensure that the criminal pays for the crime while totally neglecting the victim.

Okay, crime may not be as prevalent or as costly as I thought, but doesn't the United States have more crime than any other nation?

Your observation is somewhat accurate. The United States generally has more crime than many nations similar to it in terms of industrialization, education, poverty, and related factors. Its homicide rate is highest among all highly industrialized countries. According to a United Nations publication, the homicide rate per 100,000 people in the United States was 11.2 in 1970, compared with 4.3 in Sweden, 3.5 in Canada, 3.2 in England, and 2.5 in Japan. Clearly, the occurrence of violent deaths in the United States is several times more frequent than in other developed countries. Still, the U.S. homicide rate is not the highest found in the world. Of the countries for which data exists, the United States ranked seventh behind Mexico, Chile, South Africa, Columbia, Guatemala, and Kenya. Mexico's rate, for example, is four times that of the United States.[47]

A recent comparison of violence in Norway and the United States by William Chambliss is particularly instructive in this regard. Norway is well known for its extremely low rate of personal crime. Its official murder rate is much lower than that of the United States. Experts attribute this difference to the homogeneity of culture, strong interpersonal ties, and nonviolent traditions that persist in Norway. But Chambliss points out that Norway records the crime of murder "*only* when there has been a finding by a court that the person committing the act of violence from which death resulted did so intentionally." In the United States, any incident where a death occurs and violence can be attributed to it is classified as a murder. Furthermore, non-negligent manslaughter, which is included in the murder rate in the United States, can involve traffic deaths and other nonintentional deaths. Therefore, murder statistics in the United States include numerous acts not contained in Norwegian statistics. Violence in the two nations may be more alike than often assumed. Chambliss' comparison of National Crime Survey results supports this argument. The United States appears to have a slightly higher rate of assaults, but Norway has a much higher rate of attempted assaults.[48] Violence in the United States may therefore be more similar than simple comparisons of international statistics reveal.

Because legal definitions vary considerably, comparisons of property crime among nations are also difficult. Yet most crime experts generally agree that theft, burglary, and robbery in the United States are among the highest found in the world, particularly among highly developed countries. This phenomenon is not new. Comparatively high rates were an issue of concern in the 1920s. You may be relieved to learn that some experts believe the situation is improving. Sociologist Daniel Bell observes, "A sober look at the problem shows that there is probably less crime today in the United States than existed a hundred, or fifty, or even twenty-five years ago, and that today the United States is a more lawful and safe country than popular opinion imagines."[49] If this is true, crime may be a factor of a nation's age, requiring development of certain social characteristics and conditions found only in more mature societies.

CHARACTERISTICS OF THE VICTIM

If criminal victimization is not a random social event but is more likely to affect people with certain characteristics, are individuals physically more vulnerable, such as the elderly and possibly women, more likely to be victimized?

This idea, which is Crime Myth 3, "People who are the most vulnerable—particularly the elderly and adult women—are the favorite victims of criminals," is part of the popular belief about criminal victimization. It is not an accurate perception of victimization patterns.

Crimes against the elderly are relatively infrequent compared with other age-groups. In only one crime category, larceny with contact, are people over the age of sixty-five more often the victims than younger people, yet larceny with contact is one of the least frequent offenses. With all other crimes, the rate of elderly victimization is substantially lower than for younger people. People under the age of sixty-five are five times more likely to suffer a violent crime or have property stolen without contact with the offender. The cars of the elderly are four times less likely to be stolen, and their homes are only half as likely to be burglarized.[50]

In terms of frequency, these statistics indicate that crime is less of a problem for elderly people than often believed, but one

must not overlook the differential impact that criminal victimization may have on people. The trauma an elderly person experiences may exceed that of a twenty-two-year-old. Benjamin
Renslaw, acting director of the Bureau of Justice Statistics, points
out, "Behind the statistical conclusion . . . is the inescapable realization that the trauma and economic impact of crime may
weigh far more heavily on the elderly, leading them to take
precautionary measures that can only impoverish their lives."[51]
The age-group most likely to be criminally victimized for both
theft and crimes of violence is young people between twelve
and twenty-four years old. Frequency of victimization drops
with age.[52]

The belief that females, who are supposedly physically more
vulnerable, are victimized more often is also inaccurate. Aside
from rape, the only personal crime for which women are victimized more than men is larceny with contact. Men are twice as
likely to be the victim of an assault or a robbery and 50 percent
more likely to experience some crime of theft. Men are also the
victims of strangers more than females. Some 72 percent of all
personal crimes of violence against males involve strangers,
compared with only 57 percent of the violent crimes against
females. This relationship holds for property crimes as well.[53]

Thus, the idea that physically weaker people constantly fall
prey to the criminal has no foundation in fact. Neither women
nor older people are particularly prone to criminal victimization.
On the contrary, they are considerably less likely to be victims
than their counterparts. Still, the lifestyles of these social groups
may explain this phenomenon better than their actual vulnerability to criminals.

*Besides age and gender, what other factors play a role in who is
victimized?*

Age and gender are the two personal attributes most closely
tied to criminal victimization. Marital status, economic situation,
and race are also related. Married or widowed people are less
likely to be victims of personal crimes than persons who are
divorced or have never been married. For violent crimes, the
differences in rates among marital classes is marked. In 1981 the

victimization rate per 1,000 for divorced persons was 66, and for the never married it was 62, compared with only 20 for the married and 11 for the widowed. For property crimes, similar but less striking rate differences were observed: never married, 129; divorced, 120; married, 63; and widowed, 35.[54] To an extent these variations result from the relationship between age and marital status, but they are also strongly associated with different lifestyles.

Turning to family economics, people from the poorest families experience the highest rates of victimization for most crimes. Household larceny and motor vehicle thefts (where wealthy families are more likely to be victimized) are the two exceptions to this pattern. The poor are much more vulnerable to violent crime. Individuals from the highest income levels are victimized only about half as often as members of the poorest families. This is true for all violent crimes except rape, where women from poor families are nine times more likely to be attacked than women from wealthy families. Another important difference among income categories is that poor persons are much more likely to be seriously injured when robbed or assaulted than more affluent people.[55]

A final demographic characteristic related to victimization patterns is race and ethnicity. Contrary to what one might expect, the differences among groups are not dramatic. Blacks are more frequently victims of violence than others, while whites experience property crimes at higher rates than other ethnic and racial groups. For crimes of violence, robbery accounts for the higher rate experienced by blacks. Blacks are almost three times more likely than whites to be a robber's victim. For property crimes, blacks are more vulnerable to purse-snatching and pocket-picking than whites, but whites experience higher rates of larceny without contact. This general pattern of victimization is consistent across ethnic lines. Persons of Hispanic background are more prone to violent victimization but less likely to suffer property crime than non-Hispanics.[56]

These statistics indicate that the young, male, unmarried or divorced, and poor face higher risks of criminal victimization. According to criminologists, people characterized by more than one of these variables have exceedingly high victimization rates.

When we look at only three of the variables, some striking differences can be observed. Only 24 white females over age sixty-five out of every 1,000 are the victims of a personal crime (violence or theft), compared with 250 out of 1,000 black males between the ages of twenty and twenty-four. Young black males are thus victimized at a rate over ten times that of older white women.

If physical vulnerability does not determine who experiences crime, what does?

Criminologists Michael Hindelang, Michael Gottfredson, and James Garofalo suggest that lifestyles and daily routine determine exposure to criminal victimization. The places frequented, the people with whom one associates, and the time of day a person is out all influence the chances of encountering a criminal. For instance, the lifestyle of teenagers compared with that of older adults places them in locations and situations where the opportunity for criminal victimization is much higher. Teenagers associate with other teenagers, the age-group known to contain the largest proportion of criminal offenders. Mobility and inclination to be out at night also contribute to higher levels of teenage victimization.[57]

The relationship between demographic characteristics and the life consequence of criminal victimization is observed for other events: life expectancy, mobility, automobile accidents, and suicide. Lifestyle makes it possible to experience various life consequences.[58]

Five demographic factors have been identified above as related to victimization: age, sex, marital status, economic situation, and race and ethnicity. These factors affect lifestyles. By age, people differ in mobility, exposure to others, and time spent outside the home. Very young children are not often exposed to criminal victimization because few activities involving that age-group occur outside the home. They are under the constant supervision and protection of an adult. This pattern begins to change when a young person starts school. The child spends greater amounts of time away from home with nonfamily members. With adulthood, lifestyle shifts again. Job and familial responsibilities buffer a person from criminogenic environments. As one progresses through adulthood, mobility, interpersonal contacts, and the external world become more and more restricted. Fear of crime also increases with age, contributing to the further reduction in exposure to victimization as older adults avoid unsafe places. As Hindelang and his colleagues suggest, "By virtue of adaptation to role expectations and structural constraints that vary as a function of age, age itself [is] an important indication of lifestyle."[59]

With regard to gender, traditional sex roles and expectations (despite movement toward sexual equality) dictate different lifestyles for men and women. As adolescents, females are more closely supervised and allowed less freedom to come and go than their male counterparts. As adults, women often assume housekeeping responsibilities, which take them less often from the protective confines of their homes. Females are apt to avoid the aggressive acting-out behavior that young males of many species undergo. For human males, such behavior is often linked with criminality.[60] As sex roles become more similar, we expect that victimization rates for men and women will converge.

Marital status is also an indicator of when, where, and with whom people will spend their time. Whereas a single or divorced person is more likely to spend time outside the home and in the company of strangers, the cohabitation associated with married life, or a history of married life in the case of a widow or widower, increases stability and the number of at-home responsibilities and thus isolation from crime.

Similarly, the cultural ties associated with family income, race, and ethnicity also affect with whom one associates and the places of those associations. Housing, transportation, privacy, and leisure-time activities are related to income as well as to racial and ethnic segregation. To the extent that crime varies according to place and event, people from different income levels and racial and ethnic groups will experience crime to varying degrees.[61]

The chances of criminal victimization appear to vary according to the time a person spends in public places, particularly at night, the proportion of time spent with nonoffenders, and degree to which a person shares demographic characteristics with offenders. Each of these three elements varies with lifestyle and determines the "convenience, the desirability, and vulnerability of the person as a target for personal victimizations."[62]

CHANGING PERCEPTIONS OF CRIME

Despite what you claim victimization statistics indicate, I still believe that more crime occurs now than in the past. Once I knew no one who had been victimized, now I am acquainted with several people who have personally experienced crime. How do you reconcile this discrepancy? Your numbers indicate that everything is okay, but I sense that things are not okay. There must be more happening than propaganda by the media and the law enforcement establishment.

You have raised several issues that all stem from a single question: "Why do I have the perception of crime that I do?" By focusing on this central issue, the other issues you raised can be resolved.

In recent years three factors have played major roles in shaping public opinion about crime. The first, the distortion of information by the mass media and the law enforcement establishment, was discussed earlier, but their role in this should not be interpreted as conspiratorial. The editors do not get together and decide to overrepresent violent crime. Instead, the marketing and sales analysts from one newspaper discovered that sensationalized violence increased sales, so it became editorial policy to concentrate on reporting the more sensational crimes. To remain competitive, other papers were forced to do the same. Likewise, the manner in which crime statistics will be manipulated for a given year is not an item on the agenda at the annual meetings of the International Association of Chiefs of Police, or even a subject of polite professional conversation. This sort of collusion does not exist. What happens is that a police department receives a large federal grant to reduce crime and finds it politically advantageous to show a reduction to convince the public that their tax dollars are well spent. The reduction in official statistics is accomplished by simply changing the techniques for recording complaints. When the same departments are faced with budget cuts and fierce competition for scarce resources with the fire department, sanitation workers, and other local agencies, indications that crime is increasing and law enforcement is imperative becomes politically advantageous. The media pick up on fluctuations, particularly when they are upward, and often sensationalize the figures by presenting them in doomsday trappings. Even though no conspiratorial effort among the elite of the national media and the law enforcement establishment may have taken place, the aggregate effect of their independent actions does much to shape an inaccurate public image of crime.

But their combined effect alone is not sufficient to explain such universally and strongly held perceptions of increased criminality. Another important factor arises from changes in population density. If you lived in the 1930s, 1940s or even the 1950s, you probably resided in a less densely populated area. In the 1930s and 1940s almost half the nation's population lived in rural areas, and those who did not often resided in stable and isolated urban neighborhoods. Only 1 person in 4 now lives in a rural setting. Migration to urban areas with high population density has contributed to the distorted view of crime.

Let's say that as a teenager you lived in a town with a population of 2,500. Given the current murder rate of 1 victim out of every 10,000 people, a city of 2,500 should experience one murder every four years. For the contemporary city-dweller it would be a pleasant experience to pick up the local newspaper every morning and not have to face yet another gruesome homicide. Infrequent exposure to violent crime would leave you feeling secure and isolated from crime. Along similar lines, at current incidence rates no more than one rape each year should be reported to the police of your town of 2,500 (reported crimes rather than victimization rates are used because they are the crimes that people are aware of—they are reported by the newspapers). Only 6 or 7 robberies and aggravated assaults would be reported each year and only 2 or 3 of those assaults would involve physical injury. At these rates, only once every month or two would the local newspaper report that a violent crime had occurred. In contrast to these patterns, given current crime rates, the small town of your adolescence would experience significantly more property crime: approximately 42 burglaries and 80 thefts would be reported to local law enforcement authorities.

Still, less than 1 burglary and 2 thefts of any value would be reported each week. If reports of crime came to your attention so infrequently, would you not feel safe and believe your community to be crime free? Furthermore, if this was the environment of your youth it would serve as the basis for all future comparisons. Your safety in any future community would be evaluated based on your recollection of that time.

Now, let's assume you migrated as an adult to a large urban area with a population of 1 million (about 75 percent of the nation's population now live in urban areas). Given the *same rate of crime*, the city where you now reside would experience 100 murders each year rather than 1 every four years. You now face the account of 2 murders in the daily news each week! Some 365 rapes (one per day), almost 7 robberies (2,430 each year), and just over 7 aggravated assaults (2,900 each year) will be reported to the police *each day*. Some 46 burglaries and 86 thefts per day would also be reported.

Would you feel safer in the city with 2 murders each week and 7 serious assaults per day, or in the town with 1 murder every four years and an assault every two months? Because the rates used in this example for each location were exactly the same, the chances of victimization are also the same in each area. What is different is the perspective. The context in which you are formulating your attitude changed. As an adolescent you lived in an area with only 2,500 potential victims, but as an adult you live in an area with 400 times that many. By expanding the size of what you consider to be your community from a small town to a megapolis, you expose yourself to more crime. This in turn influences your perception of how extensive the problem really is. As the nation's population migrated from rural areas to urban areas, the shift in perceptual context left many with a sense of an exploding crime rate. It goes without saying that the establishment of national and international news networks also contributed to the same phenomenon by expanding the exposure area. We now read and hear of crime occurring throughout the nation and the world rather than only in our neighborhood.

Another important factor contributing to a perception of increased amounts of crime is a subtle and gradual change in what is defined as crime. This change did not take place in the legislatures or courtrooms across the country; it is one of social interpretation among citizens of this nation. People's attitudes about what they consider sufficiently serious to warrant formal complaint to the police have changed. Two or three decades ago, when many Americans lived in small towns and relatively stable neighborhoods where everyone knew everyone else, many acts that were technically criminal were handled informally. For example, if a friend and I broke windows in a house a few blocks from my own the owners would learn through the neighborhood grapevine who the culprits were and call not the police but our parents. We would be disciplined and restitution would be made. High mobility and increasing population concentration has eroded stable neighborhoods and created communities of strangers. If a young person today wanders several blocks from home and breaks windows, the owner will be less likely to draw on the neighborhood grapevine for information. And even if the offender could be identified, chances are the owner will not know the young person's family. Consequently, the problem cannot be resolved informally. The solution, given that replacement costs may be several hundred dollars, is to call the police and file a formal complaint. Incidents once handled among acquaintances now become official statistics.

As the nation moved toward a society of strangers, a concomitant move toward formalization of interpersonal problem resolution occurred. This is true not only for events that could be labeled criminal but also for other everyday life situations. In a society characterized by stable family and friendship ties, an individual with a personal problem would turn to someone with whom they were close for help. Today support groups are weaker, so many people turn to more formal sources of help—for example, psychologist, psychiatrist, or social worker. The boom in civil litigation suggests that there is increased utilization of formal means of interpersonal conflict resolution. Methods for helping the poor also became more formal as neighborhood charities were replaced by bureaucratic public welfare institutions. The dramatic increase in physician office visits may even suggest further formalization of health care practices. Is it not possible that the accelerating spiral of crime is due in part to formalization and reflects an increasing willingness among the citizens to consider more incidents as criminal and to report them to the police?

Credence is lent to this position by a comparison of National Crime Survey statistics (victimization trends) and Uniform Crime Report figures (reported crime) over the past few years. The survey-measured rate, though much higher, remained stable since the early 1970s, compared with the amount of reported crime, which climbed steadily and dramatically. These differences indicate that people report to the police incidents that in the past were ignored or handled informally. What is considered criminal is changing. This may reflect an increasing inability of people to cope with the complexities of contemporary life and the resulting willingness to seek outside assistance; or it may simply imply a diminishing tolerance for criminals as well as other social parasites; or it might even suggest a growing respect for official authority and services. Regardless of reasoning, what is officially labeled as criminal is expanding to include some socially undesirable or harmful acts that in the past were not so labeled.

In answer to your original question, several factors probably contributed to your changing perception of crime. Structural changes in society, particularly increased mobility and the concentration of the population, promoted a natural distortion of perception and pushed people to modify what is considered criminal. However, these changes are totally unrelated to the actual incidence of crime. There has indeed been some increase in crime in the United States, and while I would argue that crime did not rise significantly and dramatically during the 1970s, I would not take so strong a stand about increases since the end of World War II. Because of the changes and improvements in the way crime is measured, we do not know precisely how much crime has increased. Growth occurred, but not the explosion as often indicated. Those same structural changes that created distortions in the perception of crime and modifications in its definition also weakened traditional and quite effective social control mechanisms. The breakdown of stable family and neighborhood ties and the move toward a society of strangers contributed to a rise in the number of crimes committed. This argument will be advanced in more detail later in this book.

NOTES

1. Adolfo L. Paez, "Criminal Victimization, 1983," Bureau of Justice Statistics Bulletin, U.S. Department of Justice, June 1984, p. 1.

2. Alan F. Hoskin et al., *Accident Facts, 1984* (Chicago: National Safety Council, 1983), p. 2.

3. Insurance Information Institute, *Insurance Facts, 1981–1982* (New York), p. 54.

4. Patsy Klaus, "Victims of Crime," Bureau of Justice Statistics Bulletin, U.S. Department of Justice, November 1981, p. 2.

5. Michael R. Rand, "Households Touched by Crime, 1983," Bureau of Justice Statistics Bulletin, U.S. Department of Justice, p. 1.

6. Adolfo L. Paez, *Criminal Victimization in the United States, 1981,* U.S. Department of Justice, November 1983, pp. 22, 15–16.

7. Rand, "Households Touched by Crime, 1983," p. 2.

8. Federal Bureau of Investigation, *Crime in the United States—Uniform Crime Reports, 1982* (Washington, D.C.: Government Printing Office, 1983), p. 6. Since the National Crime Survey does not report murders, the UCR probably contain the best data about murder.

9. U.S. Bureau of the Census, *Statistical Abstracts of the United States, 1984,* 104th ed. (Washington, D.C., 1983), p. 78.

10. Hoskin et al., *Accident Facts,* p. 8.

11. FBI, *Crime in the United States—1982,* p. 11.

12. Hoskin et al., *Accident Facts,* p. 7.

13. Paez, "Criminal Victimization, 1983," p. 2.

14. Michael R. Rand, "Violent Crime by Strangers," Bureau of Justice Statistics Bulletin, U.S. Department of Justice, April 1982.

15. Paez, *Criminal Victimization in the United States, 1981,* pp. 23, 44.

16. Ibid., p. 23.

17. Charles Silberman, *Criminal Violence, Criminal Justice* (New York: Vintage Books, 1980), p. 7.

18. Paez, *Criminal Victimization in the United States, 1981,* p. 23.

19. *Insurance Facts,* p. 54.

20. Hoskin et al., *Accident Facts,* p. 79.

21. Paez, *Criminal Victimization in the United States, 1981,* p. 60.

22. Ibid., p. 22.

23. Hoskin et al., *Accident Facts,* p. 3.

24. Paez, *Criminal Victimization in the United States, 1981,* p. 57.

68

Crime Problem

25. National Criminal Justice Information and Statistics Service, *Myths and Realities About Crime*, U.S. Department of Justice, 1978, pp. 26–27.

26. Computed from statistics provided by Paez, *Criminal Victimization in the United States, 1981*, pp. 62, 63.

27. Ibid., pp. 62–63, 44.

28. Ibid., p. 62.

29. Paez, "Criminal Victimization, 1983," pp. 1–2.

30. Rand, "Households Touched by Crime," p. 2.

31. Paez, "Criminal Victimization, 1983," p. 3.

32. *Insurance Facts*, p. 64.

33. Computed from 1982 gross national product of $3,073 billion. U.S. Bureau of the Census, *Statistical Abstracts, 1984*, p. 448.

34. Marshall B. Clinard, *Illegal Corporate Behavior*, U.S. Department of Justice (Washington, D.C.: Government Printing Office, 1979), p. 3.

35. U.S. Bureau of the Census, *Statistical Abstracts, 1984*, p. 459.

36. Ibid., p. 316.

37. Paez, "Criminal Victimization, 1983," p. 4.

38. Ibid., p. 3.

39. Ibid., p. 4.

40. Paez, *Criminal Victimization in the United States, 1981*, p. 65.

41. Ibid., p. 23.

42. Ibid.

43. *Insurance Facts*, p. 54.

44. Sue Titus Reid, *Crime and Criminology* (New York: Holt, Rinehart & Winston, 1982), p. 247.

45. *Insurance Facts*, pp. 44, 49.

46. Paez, *Criminal Victimization in the United States, 1981*, p. 66.

47. United Nations, *Demographic Yearbook* (New York: United Nations Publishing Service, 1973), reviewed by Hugh D. Barlow, *Criminology*, 2nd ed. (Boston: Little, Brown, 1981), pp. 110–111.

48. William J. Chambliss, "The Crime Menace in the Hands of Politics," unpublished manuscript, University of Delaware, 1983.

49. Daniel Bell, "The Myth of Crime Waves," *The End of Ideology* (New York: Collier Books, 1960), p. 151; quoted in Thomas E. Cronin, Tania Z. Cronin, and Michael E. Milakovich, *U.S. Crime in the Streets* (Bloomington: Indiana University Press, 1981), p. 9.

50. Paez, *Criminal Victimization in the United States, 1981*, pp. 24, 38.

51. News release about crime and the elderly, Bureau of Justice Statistics, U.S. Department of Justice, January 17, 1982, p. 3.

52. Paez, *Criminal Victimization in the United States, 1981*, p. 24.

53. Ibid., pp. 23, 45.

54. Ibid., p. 27.

55. Ibid., pp. 29, 38, 60.
56. Ibid., pp. 25, 26.
57. Michael J. Hindelang, Michael R. Gottfredson, and James Garofalo, *Victims of Personal Crime: An Empirical Foundation for a Theory of Personal Victimization* (Cambridge, Mass.: Ballinger Publishing Co., 1978), pp. 121–124.
58. Ibid., pp. 246–247.
59. Ibid., pp. 246–248.
60. Ibid., p. 248.
61. Ibid., pp. 249–250.
62. Ibid., pp. 250–266.

5

Fear of Crime

So crime, particularly violent and predatory crime, is not as common as often thought. Then why are people so concerned? Noted social analyst and critic Charles Silberman argues that crime is uniquely debilitating because it destroys feelings of security and the sense of interpersonal trust that binds a community together. He states: "Quite apart from the physical injuries and financial losses incurred, fear of crime is destroying the network of relationships on which urban and suburban life depends."[1] But Silberman fails to reckon with the origin of these public sentiments. No genetic code determines the nature of crime. It is not innate; it is *learned*. So while Silberman's interpretation may be an accurate description of what is happening, it is not a given. Americans are taught to be afraid of violent crime, and the constant promotion of the problem by the shapers of public opinion directly influences their attitudes and beliefs. Citizens could just as easily be indoctrinated to fear and hate drunken drivers, since they kill more people each year than murderers.

So where does fear come from? How does it develop? Is it related to victimization patterns, so that those most often victimized are the most fearful?

WHO IS FEARFUL

Clear but perhaps unexpected differences have been discovered among different sex, race, education, occupation, and income groups. As might be expected, women are more afraid of crime than men; women feel less safe in their homes and walking alone at night. This is interesting, since men are twice as likely to be victims of violent crime. Women must either avoid high-crime situations out of fear or be afraid out of proportion to actual incidence patterns. The crime of rape may play an important role in this relationship. Though rape is a low-probability incident, its effect can be so devastating that it may be worthy of the fear women appear to have of it. Men, who are not raped, are not constrained by such fear.

Nonwhites and people who are less educated, of lower occupational status, or with lower incomes face much higher probabilities of victimization and appropriately are more fearful of crime. Only 1 in 7 whites report they are afraid in their own homes at night, whereas 1 in 4 nonwhites are fearful. Similar patterns hold for occupational status and income and education levels. Only about 1 in 10 of those ranked in the top status for any of the three characteristics are fearful, as compared with 1 in 4 of people ranked in the lowest status.[2]

One might argue that variations in fear depend on the sense of vulnerability, real or imagined, that people have. Women perceive themselves to be physically more vulnerable to criminal victimization, and even though their rate of victimization is not as high as that of men, they are more afraid than men. The poor and minorities are also fearful, but because they are exposed to more crime and face a greater chance of being a victim, fear is based on a true sense of vulnerability, whereas women's fear is based on *perceived* vulnerability. It follows that the elderly will be unrealistically afraid of crime because of their physical vulnerability, and that people living in larger, more crime-ridden cities will be appropriately more fearful than people living in less populated and less criminogenic areas.

But public-opinion research has not confirmed this idea. The elderly are no more fearful in their homes or walking alone at night than younger people. Similarly, people living in cities of different sizes varied little in their fear at home. In fact, slightly more people living in rural areas stated they were afraid than people living in the nation's largest cities. However, residents of larger cities are more likely to indicate there are places near their home where they are afraid to walk alone at night.[3]

Vulnerability alone, perceived or real, is not sufficient to explain why people are fearful of criminal victimization. At times, levels of fear are consistent with victimization patterns, but at other times they are not. Physical vulnerability may explain why women are more fearful than men, but not why the elderly are no more fearful than younger people. Other factors must enter into the opinion-formation process. So Crime Myth 4, "People who are most vulnerable to crime have the greatest fear," like the other myths, is more complex.

The inconsistencies in public attitudes about crime and in fear of crime are clear in the views different groups have about punishment. Women, who as a group are less likely to be victimized but who are more fearful of crime than their male counterparts, are less likely to believe the courts are not harsh enough and less likely to advocate capital punishment. Blacks, the young, and those with lower occupational status, less education, and lower income, who are both more likely to be victims and are more fearful (except for the young), also tend to be less punitive. People who can be characterized as white, college educated, professional, Republicans, or Christians—that is, people least likely to be victims—are the most likely to favor harsher sentences and to support the death penalty.[4] This defies common sense and indicates that attitudes about crime and its control are determined by factors other than the actual threat of crime.

WHY PEOPLE FEAR CRIME

Experts, as well as the general public, believe that fear of crime is individually debilitating and socially deleterious. That is Crime Myth 5, "Fear of crime is reducing social cohesiveness and deteriorating the modern urban community."

Sociologists Frank Clemente and Michael Kleiman elaborate on this idea:

[The] cost of crime goes far beyond the economic and physical losses imposed by criminals. It extends to the forced alteration of daily living habits as well as the negative psychological effects of living in a state of constant anxiety. Further, fear of crime has a deleterious effect on the general social order. As fear becomes manifest in the avoidance of strangers, sociability, mutual trust and the willingness to help others disappear. Such phenomena signify a serious erosion in the quality of life in the United States.[5]

In observing signs of fear and social deterioration, Clemente and Kleiman see a causal relationship between the two events: fear causes social deterioration. Like other social scientists, however, Clemente and Kleiman do not know the direction of causality. The simultaneous occurrence of two events may be observed and, based on experience, the direction of the relationship may be asserted, but the assertion cannot be proven correct. In the case of Clemente and Kleiman's claim, they logically propose, on initial consideration, that fear causes deterioration, but this assessment is myopic because it ignores the possibility that social deterioration may cause fear. Considerable evidence supports this possibility. And if the reverse of this generally accepted view is true, then our perception of fear is placed in a very different light.

The first hint criminologists had of this possibility came when they were studying the nature of fear. Crime researchers Hindelang, Gottfredson, and Garofalo found that people tend to depersonalize crime. They believe it to be a problem in other places but do not perceive it to affect them directly. People view crime as a nonlocal, nonpersonal issue.[6]

Using results from a survey of fear administered in eight cities along with the 1972 National Crime Survey, Hindelang and his colleagues tested the depersonalization hypothesis in several contexts. When asked whether crime is increasing, almost everyone states that it is increasing on a national level, but fewer than half believe it to be increasing in their own neighborhood. Furthermore, people view crime outside the neighborhood to be of a more serious variety—generally violent personal crime—while that within is seen as less serious property crime. In comparing crime in their own neighborhood with that of other neighborhoods in the same metropolitan area, few people, even those residing in what are considered high-crime areas, view their own community to be more dangerous. People also perceive the deleterious effects of crime as a nonlocal problem. Almost all individuals believe that people in general limit their activities out of fear, over half believe that residents of their own neighborhood alter their behavior, but fewer than half state that they personally have changed their lifestyles. People also depersonalize crime by believing that outsiders—nonresidents—commit most offenses within the neighborhood. Even victims of crime, who as expected view their own community more negatively than nonvictims, cling to the notion that crime is worse elsewhere.[7]

Based on these findings, people clearly disassociate themselves from the reality and the possibility of criminal victimization. This allows them to feel removed and thus secure from potential harm. But an interesting question arises. Do people, in depersonalizing crime, overestimate national trends or underestimate the local situations? Either possibility has liabilities. If people overestimate the national crime problem, they may support public policies to control crime that are unnecessary. If they minimize their own situation, their concern may not reflect the seriousness of the problem, and their apathy may lead to a perfunctory response to it.

Hindelang and his colleagues argue that overestimation is more likely. People are aware of what goes on in their own community, its dangers and its problems. They know what to expect and what areas to avoid. Consequently, they have a more realistic perception of the crime problem in their own neighborhood. Response patterns to the survey confirmed this idea. Regardless of age, sex, income, race, and other characteristics, people view crime as restricting the behavior of people in general, yet when asked whether they limited their own activities, important differences were found among the groups. This suggests that, as the frame of reference becomes more specific, individuals relate the issue to personal experiences and provide more accurate information about their own situation.[8]

Since people do not directly experience the situations in other communities, they rely on second parties—often the mass media—to describe what goes on elsewhere. Yet the media, as already discussed, sensationalize crime news by reporting the violent, gruesome, and provocative crimes. Since the media draws stories from all over the nation, more unusually violent incidents are reported from "other" places than from any single locality. Crime appears to be much worse in other places, and people end up with a distorted view of crime in the nation.

Depersonalization also reflects distrust of the unfamiliar, a tendency to fear that which is not understood. A similar reaction occurs whenever any unfamiliar situation is faced, whether it is attending a cocktail party where few people are known, learning "new" math or a foreign language, or finding one's way out of a dark, unfamiliar cellar. If a person does not know what to expect, his or her reaction is likely to be negative, for unfamiliarity breeds fear. Consequently, people evaluate unfamiliar places negatively.

A final factor contributing to the depersonalization of crime is a tendency to believe "it can never happen to me." Much like automobile drivers who forego the necessity of seat belts, drive while intoxicated, and weave in and out of rush-hour traffic with reckless abandon, people refuse to recognize the possibility of criminal victimization. With so many information sources describing the situation as out of control, it may be necessary to deny the possibility of personal victimization in order to cope. Otherwise, people would find it difficult ever to leave the confines of their homes and to feel safe and secure.

What these findings say to Clemente and Kleiman is that fear may not have such a great deteriorative effect after all. The public hears and reads about how bad the crime problem is throughout the nation and believes it to be so. They perceive that the American way of life is undermined by it. Since it appears that crime is out of hand, the nation must be going downhill. Consequently, the public demands that something be done, that the system "get tough" and be more punitive. But we must remember that people form these opinions on an abstract level. They feel safer in their own neighborhoods. They fear the outsider and the other neighborhoods.

On the other hand, recent changes in many communities may have contributed to unrealistic, negative perceptions of crime even within neighborhoods. Increased mobility and changes in employment patterns (particularly increasing numbers of commuters) have weakened perceptions of one's place and familiarity within the community (both as a geographic area and as a group of people related by residence). Neighbors are less likely to know one another intimately and more likely to be strangers. Social diversity, including different ethnic backgrounds, lifestyles, religious practices, and other related characteristics, have increased in many communities, so that which is unknown and unfamiliar within a neighborhood has also increased. Yet, as we just discovered, *unfamiliarity breeds fear*. Consequently, increasing numbers of people believe that they are even more vulnerable right in their own neighborhoods. The statement by Marvin Harris that "it is not the same old America"[9] is appropriate, but increasing crime and fear have not changed neighborhood environments. Changing neighborhood environments have created even greater fear and insecurity.

A study of the effect of crime on fear, by Dan Lewis and Michael Maxfield, substantiates and clarifies this argument. Residents of four Chicago neighborhoods were surveyed to determine how accurately their fear of crime paralleled official statistics. Their perceptions of dangerous areas within their own neighborhoods generally matched official records, but anomalies in perception were found when residents attempted to describe their neighborhood's specific crime problem and to ascertain the risk they personally faced. Lewis and Maxfield determined that, rather than reflecting neighborhood conditions as expressed by crime statistics, perceptions were determined by the level of *incivility* found in the community. In other words, signs of disorder, including abandoned buildings, vandalism, drug use, and loitering teenagers, exacerbated fear. Negative community attributes suggest to citizens that social controls are weak and lead them to a logical but not always accurate perception of crime. Signs of incivility may have little to do with official crime rates. Fear of crime is thus triggered by a broad range of neighborhood conditions and to a certain extent is independent of the official rate of crime. If incivility is not viewed as a problem, then people appear to be able to cope with higher levels of crime.[10]

The study by Lewis and Maxfield is important to the arguments posed in this chapter. To the extent that neighborhoods have deteriorated in recent years, fear of crime would be expected to increase. As visible signs of disorder appeared in American cities—more graffiti on buildings, buses, and subways, burned-out buildings, kids standing around with blasting radios, drunks and derelicts lying in the streets—fear of crime mounted, not necessarily because crime had increased but because the environment had changed. Indeed, it is not the same old America.

The circularity of effects should be clear. As American communities changed, fear of the unfamiliar and unknown, and consequently that of crime, rose. As a result, when people encounter illegal acts they are more likely to call the police, out of fear, whereas in the past, when the situation did not contain the element of unfamiliarity, the issue would be handled informally. So increasing fear is a cause of acceleration in *reported* crime when the actual incidence of crime has remained stable.

The relationship of fear to incivility has important implications for policymakers and law enforcers. Ways of ameliorating fear, other than directly reducing crime, should be sought. Urban cleanup and renewal may actually be more viable methods of controlling the effects of crime than an actual reduction of incidence itself. Also, those aspects of the crime problem which influence the public's sense of safety may be the aspects that law enforcement agencies tend to ignore. Local codes concerning abandoned buildings, unsightly graffiti, and other forms of vandalism are often not strictly enforced. There is little effort put into discouraging teenagers from hanging out in the streets and disturbing other neighborhood residents, and there are few attempts to reduce visible drug and alcohol consumption. Think about it for a moment. As you drive through your own city, are you more likely to lock the doors of your car in a quiet suburban neighborhood or in one with various signs of disorder? It just might be that the symptoms are the cause, rather than the indicators, of a worse situation.

CONCLUSIONS

Many people believe that crime and violence threaten the American system and their way of life. Crime and violence are

perceived to be increasing and becoming more vicious and irrational, but the crime problem is being blown out of proportion.
To an extent, these fabrications can be blamed on sensationalism
by the mass media and exaggeration by the law enforcement
establishment. But changes in communities and lifestyles have
also contributed to fear among the public.

The social upheaval of the 1960s has produced extensive
changes. Neighborhoods and life in American communities have
changed; many ethnic and racial boundaries and barriers have
been removed; with the influx of more women into the labor
force, a larger portion of the population now works outside the
home; authority is being more readily challenged, particularly
by young people; traditional values are no longer accepted, or
at least are being questioned; the underclass, though possibly
smaller, is more distinctive and firmly entrenched. Each of these
factors has changed the American community in different ways.

We no longer find the stability there once was. Neighbors are
not acquainted, ethnic solidarity with geographic areas is not
present, and fewer people are in the neighborhood during the
day. These changes have made the population feel more isolated
and increasingly unable or unwilling to deal with problems as
individuals. Now more than ever before, Americans live in a
society of strangers where interpersonal problems must be dealt
with by formal means. With this, an important basis for personal
security—familiarity—has been lost. As a result, the sense of
control has decreased and fear has risen.

Given the events that have transpired, one might hope for a
return to a way of life known in the past, but such stepping
back into history is impossible. Social changes that have occurred—many of which are positively valued by most people—
cannot and should not be undone. It is not the same old America,
nor should it be. It is important that the present status not be
evaluated with viewpoints that are no longer appropriate. Crime
is not increasing, but the sense of insecurity is. We must come
to grips with this issue and not allow it to become an issue blown
out of perspective.

NOTES

1. Charles Silberman, *Criminal Violence, Criminal Justice* (New York:
Vintage Books, 1980), pp. 16, 18.

2. Michael J. Hindelang, Michael R. Gottfredson, and Timothy J. Flanagan, eds., *Sourcebook of Criminal Justice Statistics—1980*. U.S. Department of Justice, Bureau of Justice Statistics (Washington, D.C.: Government Printing Office, 1981), pp. 172, 174.

3. Ibid.

4. Ibid., pp. 196–197, 200–201.

5. Frank Clemente and Michael B. Kleiman, "Fear of Crime in the United States: A Multivariate Analysis," *Social Forces* 56 (December 1977): 520.

6. Michael J. Hindelang, Michael R. Gottfredson, and James Garofalo, *Victims of Personal Crime: An Empirical Foundation for a Theory of Personal Victimization* (Cambridge, Mass.: Ballinger Publishing Co., 1978), pp. 153–173.

7. Ibid.

8. Ibid.

9. Marvin Harris, "Why Its Not the Same Old America," *Psychology Today* 15 (August 1981): 22.

10. Dan A. Lewis and Michael G. Maxfield, "Fear in the Neighborhood: An Investigation of the Impact of Crime," *Journal of Research in Crime and Delinquency* 17 (July 1980): 160–189.

PART TWO

Crime and the Criminal-Justice System

6

Fighting Crime

Two general perceptions about crime and its control guide the policies and activities of the law enforcement establishment and the criminal-justice system. The first perception, that crime is worse today than in the past, is fueled by official statistics of reported crime. Although most local law enforcement officials understand the problems with official statistics, they still rely on them. When the Uniform Crime Reports are published, local officials comment on the changes from the previous year and try to explain why their community experiences more or less crime than other cities. But one never hears a police chief claim that the FBI figures do not provide an accurate representation of crime in the community or the nation. That would raise questions about the accuracy of local figures. More important, the psychology and emotional circumstances of law enforcement contribute to a belief that crime is increasing.

Police departments are closed organizations whose members often become emotionally cut off from the rest of society. Many new recruits are attracted to the occupation by a sense of social responsibility and a desire to make the community a better and safer place in which to live. Those dreams are often quickly frustrated as the rookie police officer develops a cynical attitude about people which is common among other members of the force. Police officers are continually faced with human misery, cruelty, and degradation, which begin to take an important place in their world view. An officer's feelings are amplified by the isolation he or she feels as social contacts outside the department become strained. People react negatively to the occupation and its authority even when a police officer is off duty. As a result, a strong sense of a we/they dichotomy develops.

Psychologically as well as organizationally, this part of police work makes it possible to accept the suggestion that crime is worsening. It follows that one harboring a negative view of human nature would expect community life to degenerate. Many of the daily experiences of police work exacerbate this attitude: having to inform a murder victim's family of the tragedy; investigating the brutal rape of a child; arresting some people over and over, just to see them freed. Police officers are not immune to the effects of incivility either. As they patrol an area and observe it succumbing to urban deterioration, or face teenagers who progressively defy their authority, they feel the effects of these visible signs and because of their orientation are inclined to view them as indicating that control is being lost. It follows that there would be a corresponding increase in crime.

Despite these opinions, members of the law enforcement establishment as well as others in the criminal-justice field cling to a belief that improvements can be made. This is the second perception that plays a significant role in guiding the system. It is expected that if "appropriate" actions are taken the system will be able to stall the tide of rising crime and make communities safer. Police officers believe that the system, if given the necessary resources and allowed the freedom to attack the problem as seen fit, can fulfill its mission of crime control. This expectation is based on a possibly unrealistic assumption that crime is a solvable problem for which some action or change can be taken to reduce or preclude criminal acts.

What is gained by constantly stating that the criminal-justice system is failing to control crime while at the same time claiming that with appropriate incentives and new directions it can succeed? Would criminal-justice officials consciously deceive the American public, or do they also deceive themselves? One thing is certain, that Crime Myth 6 "Criminal-justice officials understand the causes of crime and are motivated solely by a desire to attack those problems to reduce crime," is at best an oversimplification.

HOOVER AND THE DEVELOPMENT OF THE FBI

A look at how the Federal Bureau of Investigation changed from a meager law enforcement agency with limited responsibilities at the turn of the century to a major federal institution with tremendous powers may help us understand why the criminal-justice system fosters the crime myth. With offices in almost every city throughout the nation, the FBI operates on an annual budget of about $800 million.[1] For many Americans, the Bureau represents the apex of law enforcement. Its personnel are considered to be unrivaled as crime fighters. Agents undergo extensive training and achieve the highest levels of law enforcement professionalism. The Bureau avails itself of the latest and most scientifically sophisticated technological advances. Yet the immortalization of its activities may be owed more to the image created by Efrem Zimbalist, Jr.'s portrayal of its activities on television than to a realistic assessment of its successes.

The Bureau of Investigation, which did not change its name to the Federal Bureau of Investigation until 1935, was established by Congress in 1908 as an agency to control interstate commerce and to enforce the Sherman Antitrust Act.[2] The prevailing belief at its inception was that law enforcement was a state and local prerogative in which the federal government had no role, yet interstate commerce and antitrust activities were considered to be sufficiently unique to warrant federal intervention. The agency was established to enforce laws that had to do with fair business practices whose effects were national in scope. The Bureau's jurisdiction was created by federal legislation, and the laws it enforced were different from those with which state and local agencies were commonly concerned. Yet it was not long before the Bureau began to transform its role by continually expanding its jurisdiction to include a range of offenses. The first opportunity for such a step came in 1910, when Congress passed the Mann Act (popularly known as the White Slave Traffic Act), outlawing the transportation of females across state lines for immoral purposes. When the Mann Act was passed, no agency was given responsibility for enforcing it, but the Bureau quickly accepted the challenge and requested funds from Congress to proceed. There was opposition to this move by some members of Congress, who argued that the Bureau's activities would duplicate the work of state and local officials. The director of the Bureau informed Congress that states and localities were lax in their enforcement efforts and that only the Bureau could get the job done. Funding was secured, and the agency's operations were expanded to every city where vice was found.[3]

Even during these early years, the Bureau did not restrict its enforcement activities to interstate prostitution but became involved in the investigation and enforcement of various vice offenses. By volunteering its assistance to local agencies, it extended its function even further. The Bureau slowly carved out an advisory role, often taking an active part in the investigation of crimes but urging local departments to make actual arrests because federal laws may not have been broken.[4] In this way the agency gained the acceptance and support of local law enforcement officials and did not threaten their sense of territoriality. The Dyer Act of 1919, making interstate transportation of stolen vehicles a federal crime, broadened the scope and consequently the power of the Bureau by expanding its jurisdiction beyond business crime and vice to include theft. This legislation set the precedent for the FBI's claim to a legitimate responsibility to enforce any law concerned with a criminal act involving more than one state.

Perhaps the single most important factor in the development of the fledgling Bureau was its wartime involvement in the investigation of individuals and groups thought to pose a threat to domestic security. As an existing federal agency with investigative experience, it was the logical choice for the task of counterespionage at the onset of World War I. The Bureau willingly took on the responsibility, but it did not limit its activities to catching international spies and instead sought to quash any threat to the war effort. It carried out raids on various radical groups and seized membership lists and official publications of such groups. This responsibility allowed the Bureau to grow substantially. Upon the signing of the armistice in 1918, an agency spokesman assured Congress that the Bureau's budget could be reduced to its prewar level. Its wartime responsibilities were ended, and the interstate commercial operations in vice had been brought under control. It could resume its position as a modest agency with limited enforcement activities, and primary responsibility for law enforcement would be left to state and local authorities.

This, of course, did not occur. Diminution was checked by the advent of peacetime radicalism.[5] A Bureau agent, Archibald E. Stevenson, informed congressional leaders and citizens that radicals were "agitating on the subject of war and peace and undermining what the American Army accomplished on the battlefield."[6] A series of bombs sent through the U.S. mails to government officials and private citizens legitimized these claims and showed that there was a need for the Bureau. The antiradical division was created in August 1919, and J. Edgar Hoover was appointed as its chief (a post he occupied until 1921, when he became assistant Bureau director and then, in 1925, chief).[7]

To track the bombers, the Bureau undertook its most ambitious manhunt, which eventually extended into six foreign countries. Rather than reducing the Bureau's budget, as predicted, Congress was asked to increase appropriations in 1919. The following conversation took place during the budget hearing:

Attorney General Palmer: . . . Please do not cut this appropriation down even if you think it is too big. . . . We must let these people know that we mean business.

Congressman Vare (Pennsylvania): . . . You believe that the moral effect of a large appropriation will have considerable value at this time?

Palmer: I do. It will show these men that we are going to the limit.[8]

The "Red Scare" of the 1920s was the first time the Bureau contributed to and played on public hysteria regarding domestic tranquillity. Its intelligence system fed the public with information suggesting that radicalism and radicals threatened the American way of life. Pacifists, socialists, anarchists, and Bolsheviks became targets of investigation. Even the National Civil Liberties Bureau (later to become the American Civil Liberties Union) was raided for supporting the right of radicals to agitate.[9]

The Bureau did not hesitate long before moving beyond track-ing mail bombers to investigating other organizations thought to foster unrest. Labor unions, particularly the Industrial Work-ers of the World (IWW), were foremost among these groups. From 1921 to 1924, the General Intelligence Division of the Bu-reau focused on the American labor movement, maintaining close surveillance of its activities and actively opposing and sup-pressing strikes.[10] It is ironic that an agency created to control illegal business activities would realign itself in just over a decade with industrial leaders and under the guise of combating com-munism seek to suppress the labor movement.

To suggest that Bureau officials fostered the belief that the Communist movement posed a threat to American life solely out of self-interest would be an overstatement. Organizations already in place and currently employing people are capable of finding tasks to occupy their attention, and the FBI is no excep-tion. At the end of World War I, it sought something—some cause, some activity—to investigate and enforce, since that is what the people who worked for the Bureau knew how to do. This function was consistent with the Bureau's self-concept as the national law enforcement agency dedicated to protecting the morals and beliefs of American society. Given the Bureau's his-tory with subversives, peacetime radicals of the 1920s were a perfect subject, and it was an easy transition to investigating noncriminals believed to pose a threat to national security.

The Bureau's free investigative rein did not go unnoticed and unchallenged. Opposition to its increasing assumption of secret operations to check political opinions of the citizenry steadily mounted during the early 1920s. Congress initiated an investi-gation of the Bureau's activities but later discovered that the Bureau, in retaliation, had initiated its own counterinvestigation into the private lives and activities of senators and representa-tives. The affairs of congressmen in Washington as well as in their home states were monitored. Agents kept these men (an unknown but probably sizable number) under surveillance and trailed visitors to their congressional offices, investigated them for official misconduct and moral impropriety, and even ex-amined their mail, personal papers, and files. It became clear to a senate committee that this activity was intended to intimidate

Congress and enemies of the Bureau who might threaten its power and survival.[11]

The appointments of J. Edgar Hoover as director of the Bureau and Harlan Stone as U.S. attorney general in the mid-1920s appeared to change the direction of the Bureau. After an awkward beginning characterized by internal corruption and poor leadership, the FBI sought to enhance its public image and to gain congressional support for its activities. Hoover achieved this by professionalizing the agency, and through his relationship with many national leaders he made the Bureau one of the most powerful agencies in the federal government.[12]

Hoover created the most professional police force in the world, rivaled only by Scotland Yard in reputation. The Bureau became the best equipped, best trained, and best financed police bureaucracy. Through Hoover's leadership, numerous innovations in law enforcement techniques were made. A training academy unsurpassed anywhere was established, and the Bureau got considerable recognition from such programs as the Uniform Crime Reporting Program, the "ten most wanted" list, and comprehensive criminal statistics.[13]

Hoover had a strong sense of moral indignation and individual responsibility, and he incorporated this into his work to improve the FBI. He viewed criminals as the lowest form of human existence, describing them as "scum from the boiling pot of the underworld," "public rats," "lowest dregs of society," and "vermin in human form."[14] Hoover wanted to rid the nation of criminals, believing that citizens should be free from the degradation and exploitation of vile criminal behavior. He stated that the FBI was there to aid in this war: "For those who deliberately step over the boundary into the realm of viciousness, I can only repeat that the F.B.I. stands ready and willing to give its utmost aid to the other law enforcement bodies of the nation, to pursue relentlessly and prosecute fully—and to fearlessly meet the challenge of the underworld even though it means a war to the death."[15]

Some less noble and more self-centered activities of the FBI under Hoover's leadership should be recognized. Hoover was aware of the politics involved in running a large federal agency, and he stopped at nothing to preserve its well-being. Numerous examples of when survival and growth replaced crime control as the primary goal of the agency are evident in Hoover's tenure as director.

One way the FBI maintained a favorable image under Hoover's administration was by selecting enforcement activities that brought public attention to the agency. In the 1930s it activities were focused on a few desperate but relatively successful bank robbers who roamed the depression-ridden country. People like "Ma" Barker and "Pretty Boy" Floyd became famous not only by their own exploits but by the massive manhunts engineered by the FBI to track them down. With dramatic flair, Hoover left his administrative duties to take charge of some investigations. The Bureau's involvement and success in these cases drew attention to it. Interviews by the national media gave Hoover an opportunity to recount the need for the FBI's expertise and to praise its successes. As a result, the agency flourished and achieved a reputation as the nation's elite law enforcement agency.

At the onset of World War II, domestic security surfaced once again as an issue of national law enforcement, and the FBI began to track Nazis. This involvement led to renewed surveillance and investigation of various radical organizations. A set of files (referred to as "noncriminal" and "civil" files), which contained information and fingerprints of people with no criminal record, were established. Employers were encouraged to fingerprint employees and send their prints to the FBI, fingerprints from the public were solicited in local campaigns, and the police were encouraged to send fingerprints taken not only from criminals but also from arrested strikers and those taken into custody for public intoxication, brawling, creating a nuisance, and vagrancy. The agency tried to obtain access to the 1940 census information but failed. This time, even the postal inspectors and Treasury enforcement agencies expressed disapproval of the Bureau's attempt to increase its dossiers.[16]

A Senate investigative committee in 1941 cited the FBI for two forms of wrongdoing: maintenance of a spy system over persons who had committed no crime but whose political beliefs and activities were intolerable to Bureau officials, and the use of illegal practices against individuals accused of crimes.[17] Little came of this report because the demands of World War II drew attention from the Bureau's improprieties and allowed it to increase its covert activities even further. These practices continued throughout the 1950s, when Hoover and the FBI aligned themselves with Senator Joseph McCarthy to create a national hysteria over communism, and the 1960s, pursuing civil rights leaders and campus radicals.

The Bureau's self-centeredness is revealed in Hoover's refusal to recognize the existence of a national crime syndicate. He was adamant throughout the 1930s, 1940s, 1950s, and most of the 1960s that organized crime did not exist in the United States. As Hank Messick reports:

In the twenties, when city gangs were transformed into regional crime syndicates, Hoover rounded up alleged Reds. In the thirties, when gangsters began bankrolling businessmen and politicians, Hoover chased "Ma" Barker and "Pretty Boy" Floyd. In the Forties, when the National Crime Syndicate operated black markets and established regional gambling centers, Hoover hunted Nazi spies. In the Fifties, as the crime syndicate expanded to Havana and London, Hoover helped [Joe] McCarthy create a national hysteria. In the Sixties, as the syndicate began its crucial transition to respectability, Hoover turned back the clock thirty years and "discovered" La Cosa Nostra.[18]

It was not until 1969 that Hoover aligned himself with Richard Nixon's war on crime, recognized organized crime, and requested 500 additional agents to combat the problem. The following year, Congress authorized an additional 1,000 agents. The FBI grew more under Nixon's administration than ever before, yet an investigation by the *New York Times* discovered that most of the new agents were assigned to college campuses and to investigate bombings and hijackings, not to fight organized crime.[19]

Under Hoover's leadership, the FBI became the most elite police force in the world, but it was also involved in some shady activities. Included among these were the suppression of political activities among groups that Hoover found obnoxious, especially those to the left; interference in labor conflicts; the collection of extensive files on thousands of citizens not convicted of any crime; and participation in illegal activities. Why would a revered law enforcement agency become involved in such activities? It served the agency's interest in that it protected the FBI from outside interference and promoted its growth. As suggested by Chambliss and Seidman, "an organization and its members tend to substitute for the official goal and norms of the organization, ongoing policies and activities which will maximize the rewards and minimize the strains for the organization."[20]

This history of the FBI reflects a curious mixture of public service and self-interest. To ensure its survival and growth, the Bureau investigated sensational crimes that would draw public attention, aligned itself with business instead of labor, and bullied congressmen with damaging information collected through secret surveillance. It became the best-trained, best-equipped, and best-financed law enforcement bureaucracy in the world.

Despite its growth, crime has not been reduced. According to the Bureau's own statistics, crime increased steadily throughout Hoover's tenure. This might lead one to conclude that the Bureau had failed in its mission, but throughout his career Hoover consistently identified two problems that prevented a reduction of crime: leniency and lack of resources. A revealing interchange between Senator McKellar and Chief Hoover occurred at a budget hearing in 1935:

McKellar: . . . Do you not think we ought to reduce the amount that we have allowed you? . . . In 1936, you asked for $15,000,000, which is almost double what you spent in 1934, and a tremendous increase over the budget estimate of 1935. . . . It seems to me your Department is just running wild, Mr. Hoover.

Hoover: May I point this out, Senator? There were a series of crime bills—the kidnapping statute, the extortion statute, the bank robbery statute, the fugitive law, the stolen-property law, and several others enacted by Congress, which have greatly increased our work.[21]

Perhaps it is coincidental that Hoover actively supported this legislation. One cannot help but wonder whether crime control is subordinate to the goal of organizational survival.

A BUREAUCRATIC EXPLANATION OF
INCREASING CRIME

Self-interest is seldom recognized as a motivation of those charged with control of crime. It is assumed that *criminals* act out of self-interest, out of a desire for economic gain, but a similar motive is seldom attributed to law enforcers.[22] Yet our review of the history of the FBI reveals that organizational self-interest was an important theme in the agency's development. Its steady growth and expanded responsibilities and powers can be attributed partially to its successes, its professionalism, and its ability to stay at the forefront of the field technologically, but throughout its history officials fought to protect the agency and to maintain a favorable public image.

The recognition of self-interest as an important motivational factor is not new. To the English philosopher Thomas Hobbes, self-interest was the most important factor in motivating people, because the instinct for self-preservation lies behind all human activities. Hobbes saw life as precarious and a constant struggle for survival. Since any security that may be achieved can quickly be lost, Hobbes argued, there is "a perpetual and relentless desire for power after power" to assure some self-protection. Security is the desired result of self-interest, but because of its own tenuous nature it can never be fully achieved and therefore acts as a constant and ongoing source of motivation.[23]

This perspective is particularly appropriate to an analysis of criminal-justice policy. It could be argued that the system's position is secure because it has a monopoly on the use of force. Since police departments, courts, and penal agencies have few competitors for their responsibilities, this is somewhat true, but the feeling of insecurity is still there. Budgets may be cut, prestige and respect may be lost, and jobs could be eliminated. If the public comes to perceive that the system cannot fulfill its responsibilities, they may advocate its replacement or significant changes in its structure. For this reason, criminal-justice agencies embody the instinct of self-preservation found in most human activities.

This sense of insecurity may be felt most strongly by the law enforcement establishment. As Jon Christensen, Janet Schmidt, and Joel Henderson noted, "The police have recognized that they will grow and be nurtured if they are perceived as crime-fighters but will not if their inability to protect people is revealed."[24] To buttress a tenuous position as a public-service organization, the police consciously create a positive media image by magnifying the importance of their work.

In a case study of police sweeps in San Diego, Christensen and his fellow researchers documented how law enforcement and the newspapers work together to convince the public that the police control crime. From February through August 1977, in what the media labeled a "crime suppression detail," the San Diego Police Department had conducted a series of mass arrests of drug users and sellers, the stated purpose of which was to reduce crime by bringing open drug dealing and drug use under control. The program received considerable media attention, which according to Christensen and his colleagues "gives the appearance of an almost coordinated strategy" between the press and the police. "Large impressive articles introduced the sweeps; then low-key but constant stories tucked in between large photo stories emerged until the press reached its peak. With little new information to milk from the sweeps, the appearance and substance of the articles diminished. The whole process was then terminated on a positive note of police claiming victory and ending the sweeps."[25] The reader was left with the impression that the sweeps were successful, that the city was safer, and that the police were actively controlling crime.

A look at who was arrested during the sweeps leaves one with a very different impression of what was accomplished. Of the 430 arrests made, only 3 were for serious felony crimes. There were 22 people arrested for selling hard drugs. So, in all, only 6 percent of the arrests were for crimes that the sweeps were intended to control. Of the remaining, 21 percent were for selling marijuana, 54 percent were for possessing marijuana, and 11 percent were for other misdemeanors, such as resisting arrest. The rate of serious crime showed absolutely no change because of these efforts. These facts never became an issue in any newspaper report.[26]

Collective interests within organizations are important, but individuals are also motivated by self-interests. As Anthony

Downs suggests in his study of bureaucracy, "We assume that every official acts at least partly in his own interest, and some officials are motivated solely by their own self-interest."[27] Even when some organizational security exists, uncertainty may be created by competition among individuals in an organization. When official crime statistics were manipulated in Washington, D.C., the police department was not threatened, because the department would not be eliminated if the crime rate did not fall. But the people within the organization were insecure; they knew that if crime was not reduced their jobs might be in jeopardy.

This is not to suggest that criminal-justice personnel are devoid of human compassion or motivated solely by self-interest. Police officers risk their lives to arrest violent offenders, public defenders work overtime to represent their clients, jurors deliberate in stuffy rooms for days to arrive at proper verdicts, and probation officers loan clients their own money to help them through troubled times. Altruistic concern is important in determining behavior within the system, yet self-interest is also a factor.[28]

The goal of self-preservation is evidenced by activities that promote organizational survival and expansion. Continuation of the agency to ensure jobs, positions, and continued service delivery is the objective of survival activities. Growth takes us back to Hobbes' observation that self-protection necessitates constant and perpetual search for "power after power." Expansion protects agencies from external threats from larger public bureaucracies that have more political power. This tendency toward growth is evident in the yearly budget requests of criminal-justice agencies. Seldom is an equivalent budget requested; instead, funds for additional personnel and supplies and new programs and projects are included in each year's proposal. This approach to public finance produces growth: the agency becomes larger, its functions are broadened, and greater public dependence is slowly fostered. Over time, these trends firmly establish the organizational function as a public priority, ensuring the power of its officials and the survival of the organization.

In embodying a strong sense of self-preservation, organizations may displace their original purpose with the means to obtain organizational goals. An excellent example of this was provided by David Sills in his study of the National Foundation for Infantile Paralysis. When its original objective of finding a cure for polio was achieved, the foundation turned to a new set of objectives—helping fight birth defects.[29] It survived because people were committed to it as an entity and dependent on it as a source of both self-fulfillment and employment.

Within criminal-justice agencies, goal displacement takes the form of a less aggressive approach to responsibilities in order to maintain organizational strength. To avoid public resentment, police departments refrain from full enforcement of laws. Laws affecting the poor criminal are more often vigorously enforced than those directed toward wealthy embezzlers, polluters, fraudulent investors, and other white-collar criminals. Losing sight of original objectives because of preoccupation with administration issues is not unique to criminal-justice agencies; in fact, it appears to be a common organizational response. Political parties, unions, and other government agencies are similarly burdened.[30]

Organizational self-interest intensifies as an organization is threatened in some way. Peter Blau and Richard Scott suggest that "as long as its very survival is threatened by a hostile environment, [an organization's] officers will seek to strengthen the organization by building up its administration and searching for external sources of support."[31] This position is one in which criminal-justice agencies often find themselves. An excellent example is seen in the reaction of the Los Angeles Police Protection League to Proposition 13 in California. The first Sunday after its passage they ran an $11,678 full-page ad in the *Los Angeles Times* claiming that layoffs "would make it impossible to effectively police [the] city, and as a result, lives will be lost."[32]

Criminal-justice agencies also function within uncertain and often politically precarious environments. Their fates are often decided by politicians who do not have the same interests as members of the organization. In studying the Indianapolis police department, William Selke and Harold Pepinsky found that the department often became caught in a losing situation when politicians made exaggerated claims about how they would control crime. Political candidates who emphasized crime control and a "get tough" approach from 1948 to 1978 (the period studied) consistently created an intractable problem for the police. When such individuals were elected, according to Selke and Pepinsky, a typical scenario follows:

A new disciplinarian chief or public safety director is appointed and the vicious cycle of failure is put in motion again. Fear is rekindled among the public and increased reporting ensues, officer morale sags because of departmental changes, arrest/clearance rates plummet, and citizens and the media are angered and become even more cynical.[33]

The politician may survive the ensuing political turbulence by turning to other issues, but the police always come up losers.

Because criminal-justice agencies are funded within political environments, they must compete with other public organizations for resources. If the public and government officials are convinced that the services of the sanitation or fire department, the educational system, the zoo, or even the providers of defense are more important than criminal justice, then the justice system may suffer fiscal cutbacks. Resources may be reduced, personnel may be laid off, and new equipment may not be provided. These factors contribute to uncertainty within criminal-justice agencies. Officials strengthen their organizational position by showing people that crime is a serious threat to their well-being but that the system can provide needed protection if supported.

To convince citizens that its services are required, the crime control establishment is one of the few organizations that admits and even fabricates its failure. No other public organization gets away with this tactic. If welfare stated publicly that it was unable to help those in need, or the fire department claimed it could not fight fires, the political backlash would be intense, and there would be an investigation, cuts in the budget, major shifts in personnel, and perhaps even elimination of the agency. But the criminal-justice system uniquely utilizes fear. Its failures are qualified by explanations: the courts handcuff the police with procedural safeguards, the system does well with the resources available but the volume of criminal activity exceeds its ability, new methods or programs hold the answer to the problem. Since few alternatives are available to citizens, they cling to the assurances of the system. Most Americans have no direct and personal interest in welfare, so its failure is met with resignation, but because fear of crime is so intense the public is willing to invest further in the potential of law enforcement.

Growth ensures the system's strength as a community agency. Since the volume of criminal activity exceeds the system's ability to control it, increasing the size of the system may improve its ability to fulfill its role. But the criminal-justice system is unique even in this situation. If through expansion the system detects more crimes, the rate of reported crime may increase, producing an image of more rather than less crime. To deal with this problem, agencies that receive additional funds for special programs to control crime manipulate statistics to indicate their success. Pepinsky pointed out that when the federal government was pumping large amounts of money into local anticrime programs (specifically between 1976 and 1978, as the Law Enforcement Assistance Administration [LEAA] shifted its policy from technological development to community crime-prevention assistance), the rate of reported crime dropped.[34] To regenerate the system's ability to expand, the need had to be rekindled by "allowing" the crime rate to increase once again.

Growth within criminal-justice agencies is desirable for other reasons. It increases the power, prestige, and occasionally the income of organizational leaders. Expansion produces new vitality, personnel can improve their status, and new and often more capable people are attracted to the organization. When new opportunities arise, internal conflicts are minimized and morale is maximized.[35] Consider how demoralizing it would be to work where few new ideas are tried, little change occurs, and advancement is unlikely. Such situations generate stagnation and resentment among personnel, and consequently an inferior product or service may be produced. For this reason there is a strong impetus for growth to maintain organizational energy.

The most important factor encouraging growth may be the need to resist external pressure and to control the environment rather than being dominated by it. Large organizations are more resistant to external pressures because they can impose their own will.[36] Given the tremendous size and long traditions of the crime control establishment, it is unlikely that it will be abolished and that something new will be tried. Prisons are a good example. Shortly after the first penitentiary was built during the late 1700s, it was possible to forsake it as the primary method of criminal punishment, but 200 years later, when there are over 1,000 institutions (even though most experts agree they are failures), the investment is too great to abandon them.

As criminal-justice agencies grew, people came to rely on them as means of social control and problem resolution. This in turn allowed the system to make greater demands on the political environment for resources and favorable policy.

CRIME CONTROL IN A COMPETITIVE FISCAL ENVIRONMENT

Given the tendency of the criminal-justice system to act in its own self-interest, like any large bureaucracy, we must ask whether the current public fiscal crisis is creating pressure on agencies to promote their survival. Inflation, by decreasing buying power, hurts criminal-justice agencies just as it hurts a family's budget. If the police department receives the same budget as the year before, adjustments will be necessary: salary increases will not be possible, some people may be laid off, and fewer supplies and equipment can be purchased. Such economic exigencies are painful for any organization; they are demoralizing and reduce the quality and quantity of service delivery. For these reasons they are to be avoided. Like inflation, tax cuts also threaten the economic well-being of criminal-justice agencies. Proposition 13, state budget cuts, and Reaganomics reduce the amount of money allotted to agencies, bringing about the secondary losses noted above.[37]

Since criminal-justice agencies exist within a myriad of public-service organizations, including fire protection, ambulance services, welfare, sanitation, parks and recreation, highways and streets, and health and education, their survival and growth is determined by the competition with these agencies for scarce and relatively fixed resources. If criminal-justice agencies fail to convince government and political decision-makers that their services are needed and that they can protect the public, their ability to compete in this struggle for resources will be limited and they will not fare well in annual budget hearings.

So is it surprising that the crime rate started to go up at the same time public fiscal retrenchments began? Is it difficult to explain why national law enforcement leaders now claim that violence is out of hand and is more random and senseless than ever? Do you wonder why the chief justice of the U.S. Supreme Court recently told Americans that crime control is as important to national defense as the Pentagon's budget? Is it a surprise that criminal-justice personnel are suddenly endorsing a conservative hard-line approach to law enforcement, a direction popular with the public, after being so liberal for so long? Is it possible that criminal-justice officials are afraid that after all these years someone might question whether they really can control crime and would take away their power, prestige, personnel, and position and try something new?

FBI Director William Webster's reaction to the stabilization of crime statistics in 1981 is revealing in this regard:

As we entered the decade of the 1980s the amount of crime reported to law enforcement rose to an all-time high. During 1981, this value remained at the same level. While the stabilization may be interpreted as a social message that law enforcement is holding its own, we must concede that we still have a serious crime problem and one that requires new and better methods to combat.[38]

Even at a time when crime statistics were leveled off, Webster would not allow the American public to be optimistic, choosing to allude to the need for further resources if the law enforcement establishment is to do more than hold its own. The desire for organizational survival and growth cannot be denied.

NOTES

1. Office of Management and Budget, *Budget of the United States Government, Fiscal Year 1983* (Washington, D.C.: Government Printing Office, 1982).

2. Hugh D. Barlow, *Criminology*, 2nd ed. (Boston: Little, Brown, 1981), p. 362.

3. Max Lowenthal, "The Beginning of the Crime-Control Bureau-

cracy," in Isidore Silver, *The Crime-Control Establishment* (Englewood Cliffs, N.J.: Prentice-Hall, 1974), pp. 23–24.

4. Ibid., p. 24.

5. Ibid., pp. 25–27.

6. Ibid., p. 26.

7. Ibid., pp. 27–31.

8. Quoted in ibid., pp. 28–30.

9. Ibid., pp. 26–27.

10. Ibid., pp. 29–31.

11. Ibid., pp. 31–37.

12. James P. Levine, Michael C. Musheno, and Dennis J. Palumbo, *Criminal Justice* (New York: Harcourt Brace Jovanovich, 1980), p. 171.

13. Barlow, *Criminology*, pp. 407–408.

14. Quotations from speeches of J. Edgar Hoover as reviewed by an editorial in the *Journal of Criminal Law and Criminology*, January–February 1938, p. 627, and quoted in Harry Elmer Barnes and Negley K. Teeters, *Criminology* (New York: Prentice-Hall, 1945), p. 634.

15. Speech by J. Edgar Hoover as quoted in Barnes and Teeters, *Criminology*, p. 634.

16. Lowenthal, "The Beginning of the Crime-Control Bureaucracy," pp. 33–35.

17. Ibid., pp. 34–35.

18. As quoted by Jeff Gerth, "The Americanization of 1984," in Richard Quinney, ed., *Criminal Justice in America* (Boston: Little, Brown, 1974), p. 224.

19. Ibid., pp. 224–225.

20. William J. Chambliss and Robert B. Seidman, *Law, Order, and Power* (Reading, Mass.: Addison-Wesley Publishing Co., 1971), p. 266.

21. As quoted in Lowenthal, "The Beginning of the Crime-Control Bureaucracy," pp. 45–46.

22. Levine et al., *Criminal Justice*, p. 171.

23. Thomas Hobbes, *Leviathan*, chap. 11, dicussed in ibid., p. 10.

24. Jon Christensen, Janet Schmidt, and Joel Henderson, "The Selling of the Police: Media, Ideology, and Crime Control," *Contemporary Crisis* 6 (July 1982): 237.

25. Ibid., p. 234.

26. Ibid., pp. 234–235.

27. Anthony Downs, *Inside Bureaucracy* (Boston: Little, Brown, 1967), p. 83, as quoted in Levine et al., *Criminal Justice*, pp. 9–10.

28. Ibid., p. 11.

29. See Peter M. Blau and W. Richard Scott, "Organizational Development," in Merlin B. Brinkerhoff and Phillip R. Kunz, eds., *Complex*

Organizations and Their Environments (Dubuque, Iowa: William C. Brown Co., 1972), pp. 170–173.

30. Ibid.

31. Ibid., p. 173.

32. Christensen et al., "The Selling of the Police," pp. 235–236.

33. William L. Selke and Harold E. Pepinsky, "The Politics of Police Reporting in Indianapolis, 1948–1978," *Law and Human Behavior* 6 (1982): 341.

34. Harold Pepinsky, *Crime Control Strategies* (New York: Oxford University Press, 1980), p. 100.

35. Downs, *Inside Bureaucracy*, pp. 18–20.

36. Ibid., p. 20.

37. See Kevin N. Wright, "Economic Adversity, Reindustrialization, and Criminality," in Kevin N. Wright, ed., *Crime and Criminal Justice in a Declining Economy* (Cambridge, Mass.: Oelgeschlager, Gunn & Hain, 1981), pp. 51–68.

38. Federal Bureau of Investigation, *Crime in the United States—Uniform Crime Reports, 1981* (Washington, D.C.: Government Printing Office, 1982).

7

The Efficiency of Punishment to Control Crime

Crime control policy in the 1980s stands in sharp contrast to that of the 1960s. Growing fear on the part of the public, the unsuccessfulness of the liberal programs of the previous two decades, and the conservative swing in political mood have produced a dramatic departure from a policy of improving the justice system and rehabilitating convicted offenders to concern about violent crime and attitudes that favor punitive policies. Federal, state, and local governments have reacted to public sentiment by passing legislation that provides for longer sentences for violent criminals, and legislative, executive, and judicial bodies are streamlining due-process rights to protect the innocent rather than the guilty.

What is striking about these trends is the relentless dedication to a belief that something more, or new, can be done about the crime problem. During the past two decades, even though the focus may have been different, the intent was the same—to make the system work. In the 1960s, both institutional change and individual change were the primary stated objectives of crime control policy. Today control of the violent offender occupies the attention of criminal-justice policymakers. The system's endorsement of such major policy orientations leaves one with the initial impression that the system is dedicated to goal accomplishment and is willing to take decisive action. But given the effect of self-interest on policy-making, discussed in Chapter 6, one wonders about the motivation behind this current war on crime. Apparently, no one in the crime control establishment questions whether the system should so wholeheartedly redirect itself to fight violent crime. Nor does anyone bother to consider whether the criminal-justice system can do anything more about the problem. In an unrestrained reaction to public sentiment and pressure, the system's role as crime controller is blindly accepted. High-level government officials, police chiefs, judges, and academics willingly jump on the bandwagon of public sentiment to ride out this new wave of interest.

THE MOMENTUM OF CONTEMPORARY
PUNITIVE TRENDS

Nationally known news commentator James J. Kilpatrick outlines the reasons for punitive reform in criminal justice today and states: "There are steps that can be taken—practical, specific steps—that will help. . . . We begin by recognizing the enemy. He is the willful, deliberate criminal, to whom crime is in fact a way of life. If he can be caught and convicted and punished by a significant period of incarceration, some of the dreadful atmosphere may be dispelled."[1]

Consider the strength, the resignation, and the pragmatism in Kilpatrick's remark. Crime is a problem facing the nation, but one for which a solution exists. It must be met head-on with a hard-line approach. The criminal offender is an "enemy" who deserves condemnation and retaliation. The answer lies in the ability of the criminal-justice system to catch, convict, and punish the violent criminal. And while the system has not been very successful in the past, it can be. Kilpatrick's words contain that undaunted belief of Americans that the problem can be "fixed." "If we believe that present levels of violent crime are intolerable, let us tolerate these levels no longer. An apathetic people can accomplish nothing, an aroused people in time can win this war."[2]

Other nationally recognized experts advocate a similar hard-line, punitive approach to crime control. Harvard Professor of

Government James Q. Wilson agrees that the purpose of criminal justice should be to isolate and punish, because "at a minimum, society must be able to protect itself from dangerous offenders and to impose some costs on criminal acts." He suggests that we have no other option, that it is all we know.[3] Wilson's contemporary, psychoanalyst and social critic Ernest van den Haag, argues that efforts to reform criminal offenders make sense and will work "only if offenses are made unrewarding, self-defeating, irrational, and ultimately painful."[4] According to van den Haag, punishment is the only method that will work. So strong are his beliefs in the viability of punishment that he suggests we may be forced to give up justice to preserve social order: "The preservation of society and of the social order may require that we subordinate clarity, and sometimes even justice, to punish most severely what most endangers society and the social order, even when there is little guilt or none."[5] This last thought appears to guide much of the movement toward reduction of procedural safeguards today. To many, the defendant's rights have long been placed above society's safety, and it is time to reverse this practice and protect the rights of the innocent.

Throughout his long career in law enforcement, J. Edgar Hoover claimed that a tough and punitive approach was the only workable solution to crime. Shortly before his retirement and subsequent death he stated: "I think more and more Americans are beginning to realize that quick apprehension, prompt trial and substantial punishment commensurate with the crime is the basic method of dealing with criminality. Too frequently, soft justice and the abuse of judicial leniency have increased and not decreased crime."[6]

Ideas like those expressed by Kilpatrick, Wilson, van den Haag, and Hoover guide current reforms within criminal justice. The intent is to impose some costs on offenders, particularly violent criminals, for their transgressions, to get them off the streets as quickly as possible, and to keep them off longer. The goal is the safety of the public and restoration of social order within cities. This brings us to Crime Myth 7, "A no-nonsense approach to crime control where violent and predatory criminals are made to pay for their offenses will reduce crime."

In the first half of 1981 alone, approximately every fifth bill introduced in the California legislature (about 350) was crime-related, and in Texas about 500 crime bills (about 1 in 7) were introduced. Similar patterns were found in state legislatures across the nation—bill after bill aimed at getting tough has been introduced.[7]

One target of reform efforts is the release of arrested but not yet convicted violent offenders on bail. According to the U.S. Constitution, a person accused of committing a crime has the right to be free after arrest to prepare a defense but can be required to post bail to guarantee presence at the trial. This practice sometimes leads to the release of violent and often known repeaters back into the community to prey on unsuspecting citizens. Police officers often claim that the criminal is back on the streets before they have finished doing the required paperwork. One study found that 25 percent of the serious crimes in New York City are committed by persons arrested and on bail awaiting trial.[8]

For this reason, stringent conditions for bail, allowing judges to consider the seriousness of the offense and the probability that the criminal will reoffend if released, a practice known as preventive detention, has been proposed and supported by several respected authorities. Chief Justice Warren Burger has suggested adding to "all bail release laws, state and Federal, the crucial element of future dangerousness, based on the evidence before the court and the past record of the accused, to deter crime while on bail."[9] This proposal is supported by New York City Mayor Edward Koch, President Ronald Reagan, and Massachusetts Senator Edward Kennedy. A bill to allow federal judges to consider "dangerousness" has been approved by the Senate Judiciary Committee.[10]

Preventive detention has been debated for many years. Its proponents argue that it would prevent crime by incapacitating those likely to reoffend. Its opponents claim that it is fundamentally unfair because it allows a judge to make a decision about a person's future behavior. Since no one can accurately predict behavior, particularly criminality, the chances of mistakes are high. It is also considered to be a dangerous step toward punishment without trial. Since most of the nation's jails are already overcrowded and in disrepair, it is pragmatically an unworkable solution.

Another component of the current punitive trend is tougher sentencing laws, particularly for serious crime and repeat offenders. Within the past few years at least three dozen states have enacted stricter sentences. Most of the remaining states introduced but have not yet passed similar legislation.[11] These new laws have lengthened the time offenders spend in prison.

During the heyday of rehabilitation, the form of sentencing most often used was the indeterminate sentence. Legislatures set wide ranges for sentencing, and judges meted out minimums and maximums that also had a wide range. This allowed correctional personnel the discretion of releasing offenders when they were reformed. No one, other than correctional authorities, paticularly cared for this system. Inmates did not like it because their release depended on the whims of the parole board and because offenders never knew exactly when they would be released. Judges and the public did not like it because the term served never resembled the actual sentence given and was almost always shorter.

Recent legislation in many states replaced the indeterminate sentence with more determinate forms of sentencing. Discretion has been taken away from correctional personnel and assumed by legislators and judges. New laws specifying set lengths of sentences for particular offenses allow modifications of the time served based on the specific circumstances associated with a given incident. Judges then sentence according to the prescribed scheme and set a specific time for a person to remain incarcerated, which correctional officials can do little to modify. This change lengthened sentences, particularly for serious and repeat offenders. In many states, third-time convicted felons automatically receive a life sentence, and second-time felons receive automatic prison sentences with no chance for probation.

Restriction of the opportunity for probation and parole often accompanies new sentencing legislation. Many states made it more difficult to be placed on probation for certain offenses and impossible for certain serious ones. Parole, which is the conditional early release from prison under supervision in the community, has also been restricted in many states. In theory, a return to determinacy and the abandonment of rehabilitation eliminates the need for parole, which was designed to help the offender prepare to reenter the community. Yet parole serves another important function of controlling inmates in prison and is one of the few rewards that can be manipulated. For this reason, most states have retained it. Still, the administration of parole has been modified so that the parole date is determined by the sentence rather than by the paroling authority.

Good time—receiving extra credit for time served while maintaining good behavior in prison—is another major form of reward used in prison to control inmates. Because it reduces the total amount of time an individual will serve and modifies the original sentence, several states have considered eliminating it. However, heavy lobbying against the legislation by correctional personnel has prevented its elimination.

These punitive reforms produced dramatic changes in prison populations. Between 1975 and 1980 the number of people incarcerated jumped by more than 50 percent, forcing many prisons beyond their capacity. In Tennessee, inmates were housed in a large recreation room to cope with overcrowding, while Texas inmates slept on the floor and in tents set up on the prison grounds. The acceleration of population forced many states to undertake costly prison construction, and several cities and counties to increase jail space.

Reinstitution of the death penalty is another good example of the punitive trend in U.S. criminal justice. In the early 1970s only about half the population favored capital punishment, but by the 1980s 4 out of 5 citizens favored execution. The landmark Supreme Court case *Gregg v. Georgia* allowed in 1977 that capital punishment is constitutional and permissible. Since then, several people have been executed and over 1,000 await punishment on death row. All but twelve states (North Dakota, Kansas, Minnesota, Iowa, Wisconsin, Michigan, Ohio, West Virginia, New York, New Jersey, Connecticut, and Maine) now provide the death penalty for some offenses.

Under current reforms, treatment of juvenile offenders is also becoming more and more punitive. Once regarded as naive and needing guidance and protection, juveniles are now considered by many to be willful, malicious, and dangerous predators of the community. James Kilpatrick suggests: "Today's juvenile criminals are a different breed of young punks and hoodlums. The 17–year old gunman is still a gunman. The 15–year old mugger is still a mugger."[12] Consequently, more young people are tried and punished as adults today. Several states have lowered the age at which a juvenile can be certified, tried, and punished as an adult.

The reason politicians endorse punitive reforms is obvious: it is what the public wants. People are afraid of crime. They are tired of being the victims of theft and violence, and they want action. They want government to solve the problem. The accuracy of the public's image of crime is irrelevant. If the public believes that a problem exists and wants changes, then responsive government must respond.

There are two reasons for the direction of current punitive trends. First, it is a reaction to the perceived failure of liberal ideas tried during the 1960s and 1970s. Programs providing opportunities for the disadvantaged and programs for rehabilitating criminals did not reduce crime, so penal philosophy followed the general swing back toward conservatism. Second, it is a reaffirmation of three goals of criminal sanction: deterrence, incapacitation, and retribution. The fourth recognized goal is reform, from which the system is moving away. Deterrence, simply, is the use of punishment to prevent illegal behavior and may be directed toward two different populations. Offenders are punished to prevent them from repeating their crimes in the future; this is known as specific deterrence, a practice that embodies the principle most American families use in disciplining. When children engage in undesirable behavior, they are punished. This is repeated whenever the behavior occurs until the punishment is associated with the act. To avoid the punishment, the child learns to refrain from the act. Punishing criminals has the same purpose. We want the individual to associate the punishment and its related pain and unpleasantness with commission of the illegal act so that in the future, to avoid the punishment, the individual will refrain from repeating the crime.

Besides the benefits of specific deterrence, secondary effects known as general deterrence accrue. Punishment serves as a warning of what will happen to anyone who commits an illegal act. In this way, the criminal sanction should have a restraining effect on the entire population, and even though most do not directly experience its unpleasantness, they come to associate it with illegal behavior.

Along with deterrence, incapacitation is considered to be an important aspect of the current reform efforts. Rehabilitation had as its objective the return of offenders to the community as cured and viable members of society. But the rehabilitation efforts of the 1960s and 1970s were to a large extent unsuccessful. No program appeared to be any more effective in changing criminals than any other program, so a sizable portion of the people released from prison continue to return. This has led many to conclude that the best and possibly only alternative is simply to remove offenders from the community, precluding any further vexation and exploitation by them. An article in *New York Magazine* summarizes these conclusions: "The most important lesson research has taught is that there is only one thing government can surely do about criminals. It can lock them up—and then be secure in the knowledge that while in jail they are not out committing more crimes. And that's about all government can know."[13] Or as James Q. Wilson tells us, "Wicked people exist," we have no alternative but to remove them from the community so other people can go about their lives and enjoy the freedoms they deserve.[14]

Incapacitation will be effective if the "right" people—those likely to commit crimes—are locked up. Since criminals are thought to be more likely to commit crimes than those never convicted of a criminal act, it follows that some benefits will be derived from incarcerating convicted criminals. Incapacitation has the greatest potential as a method of crime control if it is a few hardened criminals who commit most crimes. If they can be identified, convicted, and incarcerated for long periods, a significant reduction in crime would be realized.

Most advocates of punitive reform have this perspective on the criminal population. Blame for the majority of crimes committed is placed on a relatively few compulsive, predatory individuals thought to commit hundreds if not thousands of crimes each year. A study conducted by the late Samuel Yochelson, a psychiatrist, and Stanton E. Samenow, a psychologist at St. Elizabeth's Hospital in Washington, D.C., supports this perspective. The fourteen-year study was based on clinical interviews with 240 men assigned to St. Elizabeth's because they were believed to be criminally insane (John Hinckley, who attempted to assassinate President Reagan, was assigned to St. Elizabeth's after he was found to be not guilty by reason of insanity). Almost all of the 240 subjects were violent offenders, but according to Yochelson and Samenow none was actually insane. Instead, they were habitual criminals who committed thousands of crimes of various types, including rape, assault, burglary, robbery, and even murder, but who were capable of feigning mental illness and convincing a jury they did not appreciate the consequences of their acts. These habitual and predatory offenders have distinctive criminal personalities characterized by unique thinking patterns. Such individuals are persistent liars who have little capacity for love or friendship. They commit brutal acts with little remorse, totally disregarding the rights of other people to live safely, and they find the restraints of responsible living contemptible. These characteristics do not develop during the course of the individual's life experiences but manifest themselves early in the individual's life.[15]

This study has been severely criticized by other criminologists. It is methodologically defective because the only criminals studied were those assigned to St. Elizabeth's, yet Yochelson and Samenow generalize their findings to all criminals. Still, if the study is valid, incapacitation may be an extremely effective method of controlling crime, particularly violent crime. Society need only lock up those few social misfits incapable of participating in productive lifestyles.

The final goal behind the punitive reform movement is the reestablishment of retribution. Of all penal goals, retribution is the most moralistic. It contains an element of revenge because the victim deserves to be repaid with pain for the harm suffered. But retribution goes beyond simple revenge. Justice is achieved when the punishment given the offender is equivalent to the harm accruing from the criminal act. Consequently, a social balance or equity is reestablished and maintained within society. People can see that productive contributions to society are rewarded and that noncompliance with generally accepted rules and the victimization of others is punished.

The liberal orientation of the 1960s and 1970s, along with the strong concern for procedural safeguards within the courts, produced a common assumption that the system is too lax and that criminal sanctions are not sufficient to reestablish any sense of social balance. Plea-bargaining, provision for "good time," and parole heightened the public's opinion that punishments were inadequate. That criminals are getting away with murder, even literally, came to be accepted by growing numbers of people until it reached a critical stage in the 1980s. Now people are demanding longer sentences, pushing for the death penalty and for making inmates serve their entire sentence, and advocating the removal of protections that prevent punishments from being administered.

THE EFFICACY OF A PUNITIVE ORIENTATION

An important question is whether these new efforts will more effectively control crime. Will a no-nonsense approach to crime control, where violent and predatory criminals are made to pay for their offenses, reduce crime (Crime Myth 7)? Will increased financial support for crime control methods reduce crime? The answer is an emphatic *no*. Current trends, the proposed changes, or any changes in the criminal-justice system for that matter, will not and cannot produce significant reductions in the actual incidence of crime in the United States. In principle, James J. Kilpatrick may be right in stating that "an aroused people in time can win this war,"[16] but in orientation he is wrong. He, like others, turns to the criminal-justice system, the government, to solve the problem. It is fascinating that conservatives, who generally shun government intervention and argue that it is an ineffective and inappropriate source for handling social problems, look to government for crime control, just like liberals. Liberals want government to help, conservatives want government to punish, but both want *government* to solve the problem. The truth is that regardless of the financial investments in crime control made by federal, state, and local governments, the system will not reduce crime.

Let us look at why. As indicated above, deterrence is one method held to have great potential for reducing criminal behavior. It is predicated on two important factors: (1) that there be a relatively high degree of certainty that the person will be caught and convicted so the costs will outweigh any potential benefits, and (2) that offenders will be rational enough to recognize the potential losses and benefits that might result from commission of a crime. Unfortunately, the realization of each factor is limited, to a degree that renders deterrence virtually impotent as a crime control strategy.

In considering the certainty of detection and sanction, less than 1 serious crime in 3 is ever reported to the police. For the personal crimes of violence, rape, assault, and robbery, the rate is somewhat higher, but still only a surprising 45 percent are ever reported. Less than 1 in 4 personal thefts is ever reported.[17] There are a number of reasons why people do not call the police. In some cases the crime is never completed or the loss or danger is considered too minor. Some people do not believe the police can do anything. Others—rape victims, for example—want to avoid any further embarrassment and humiliation. For whatever reason, victims themselves create a situation in which criminals face only 1 chance in 3 that the police will ever learn of their illegal acts. This provides good up-front odds of getting away with a crime; coupled with the system's inability to catch and convict, the odds are even better.

For all crimes reported to the police, only about 1 in 5 is cleared by an arrest. Once again, this varies with the crime committed. Most murders are solved, since arrests are made in more than 70 percent of the cases known to the police. Burglary, on the other hand, results in an arrest only in about 15 percent of the crimes known.[18] These figures are known to be inflated. Police departments are evaluated by their arrest records. One way to assure high rates is to encourage offenders who plead guilty to one offense to also plead guilty to several other recent and similar offenses in exchange for leniency. This practice makes the department look good, because it can claim to have solved a high proportion of the crimes brought to its attention, and in return the offender gains special considerations.

Regardless of its bias, we will use the 1 in 5 figure. Since only

1 in 3 crimes are reported and only 1 in 5 of those result in an arrest, offenders face 1 chance in 15 of being arrested. Those are excellent odds for someone evaluating the potential benefits of committing a crime against the possible losses. But the odds get even better—for the criminal.

Of those arrested, only about half are ever formally charged by the prosecutor.[19] Others are simply released without further inconvenience. Why? In some cases the police have violated the offender's rights and the prosecutor knows the case will be thrown out of court, but this situation is rare. (In Chapter 8 we will see instances of this.) In other cases, the prosecutor may determine that the evidence is unlikely to produce a conviction. A witness's testimony may not be corroborated, or the physical evidence may be insufficient. The most frequent reason for dismissal of charges occurs because victims and witnesses are unwilling to testify. A study conducted in New York City found that 60 percent of all dismissals resulted from noncooperation on the part of the *victim*.[20] People may be afraid or feel they have undergone enough, or simply cannot afford the time off from work to testify. For whatever reason, they fail to assist the prosecutor, making it impossible to obtain a conviction; there is no choice but to drop the charges. An offender's chances of being charged for a crime committed are up to 1 in 30.

The next step in criminal processing is the attempt to obtain a conviction. It will be surprising to many that almost all criminals charged are convicted, sometimes for lesser offenses, but they are nevertheless convicted. Only about 1 person in 10 formally charged subsequently gets off.[21] The reason is that most people plea-bargain. Somewhere between 90 percent and 95 percent of those convicted plead guilty in order to receive a lesser punishment.[22] Of those actually tried, either by a judge or by a jury, the vast majority are convicted, with only 1 of every 4 tried acquitted. The pivotal point of the criminal-justice process in almost everyone's mind is the trial, which is believed to be the point at which guilt or innocence is decided and where justice is done. In reality, however, the trial is of little consequence in determining the outcome of the criminal-justice process. By the time of the trial, it is simply a matter of negotiating the details.

Sanctions for those convicted are basically of two types: probation and incarceration. A few criminals receive fines with no other sanction, but this is rare for serious offenders. Approximately half those convicted go to prison, while the remaining half are released on probation.[23] Because probation may be considered more of an inconvenience than a true punishment, only about half those convicted will be considered to have been truly punished. The average sentence for offenders tried in federal courts is just over three years, yet the average time served is about half that, just over eighteen months.

In sum, an individual's chances of being caught, convicted, and sanctioned are as follows:

1 out of 3 offenses are reported (1 chance in 3).

1 out of 5 reported offenses result in arrest (1 chance in 15).

1 out of 2 people arrested are formally charged (1 chance in 30).

9 out of 10 people charged are convicted (3 chances in 100).

1 out of 2 people convicted receive prison sentences (3 chances in 200 or 1 chance in 67).

So a criminal faces 1 chance in 67 of ever being incarcerated for committing a serious crime. Wouldn't you like to have those odds in the Irish Sweepstakes or the state lottery—only 1 chance in 67 of losing? There are variations in these odds, depending on the crime. A murderer faces a greater chance of sanction, since most offenses are reported, arrests are usually made, most are charged and convicted, and almost all receive prison sentences. But for robbery, rape, burglary, and larceny, this is not the case. An offender should worry little about the costs of criminal activity since punishment is so improbable.

But is this not what concerns politicians and criminal-justice officials? Are they not claiming that the responsiveness of the system must be improved? That is exactly what they argue, but try as they may, the certainty of punishment cannot be enhanced to the point that it will have a significant effect on criminal offenders. For example, if the size of the nation's police departments were to be doubled and they would therefore be able to arrest twice as many offenders, the cost would be tremendous but the result would be insignificant. A criminal's chances of sanction would be improved to 1 chance in 33!

Another frequently suggested way of improving the deterrent effect is elimination of probation, causing every convicted criminal to experience the punishment of incarceration. Because this change occurs at the very end of the criminal process, it too would increase the chances of sanction to 1 in 33. The expense of incarcerating twice as many offenders would be substantial, to say nothing of the added burden on the courts due to the loss of the incentive to plea-bargain.

For deterrence to be effective, the criminal must perceive that there is some chance of being caught. No one knows exactly what point that is, but it certainly is higher than 1 chance in 67, or 1 in 33 for that matter. One study, among the voluminous research on deterrence, found in examining the differences in arrest rates across geographic areas that a deterrent effect occurred when the arrest rate reached or exceeded 50 percent.[24] But causes and effects cannot be isolated, and no firm conclusions are possible. A high arrest rate and the seeming deterrent effect (less crime) may be the result of a naturally low crime rate or a strong sense of social responsibility within the community. Since fewer crimes occur, local police can be more efficient in solving cases, giving the impression that crime is reduced when in fact the low crime rate causes the efficiency. It is paradoxical, but as a sense of moral obligation increases among people, legal threats are needed less.[25]

There appears to be little hope for effectively meeting the first requisite of deterrence—certainty. The police are limited in what they can do. Their primary method of promoting deterrence is to provide patrols intended to pose a threat of detection to potential offenders and allow officers to respond quickly to calls of crimes in progress. It would seem that adding additional patrols might enhance the deterrent capability, but research has not supported this presumption.

Cities are simply too large to maintain effective surveillance. Adding personnel has meager, if any, effects on the certainty of detection. A study in Kansas City, Missouri, conducted by the Police Foundation, found that individual officers achieve an average of 1 felony conviction for every 14,720 hours of patrol, or 1 conviction during every 7 years of patrol.[26] With such a low detection rate, significant improvement is unlikely. The findings of several studies about police patrols generally supported this conclusion. In the Police Foundation study, the effect of an increased patrol was evaluated by allocating four times the usual number of squad cars to particular areas and measuring the reduction in crime. No effect was found. The presence of more patrols did little to increase the deterrent effect.[27]

Courts face similar problems in improving the certainty of punishment. Considerable public funds have been expended to improve court efficiency, trying to alleviate delays and bring about swifter justice. Speed of sanction is an important factor in specific deterrence, but if so few offenders are caught and sanctioned, improved swiftness will have little effect on the crime rate. Besides, a method to maintain swiftness has developed naturally, without large federal grants—plea-bargaining. Because 19 out of 20 people convicted plead guilty, courts are able to convict and sanction most offenders quickly and preclude further delays associated with appeals, since there are few grounds on which to contest a guilty plea.

Another possible improvement in judicial processing would be the establishment of support programs to encourage and aid victims and witnesses in pressing charges and bringing cases to trial. But, once again, this would not greatly affect the low probability of getting caught, and the overall effect would not be substantial.

Even if the police and the courts can do nothing to enhance the deterrent effect, one might ask whether punishments might be changed in some way. If punishments were more severe, offenders might think twice about committing crimes. More important, others might reevaluate the benefits to be derived against the more extreme costs. There are several problems with this idea. Researchers have found that the certainty of sanction is more important in establishing the deterrent effect than the severity of the sanction. In fact, a direct link between severity and lower crime rates has never been empirically established. Some evidence suggests that at the low end of the scale increasing punishments (such as doubling the fine for speeding) may be effective, but that increasing maximum sentences from 20 years to 30 years appears to have little effect.[28]

Problems with the second requisite for deterrence—the ability to recognize and evaluate the potential losses and benefits faced when one commits a given offense—are also apparent. Since as a reader of this book you are probably intelligent and more affluent, you will argue that your behavior is or would be affected by the fear of punishment. If you drive in the Northeast, you probably drive nearer to the speed limit in Pennsylvania because you know you are more likely to be caught if you speed and that fines are greater there than in other states, and you may claim you would not consider stealing because you are afraid of getting caught. But remember, you have something to lose—your home, your car, your family, your respect in the community.

Now consider Baby Love's life. He is a fourteen-year-old, sixth grade dropout who can barely read or write, a skinny black kid who lives in Brooklyn's Bedford-Stuyvesant section and inhabits a world one reporter described as "a Dickensian hell of cheap thrills, senseless deaths and almost unrelieved hopelessness." Because he is nearly illiterate and has been running free in the streets for so long, it is next to impossible that Baby Love will ever be gainfully employed. He survives by stealing. His favorite method is to snatch gold chains, especially from passengers in buses pulling away from the curb. Baby Love leaps in the air, grabs the jewelry through an open window, and is gone before anyone realizes what happened. But he also engages in shoplifting, pocket-picking, and mugging. He has been caught numerous times and has served six months on probation.

Baby Love's life is well integrated with the street life of the ghetto. He lives in a decaying tenement with his aunt, two cousins, two sisters, and occasionally his mother, but most of his time is spent on the streets—hanging out, getting high, and gambling. Violence is common in his world. When he was thirteen, he saw a man blown away by a shotgun blast. Several friends have been killed. Because he is small, Baby Love was often beaten up until he could steal enough to bribe his assailants with drugs.[29]

To lawmakers, the middle class—people with stable, "normal" lifestyles, you and I—it is logical that threats of punishment should deter and that a more severe threat should deter even more. But Baby Love's life situation is different. He is growing up in an environment that encourages criminality. He learned how to commit crimes and how to get away with them. The threat of sanction adds only excitement. If caught, punishment will bolster his status in the neighborhood. Incarceration would not be so bad—friends from the neighborhood would be there, along with three meals and a place to sleep. Prison temporarily relieves the pressures of hustling and provides a relatively safe place to stay for a while.

I know from my own adolescence that the threat of punishment was not always evaluated rationally. When I was in college, several friends and I stole some expensive hubcaps of felony value. We did not need them, but stealing them was exciting, and not once did I or my friends ever consider that we might be caught or think about the consequences we might face. The process is analogous to driving without a seat belt. It is not a matter of weighing the consequences; they never enter into the decision. One simpy acts on impulse.

Therefore, the second requisite of deterrence is often missing. Offenders are too young, too immature, or living in environments that support criminality, where the threat of punishment has little meaning in the context of their lives. And the criminal-justice system can do nothing to establish a rational interpretation because such methods do not exist. For Baby Love, threats of criminal sanction are at best irrelevant; at worst, they are of value in his world.

The unlikelihood of sanction raises a question each reader should consider carefully. If one's chances of apprehension and conviction are so low, why are you reading this book rather than out stealing? Theft would be more profitable, and you now know that the chances of getting caught are almost nonexistent. There must be something else restraining you from criminality. Is the criminal-justice system—that outside, formal force—influencing your behavior? I would guess not.

Incapacitation, the second highly touted crime control strategy, runs into the same problem. The idea behind the strategy is to identify and incarcerate individuals likely to continue committing crimes. As noted above, its success depends on the assumption that a small percentage of offenders commit a large proportion of all serious crimes, yet this bears little resemblance to reality when the total crime picture is considered. Predatory career criminals do commit crime after crime, piling up hundreds if not thousands of offenses, but such individuals are obscured by the flood of people who do not make crime their vocation but transgress at some point in their lives. Almost all of us commit at least one criminal act during our lifetime, generally when we are young, yet rarely are we caught.

Because information about undetected criminals is not available, little is known about the criminal population. We do not know how many Americans commit serious crimes each year. The number of crimes committed can be estimated, but some are by the same people. Virtually nothing is known about criminals who are not arrested. Are they similar to people who are caught, or are they different in some way? Are they talented or lucky? Do they commit a few crimes or many crimes? Lack of information makes it difficult to analyze and argue about the potential effectiveness of incapacitation. However, consideration of a few central issues will lend credibility to the argument that the ability to incapacitate is limited.

In considering the age structure of the criminal population, it appears that fifteen- to twenty-five-year-olds are responsible for the bulk of crimes committed. Studies asking subjects to recount their criminal histories find that most adolescents commit at least one serious crime.[30] This suggests that the criminal population is large, not restricted to a few compulsive predators. It also indicates something about career patterns of criminals. Rather than establishing lifelong commitments to criminal behavior, many younger people appear to engage in crime but move on to other things as they accept the responsibilities of adult life. The criminal population is not limited to a few hardened, vicious criminals; it contains many younger and occasional criminals. Consequently, the idea of apprehending and incarcerating this group for long periods of time is unappealing.

Statistical studies of incapacitation generally support this image of the criminal population. Based on the offense history of those who are incarcerated, David Greenberg estimated that if the U.S. prison population increased by half again there would be a reduction of from 50,000 to 333,000 serious crimes. These figures are quite impressive. It would be wonderful if the citizens of this nation were spared 300,000 victimizations. But such a reduction would represent a decrease of only 0.6 percent to 4.0 percent of the 8 million reported crimes commited each year.[31] In this light, the incapacitative effect is much less impressive. On the other hand, the cost of providing space and care for the approximately 125,000 new state charges would be substantial. Since most prisons have reached or exceeded their capacity, construction of new space would be needed to accommodate all the prisoners. At present-day costs, construction would run just under $10 billion[32]—two and a half times what the federal government now spends on all of criminal justice each year. Furthermore, a yearly outlay of approximately $2 billion[33] would be required to house, feed, and supervise these new inmates. These figures raise the question of whether incapacitation would be cost-effective. Substantial costs will accrue for at best marginal reductions in crimes committed.

Greenberg's findings also indicate that present incarceration has a limited effect on the crime rate. If prison populations were reduced to half the present level, disregarding the loss of deterrent effects from the increase of people in the community who have a history of criminal activity, reported offenses would be expected to rise by only 0.6 percent to 4.0 percent. Furthermore, Greenberg's statistics suggest that the release of all incarcerated felons would push the crime rate up by at most 8 percent.[34] From these figures, we conclude that a very small proportion of the criminal population is incarcerated, that for every criminal imprisoned there are ten to twenty others who are free in the community.

Greenberg's study is not unique among the incapacitation research and was not selected by this author to make his strongest case. Researcher Steven Clark estimated that by incarcerating juveniles only about 1 to 4 percent of all known Index Crimes are avoided.[35] Another researcher, Isaac Erlich, found that a 50 percent reduction in the average time served in prison would produce only a 5 percent increase in serious offenses.[36] Steve Van Dine, John Conrad, and Simon Dinitz, who evaluated the ability of various incapacitation strategies to identify and control chronic offenders, concluded, "It is clearly impossible to define the chronic offender in such a way that a practical basis for crime reduction can be structured." A policy requiring incarceration of all second-time felons would produce meager reductions in crime but explode the prison population. Any more-liberal criteria would be totally ineffective in identifying chronic offenders.[37] Possibly the most significant recent piece of incapacitation research was conducted by the Rand Corporation.[38] *Time* magazine notes that the findings are like a statistical "good news, bad news" joke.[39] Significant reductions in criminal activity are possible if every second-time felon is incarcerated for five years, but the prison population would triple, necessitating a $40 billion initial outlay and an additional $2 billion each year.

Another limitation of incapacitation as an effective method of crime reduction is its dependence on the ability of the system to identify people with high probabilities of committing offenses and to remove them from society. A person who committed an offense may be more likely to offend again than someone who has not, but this is not always the case. Because some people who are caught and convicted for one offense will never reoffend, incarceration is an inefficient method of crime reduction. One solution might be to allow judges to sentence according to their impression of the risk posed by the offender, yet such a practice would base an individual's punishment on the expectation of future behavior, which would be sanctioning a person for acts not yet committed. Since no judge is particulary adept at predicting the future behavior of anyone, there are substantial problems with such selective sentencing to achieve incapacitation.

A final problem with incarceration as a method to achieve incapacitation is that it does not eliminate the opportunity to commit criminal acts, it simply displaces it. Criminals are removed from the community, but they are placed in a setting where they can victimize guards and other inmates. Crime in prison is common. Inmates assault, rape, murder, and exploit one another. Crime is not eliminated, but the population of potential victims is modified and reduced in number.

The criminal-justice system's attempts to reduce crime through rehabilitation and to satisfy the public's need for retribution fail for much the same reason that deterrence and incapacitation do not work: the proportion of the criminal population touched by the system at any point is too small to have a major impact. During the 1960s, rehabilitation was held to be the answer to the crime problem. Officials claimed that by reforming convicted felons crime could be reduced. Yet as we learned with incapacitation, the prison system holds a very small percentage of the criminal population. Even if every incarcerated criminal was reformed, the system would fail to influence those who are never caught, those who are just deciding to experiment with criminality, and those who occasionally commit illegal acts. Rehabilitation, as an overall strategy, was thus doomed to fail from the start; too few criminals are brought into the system to be reformed.

But rehabilitation faced other problems. From 1965 to 1975, when the central focus of corrections became rehabilitation and there was a substantial investment of time and energy in finding methods that worked, we learned that behavior engineering is a bit more complicated than initially expected. No single method, program, or treatment emerged as appropriate and effective for all types of inmates. No cure-all was found. Yet this should not be so surprising. Medical science does not rely on one treatment for all physical maladies, so why should one method work for all behavioral problems that produce crime? Identifying the problems and coming up with an appropriate method to cure them also proved to be a difficult task.[40]

Beyond the difficulties in finding effective techniques, there were administrative problems with rehabilitation. Inmates insisted that they were not sick or in need of treatment, claiming that they had selected or learned crime as a way to get something they desired. They asked to be punished without having to participate in the hypocritical game of rehabilitation.[41] Criminologists argued that rehabilitation creates inequities because the sentence a person receives is based on some diagnosis and prognosis of behavioral problems rather than on the offense committed.[42] Today rehabilitation is still part of correctional programming, but it is no longer compulsory and there are no great hopes for its success.

Retribution, the reestablishment of social balance and a sense of justice and fair play within the public, also fails to reduce crime because the system catches and punishes so few. Predatory crimes occur every day, but in few cases are people arrested, convicted, and sent to prison. This situation defies the sense of what is fair—hardworking citizens are denied the benefits of their labors. The public has reacted by calling for stiffer punishments, but intensifying punishments will not enhance the sense of retribution because so few are punished. The vast majority of victims will not see their assailants brought to justice.

We must conclude that the criminal-justice system is limited in what it can do, but this does not mean that it serves no purpose and should be eliminated. The justice system fulfills an important symbolic function by establishing standards of conduct. It formally defines right and wrong for citizens and frees them from the responsibility of taking vengeance, thus preventing the escalation of feuds within communities. The system protects the rights of free citizens by honoring the principle that individual freedom should not be denied without good reason.

Beyond these abstract functions, the criminal-justice system serves a real function in protecting people. If you are afraid or threatened, there is a place to call. Whether the problem is fear that someone is trying to break into your house, a family fight that is getting out of hand, or someone about to get hurt in a barroom brawl, law enforcement agencies that employ professionally trained people can help with threatening events. Dangerous people should not be allowed to continue to hurt others who live in our communities, and while the system is not always effective in apprehending and incarcerating them, it does what it can.

We should not expect much more out of the system. A formal system simply cannot control the amount of crime occurring in the United States. Success could only be realized by establishing a police state in which strict surveillance of the citizenry is maintained and swift sanctions are executed with little regard for individual rights. The American people would not tolerate this. Formal controls are too far removed from the meaningful aspects of everyday life to influence our behavior directly. The attitudes of peer groups, families, and perhaps even neighbors are more influential on behavior. People do not want to embarrass themselves or disappoint those they respect. But to consider that they might get caught or even that they might be doing something wrong is too far removed from their self-perception to influence actions greatly. Consequently, the system will never effectively control crime—not through deterrence, or incapacitation, or rehabilitation.

THE BURDEN OF PUNISHING MORE

The United States is the most punitive nation in the modern Western world. More people are incarcerated in the United States than in any other modern nation. In 1980 more than 300,000 people were held in this nation's prisons. But of greater significance is the proportion of the population this number represents. In the United States, 200 out of every 100,000 citizens are imprisoned, a rate that outranks that of all other nations. Poland comes closest to the United States with a rate of 190, and Australia incarcerates 128 of every 100,000 people. All other Western nations incarcerate less than half the proportion of their populations that the United States does. This is true of Canada, England, Wales, and France. Japan's incarceration rate is about one-sixth that of the United States; the Netherlands rate is about one-twelfth.[43]

Still, many people advocate that greater punishments be applied to a larger number of people. It seems paradoxical that one of the most punitive nations continues to have one of the greatest crime problems. Why do we continue to fall back on punishment as the desired means of crime reduction? It has not worked in the past, and it is not working today. The lower crime rate in other countries must be attributable to something other than the effect of formal sanctions. Instead of trying to figure out what that might be, we rely on punishment. If what exists is not working, people want to increase it—incarcerate more people for longer periods. Prison space to incarcerate one person costs an average of $75,000. This means that if a state wants to lock up a mere 100 additional inmates, $7.5 million will be needed. The need for space far exceeds our fiscal ability to provide it.

To incarcerate one person for one year costs about $20,000, which is more than a year's education at Harvard. Does it make sense to spend $75,000 creating a new prison cell and $20,000 a year for three years to incarcerate a burglar who stole a $500 television, a $500 silver service, and $1,000 in jewelry? Even if

a cell is not needed, that is a $60,000 expenditure to show some-
one it is wrong to steal $2,000 worth of personal property. You
would expect a nation that prides itself on cultural and technological advancements to be more creative.

NOTES

1. James J. Kilpatrick, "Arresting Violent Crime," *Nation's Business*,
July 1981, p. 14.

2. Ibid.

3. James Q. Wilson, *Thinking About Crime* (New York: Basic Books,
1975), pp. 172–173.

4. Ernest van den Haag, *Punishing Criminals* (New York: Basic Books,
1975), p. 191.

5. Ibid., p. 50.

6. "An Interview with J. Edgar Hoover, F.B.I. Director," *U.S. News
& World Report*, August 26, 1968, pp. 36–37.

7. Timothy Harper, "Getting Tough on Rising Crime," Associated
Press syndicated article appearing in the *Sunday Press* (Binghamton,
N.Y.), May 17, 1981, p. 8A.

8. Michael Kramer, "Keeping Bad Guys Off the Streets," *New York
Magazine*, February 8, 1982, p. 39.

9. Warren Burger, Address to the National Convention of the American Bar Association, New Orleans, February 8, 1981.

10. Senate Bill 1722, 96th Congress.

11. Harper, "Getting Tough on Rising Crime."

12. Kilpatrick, "Arresting Violent Crime."

13. Kramer, "Keeping Bad Guys."

14. Wilson, *Thinking About Crime*, p. 209.

15. Samuel Yochelson and Stanton Samenow, *The Criminal Personality*
(New York: John Aronson, 1976).

16. Kilpatrick, "Arresting Violent Crime."

17. J. Frederick Shenk, *Criminal Victimization in the United States, 1979*,
U.S. Department of Justice, September 1981, pp. 15–16.

18. Timothy J. Flanagan, David J. van Alstyne, and Michael R.
Gottfredson, eds., *Sourcebook of Criminal Justice Statistics, 1981*, U.S. Department of Justice, Bureau of Justice Statistics (Washington, D.C.: Government Printing Office, 1982), p. 368.

19. James P. Levine, Michael C. Musheno, and Dennis J. Palumbo,
Criminal Justice (New York: Harcourt Brace Jovanovich, 1980), p. 206.

20. Vera Institute of Justice, *Felony Arrests: Their Prosecution and Dis-*

position in New York City (New York: Vera Institute of Justice, 1977), p. 20, as discussed in Levine et al., p. 210.

21. Bureau of Justice Statistics, *Violent Crime*, National Indicators System Report no. 4, September 1981, p. 46.

22. Levine et al., *Criminal Justice*, p. 214.

23. The proportion of serious offenders incarcerated is a difficult statistic to obtain. Some estimates are lower than 50 percent.

24. William Bailey, "Certainty of Arrest and Crime Rates for Major Felonies: A Research Note," *Journal of Research on Crime and Delinquency* 13 (July 1976): 145–154.

25. Levine et al., *Criminal Justice*, p. 357.

26. Ibid., p. 385.

27. Ibid., pp. 386–387.

28. Ibid., pp. 386–371.

29. "In Brooklyn: A Wolf in $45 Sneakers," *Time*, October 12, 1981, p. 10.

30. For a review and critique of self-reporting studies, see Harold Pepinsky, *Crime Control Strategies* (New York: Oxford University Press, 1980), pp. 197–244.

31. David F. Greenberg, "The Incapacitative Effect of Imprisonment: Some Estimates," *Law and Society Review* 9 (Summer 1975): 541–580.

32. Figure arrived at by multiplying 125,000 new inmates by $75,000 cost for new space.

33. Figure arrived at by multiplying 125,000 new inmates by yearly cost of $17,000 for incarceration.

34. Greenberg, "The Incapacitative Effect."

35. Steven S. Clark, "Getting 'Em Out of Circulation: Does Incarceration of Juvenile Offenders Reduce Crime?" *Journal of Criminal Law and Criminology* 65 (December 1974): 528–535.

36. Isaac Erlich, "Participation in Illegitimate Activities: An Economic Analysis," in C. S. Becker and W. M. Landes, eds., *Essays in the Economics of Crime and Punishment* (New York: National Bureau of Economic Research, 1974).

37. Steve Van Dine, John P. Conrad, and Simon Dinitz, "The Incapacitation of the Chronic Thug," *Journal of Criminal Law and Criminology* 70 (Spring 1979): 125–136.

38. Peter W. Greenwood and Allan Abrahamse, *Selective Incapacitation* (Santa Monica: Rand Corporation, 1982).

39. Kurt Anderson, "What Are Prisons For?" *Time*, September 13, 1982, p. 40.

40. For a review of the research conducted on rehabilitation effectiveness, see Robert Martinson, Ted Palmer, and Stuart Adams, *Re-*

habilitation, Recidivism, and Research (Hackensack, N.J.: National Center for Crime and Delinquency, 1976).

41. John Irwin, *Prisons in Turmoil* (Boston: Little, Brown, 1980).

42. See Norval Morris, *The Future of Imprisonment* (Chicago: University of Chicago Press, 1974), and David Fogel, *We Are the Living Proof* (Cincinnati: Anderson Publishing Co., 1975).

43. Irvin Waller and Janet Chan, "Prison Use: A Canadian and International Comparison," *Criminal Law Quarterly* 17 (December 1974): 47–71.

8

Procedural "Safeguards"

Few events spark such intense public ire as the release of a criminal guilty of a revolting and heinous offense on a procedural technicality. In the eyes of the public, such judicial decisions contradict the purpose of the justice system in that they undermine the law enforcement function and fail to set the social balance right. Accounts of such travesties appear daily in newspapers across the nation. The following example illustrates what happens:

Baltimore—There were photographs on the desk. "Anybody want to look?" asked Bill Swisker, State's Attorney for Baltimore.

They were baby pictures, only the baby was dead. In a courtroom across the hall, James McClain, the man convicted of killing the child, had just been released.

The baby belonged to McClain's girlfriend. She was out when a friend came to the highrise apartment and showed McClain a picture of his girl with another man.

In his confession, McClain said, "I carried [the baby] to the garbage opening, [laid] him in [it] and just let him go." McClain was convicted of killing the child and sentenced to life behind bars.

Almost 18 months after that confession, the Court of Appeals, Maryland's highest court, ruled in another case that a defendant had to be taken before a court commissioner within 24 hours of arrest, or the state could not use any subsequent confession. McClain was not taken before a commissioner until he had given his confession—24 hours and 12 minutes after arrest.

The Court of Appeals decided to make its ruling retroactive.

So James McClain is a free man. (Column by Michael Olesker in the *Baltimore Sun*.)[1]

Was justice done in this case? A child is dead, and a guilty man by his own confession is free. The public has been denied the opportunity to punish—to get even with—a man who maliciously and without human compassion destroyed an innocent child. The public has also been denied protection from a man for whom life holds little value. We can only wonder, and fear, who his next victim might be.

We ask, what difference does it make that some trivial procedural rule was violated? Are the rules more important than the horror of the criminal act or the reasons for criminal sanction? Are the judges who hear such cases as unfeeling as the criminals who prey on innocents? On what basis does the judiciary deny citizens the right to punish and to be protected?

The legal culprit is the *exclusionary rule,* a legal doctrine that bars illegally obtained evidence from criminal trials. The exclusionary rule is not mentioned in the U.S. Constitution or in any federal legislation. It is a rule created by judicial decision, an instrument invented by the U.S. Supreme Court to guarantee due-process rights to criminal defendants. Its origins date back to 1886, when the Supreme Court first ordered that illegally seized evidence be excluded from a federal criminal trial.[2] The inadmissibility of evidence was not fully established until 1914, when the Court reaffirmed the exclusionary rule in *Weeks v. United States.*

Freemont Weeks was arrested by federal authorities for illegal use of the mails. When federal officers took him into custody, they searched the home where he was staying without a valid warrant. Incriminating letters and materials were found and subsequently used to obtain a conviction. Upon appeal, the Supreme Court ruled that evidence was obtained illegally and must be excluded.[3] The reasoning was: "If letters and private documents can thus be seized and held and used in evidence against a citizen accused of an offense, the protection of the Fourth Amendment declaring his right to be secured against such searches and seizures is of no value and, so far as those thus placed are concerned, might as well be stricken from the Constitution."[4] The *Weeks* decision applied only to federal court cases and was not imposed on states until 1961.

In establishing the exclusionary rule, the Court decided that procedural safeguards were meaningless if they could be ignored by law enforcement officials in their zeal to rid the community of offenders, that such practices obviate the entire concept of due process. So the way evidence is obtained became as important in the trial as the relevance of that evidence to the case.[5]

Judicial review is confounded by the broad manner in which due-process safeguards are stated in the Constitution. As one set of authors notes, "Exactly what constitutes due process in a specific case depends on the facts of the case, the federal and state constitutional and statutory provisions, previous court decisions, and the ideas and principles that society considers important at a given time and a given place."[6] For example, note what initially appears to be a straightforward constitutional provision: "In all criminal prosecutions, the accused shall enjoy the right . . . to have the assistance of counsel for his defense." Does this mean that defendants may have attorneys at their trials, or does it mean that counsel must be or can be present at any time during the accusational process? If the person cannot afford an attorney, must one be provided, so that both the poor and the wealthy are equally protected by the law? Because the answers to such questions are not clear and are therefore subject to court interpretation, they evolve and change over time. Occasionally a rule will be established at a particular point in time, creating a standard for all future cases but leaving open the question of those previously tried. For example, up until 1962, indigent felony defendants who could not afford attorneys were often not represented by counsel. The Supreme Court decided in *Gideon v. Wainright* that states must provide counsel when the defendants are unable to pay for their own. This standard applied to all future cases. But what about the hundreds of defendants tried in the past under the old rule? The states had acted in good faith when they tried them without counsel; it was the accepted practice. But with the decision in *Gideon*, the rule was applied retroactively, and individuals who had not been represented by counsel were released from prison. It was the opinion of the Court that to do otherwise would be unfair, since many of those tried without counsel might not have been convicted.

This type of situation precipitated the release of James McClain in the case used to introduce this chapter. According to the Constitution, a person cannot be arrested and held for an indefinite period without being formally charged for some crime. Such a legal standard is reasonable because otherwise law enforcement officials could incarcerate people for indefinite periods without charging or trying them. Police officers could harass people they did not like, or simply never bother using the judicial stage of criminal processing. Maryland's highest appeals court defined what a "reasonable" period of time before a person had to be charged as twenty-four hours and attempted to be fair by applying the rule retroactively. But this created a legal loophole that led to the release of James McClain. Because he had been held for more than twenty-four hours before being formally charged, his confinement was illegal and his confession made during that time was also illegal and inadmissible (according to another judicially created rule known as "the fruits of the poisonous tree doctrine," according to which any evidence obtained as a result of evidence obtained illegally is also inadmissible in a criminal trial). On this basis McClain's conviction was overturned.

We are faced with a legal Catch-22 situation. In the absence of legislation, the courts must define what is a reasonable time for accused people to be held before they are formally charged. To provide some degree of equal protection, it is also appropriate that the new standards be applied retroactively. Yet law enforcement officials, acting in good faith, made a good arrest, provided the accused with the rights he was entitled to at the time, and brought him before a court official in what they considered to be a reasonable amount of time. After the fact, that amount of time was determined to be unacceptable (by twelve minutes). In working to achieve a legal system that is fair and predictable, the court ended up releasing a known murderer. Cases like this leave many people with the impression that Crime

Myth 8, "In using the exclusionary rule to dismiss cases when evidence is obtained illegally, the courts protect criminals and reduce the deterrent effect of sanctions," is an accurate description of what really happens.

THE PUSH FOR LIMITING EXCLUSION

Since a series of U.S. Supreme Court decisions in the early 1960s clarified and extended due-process rights, an outspoken group, which has grown steadily and now includes some influential political figures, has been calling for abandonment of the exclusionary rule. The push to limit, if not abandon, exclusion also came to be associated with the larger, conservative movement to "get tough" on crime.

This movement received a major boost during the 1968 campaign and subsequent administration of Richard Nixon. A prominent feature of Nixon's campaign was a pledge to reduce crime and restore safety in the streets. Nixon argued that Supreme Court decisions had significantly hindered law enforcement and prosecution and virtually precluded confessions as a means of convicting criminals. (This is contrary to fact, since most convictions result from guilty pleas that are part of a bargain.) According to Nixon, lawlessness and insecurity resulting from crime posed a significant threat to individual freedom and to society, and contrary to the popular liberal interpretation of the preceding decade, he viewed society "guilty of crime only when we fail to bring the criminal to justice."[7] The liberal view that the state poses the most significant threat to individual liberty began to be replaced by a move toward the conservative position that the criminal poses the greatest threat. The political problems encountered by the Nixon administration slowed the momentum of this movement, but widespread public endorsement of these sentiments did not die away. They resurfaced during the conservative administration of Ronald Reagan.

In a speech made to the International Association of Chiefs of Police during the fall of 1981, President Reagan emphatically stated that the exclusionary rule "rests on the absurd proposition that a law enforcement error, no matter how technical, can be used to justify throwing an entire case out of court, no matter how guilty the defendant or how heinous the crime." He urged legislation to allow illegally obtained evidence gathered by the police in good faith to be used in criminal trials.[8]

Perhaps the strongest stand against exclusion by a public figure is taken by Supreme Court Chief Justice Warren Burger. He has lashed out at the exclusionary rule, arguing that it frees the criminal but fails to prevent law enforcement officers from engaging in improper and illegal behavior. His opinion is based on a belief that "the cost to society of releasing guilty criminals mandates that the rule clearly demonstrate its effectiveness."[9] According to Burger, this condition is not met. Errant police officers are not directly sanctioned by the rule, and the offender is simply rewarded by having his case tossed out. Since clearance is the standard by which superiors and the public evaluate performance, the first objective of law enforcement is to make an arrest. Secondary to this objective is making a "good" arrest that will produce a conviction. To a police officer, a "bad" arrest is better than no arrest at all. The deterrent impact of exclusion has no effect on the officer who makes an honest mistake. The ability of police officers to keep abreast of appellate decisions, to know what procedural boundaries are applicable, is also questioned. Given these limitations, according to the chief justice, the ends do not justify the means, and the need to protect society outweighs the need to suppress information in the name of justice.[10]

The opponents of the exclusionary rule see two benefits of limiting exclusion: a significant reduction in crime and a more just outcome to the criminal process. As far as crime control goes, critics believe that many criminals escape sanction because of legal technicalities. Police refrain from arresting, and prosecutors refuse to charge and bring a case to trial, because tainted evidence prevents them from establishing a good case. It is believed that many criminals are also freed from prison under judicial review of procedural blunders. Chief Justice Burger referred to "thousands of cases in which the criminal was set free,"[11] implying that there would be a substantial drop in crime if this steady progression of criminals avoiding punishment could be curtailed by easing the rule. The second expected benefit is that justice will be served better by limiting the rule. According to the conservative view, exclusion interferes with finding out the truth in criminal trials. Without the excluded information, a full understanding of the circumstances of the alleged act is impossible and an accurate and good decision cannot be reached.

Allowing the guilty to go free undermines public faith in the courts' decision-making capabilities and the entire judicial system, which leads to a more general loss of respect for legal controls and trust in the integrity of government. When people feel that the system protects the guilty rather than the innocent victim, they may be less likely to cooperate with and support the system and in their frustration may turn to other methods of crime control.

RECONSIDERING EXCLUSION

Many Americans regard the exclusionary rule as the scourge of the criminal-justice system, but in early chapters of this book, public perceptions of crime—the threat of victimization and the capabilities of the system—were found to be distorted and inaccurate. Might this not be true of the exclusionary rule? Could it be that exclusion actually has little to do with the crime rate and that just as many examples of injustices prevented by the rule can be found as examples of injustices created by it, that its role as culprit is one created by the media and the law enforcement establishment for their own advantage and convenience?

To consider these possibilities, several questions must be answered. Does the rule actually make it difficult for the police to carry out effective investigations and to obtain confessions from criminal suspects? Or can law enforcement be conducted under stringent procedural limitations? For that matter, to what extent are the police responsive to procedural limits? Did such major decisions as *Miranda v. Arizona* (1966) actually affect police behavior? How many criminals actually get off as a result of excluded evidence? Do prosecutors fail to indict and bring a case to trial because important evidence may not be usable? How many criminals are actually freed because of postconviction appeals? We must also consider whether illegal police behavior occurs frequently enough to warrant stringent procedural safeguards. Since most police departments have become more professional, is it likely that officers would succumb to the temptation to use illegal methods? Chief Justice Burger believes this to be the case, but is he right? Finally, we should consider whether any of the alternatives to the exclusionary rule are more desirable.

Let us begin by considering whether the exclusionary rule severely limits law enforcement efforts. According to the police themselves, it does. In the 1960s, law enforcement officials voiced serious reservations about their ability to enforce the law and to apprehend criminals under the new decisions. They continued to make such claims into the 1980s. *U.S. News & World Report* stated in 1963 that police say "there is no mystery about the crime wave threatening the U.S. A basic cause: too much worry about the rights of criminals and too little worry about the rights of law-abiding citizens."[12] How many times have we read or heard that in the last two decades? The argument is even more dated than that. Judge Learned Hand wrote in 1923: "Our procedure has been always haunted by the ghost of the innocent man convicted. It is an unreal dream. What we need to fear is the archaic formalism and watery sentiment that obstructs, delays and defeats the prosecution of crime."[13]

Contrary to these claims, the exclusionary rule appears to be one to which the police can adjust and work within. As Charles Silberman states: "Arguments of this sort are rooted in ideological preferences rather than in empirical research."[14] A steady stream of studies supports this position. The federal government's General Accounting Office (GAO) released a report in 1979 indicating that the rule does not "cripple law enforcement." The study reviewed almost 3,000 federal cases from the offices of thirty-eight federal prosecutors across the nation. Defendants and their attorneys request that evidence be suppressed in only 1 case out of every 10, and the motion is granted in only 1 out of every 10 requests. This means that in only 1 case out of every 100 is any evidence excluded, and that even in these cases such action may not result in the case being lost or terminated. In only 17 of the 2,804 cases (0.6 percent) were charges dropped by the prosecutor because of anticipated exclusion problems. These figures show that federal courts drop few cases because of procedural slipups.[15] (It is interesting to note that the GAO study was commissioned by the Senate Judiciary Committee, chaired by Edward Kennedy of Massachusetts. Yet before and after the study, Kennedy supported federal legislation to limit the exclusionary rule. One wonders why he wanted the study in the first place, but we might conclude that politics run deeper than liberal beliefs.)

Since most criminal prosecutions take place not in federal courts but in state courts, does the same finding hold there? The answer seems to be yes. New York Supreme Court Justice Peter Mc-Quillas, who has heard thousands of suppression motions in his years on the bench since 1971, states, "I'm convinced that the rule causes no harm to law enforcement" because most motions are rejected.[16] A study released by the Law Enforcement Assistance Administration confirmed this conclusion. In an evaluation of the effect of the exclusionary rule on law enforcement in five cities (Los Angeles; Washington, D.C.; New Orleans; Cobb County, Georgia; and Salt Lake City, Utah), the rule was seldom found to be successfully used to suppress evidence and caused few problems for police.[17]

Research supporting this claim does not stop here. Tangential to their study of robbery in California, Floyd Feeney and Adrianne Weir sought to determine whether any of the 160 cases studied were lost to procedural technicalities. Their conclusion: "Not a single case was lost on 'search-and-seizure' grounds, not a single case involved any serious legal issues involving interrogation, no evidence was excluded as a result of the Miranda rule, and not a single identification of a suspect was lost to the prosecution because of violation of the Supreme Court's rules governing identification of suspects in line-ups."[18] Similarly, a study of what happened to every individual arrested for a serious street crime over a six-year period in Washington, D.C., found the myth that offenders escape punishment as a result of procedural loopholes to be totally false.[19] A Vera Institute study of serious crime—assault, rape, murder, robbery, burglary, and grand larceny—in New York City also failed to link the exclusionary rule with case dismissals.[20] In Los Angeles County, a Rand Corporation study found that 3 percent of the burglary arrests are dismissed because of an illegal search and seizure, unlawful arrest, or some violation of the defendant's rights.[21]

Of the 248 cases analyzed in a study of judicial practices in the Midwest, only one confession and one search were successfully challenged.[22]

Empirical studies lead to a conclusion very different from that popularly held about the effect of the exclusionary rule. It may be politically expedient to single out the rule as a culprit, but it actually plays no discernible role in the dismissal of criminal charges. As *Newsweek* writers Aric Press and Diane Camper suggest of the rule: "While police may not have learned to like it, clearly most have learned to live with it."[23]

Even more significant than finding that exclusion causes few cases to be lost is the realization that it is seldom an issue. Since 9 out of every 10 convictions are the result of guilty pleas (usually as part of a plea-bargain), the quality of the evidence is never an issue. An arrest is made, a deal is worked out, the person pleads and is sentenced. This practice may occasionally lead to the denial of due-process rights. If police officers cannot avoid it, they may make an illegal arrest or obtain "bad" evidence, and then in working with the prosecutor attempt to obtain a guilty plea through bargaining and achieve a conviction in a case that if tried would be lost. Since convictions resulting from guilty pleas preclude most grounds for appeal, exclusion does not become an issue for postconviction relief either.

We should ask why law enforcement officials and politicians are so intent on convincing us otherwise. Why do they try to focus public attention on this aspect of criminal justice when study after study indicates that it is not a problem? Why would Senator Edward Kennedy sponsor legislation that limits the exclusionary rule after a study he requested showed that it did not harm law enforcement? Why would a Manhattan district attorney in a public statement estimate that 25 percent of the cases he takes to court are dismissed because of the rule?[24] The answer to these questions, based on the discussions in the previous chapters, is obvious. Politicians benefit from their active and visible efforts to "get tough" on crime. Law enforcement personnel are acquitted for failing to control crime and are able to promote an image that they are the true protectors of the innocent public—an innovative way of diverting attention from the fact that the police may be doing about as well as they can under any circumstances.

Knowing that exclusion does not handcuff the police falls short of proving it does anything. Its primary if not sole purpose is to deter illegal law enforcement. If the rule accomplishes nothing, the fact that no adverse effects occur is irrelevant. Proponents of exclusion argue that it is "the *only* practical way to prevent wholesale violations" of the Fourth Amendment,[25] but its opponents claim that it fails to embody the fundamental elements necessary for deterrence. Police behavior is too far removed from judicial action that tosses a case out. A fundamental question to be answered, then, is whether the rule is worth having.

One way to evaluate the effect of exclusion is to compare police activities before the rule was applied and after. Police used to use whatever means necessary—even if unlawful—to obtain evidence for a conviction, including breaking into private homes and harassing suspects. But today practices are more regulated and ethical. To attribute this change to the deterrent effect of exclusion would be presumptuous. Professionalization of American law enforcement and decreased public tolerance of illegal law enforcement activities surely contributed to these improvements. Sorting out the role of the exclusionary rule is difficult.

Close examination of a few studies may help resolve this question. One project found that the rule works best in serious cases, but with less serious crimes—such as gambling, narcotics, and weapons violations—the harassment associated with a search and arrest, and the confiscation of contraband, are considered by law enforcement officers to be sufficiently punitive in themselves, so that the loss of a case because of legal technicalities does not really matter. In these cases, exclusion is not an effective deterrent of unlawful practices.[26] Research by Jerome Skolnick supports this conclusion. Police officers were found to tacitly recognize and subscribe to the obligation of obeying procedural standards, but when those standards hindered or prevented the apprehension of criminals, allegiance generally succumbed to the responsibility of reducing crime. Officers were found to occasionally fabricate the events or information after the arrest to justify their intervention, thus establishing probable cause after the fact.[27]

For most Americans, the Miranda warning is the personification of procedural due process. Many people can recite it along with the prime-time television cops and know that if stated incorrectly the arrest will be invalidated. Like most law enforcement activities portrayed on television, however, this image is not accurate. The effect of the *Miranda* decision has not been so universal or dramatic. The warning requirement was precipitated by a case involving interrogation of a suspect in a way that was later determined to be coercive. Ernesto Miranda, a twenty-five-year-old mentally retarded man, was accused of kidnapping and rape. After being arrested and identified by the complaining witness, he was interrogated for about two hours before signing a written confession. His attorneys appealed his case, claiming he did not understand that he had a right to legal counsel or that what he said could be used against him. The U.S. Supreme Court decided that many people arrested are similar to Ernesto in that they do not understand their rights and in the coercive atmosphere of the stationhouse are likely to sign confessions or make statements they normally would not. The Court decided that before interrogations take place defendants must understand their rights.

Despite television's portrayal, widespread compliance with the *Miranda* ruling is not found. Formal procedures of the more professional police departments are generally consistent with the principles of *Miranda*, but in some the practices remain basically unchanged. Outright refusal to comply generally has not occurred, but techniques to subvert its effects have been found. The warning is given, but informal and often coercive or qualifying statements are inserted, the effect of which is to undermine the warning. For instance, a suspect may be encouraged "to get information off his chest," or the importance of the rule may be diminished by reading the defendant his rights and then saying, "We have to say that before we can talk."[28] Because many suspects lack sophistication, these techniques work. A confession is obtained, the case is plea-bargained, and chances for an appeal are lost. *Miranda* has also been eroded by state appeal courts. Prosecutors are allowed to use illegally obtained statements to attack the credibility of defendants. Statements made when a confusing warning was given are allowed in trial, as well as those made when police continue to interrogate after the suspect demands that the questioning be terminated.[29] At the time the Warren Court returned the *Miranda* decision, many claimed it would undermine the ability of law enforcers to obtain a confession. As it turns out, that ability has hardly been affected.

What can be concluded about the effect of the exclusionary rule on police behavior? Law enforcement efforts do not appear to be restricted as often as suggested, but neither have unlawful police practices been eliminated. Perhaps the greatest value of the exclusionary rule is that it sets a high standard for police practice and serves as a check on abuses of official authority. As such, it defines judicial and government integrity. If government should engage in illegal behavior, it invites disrespect and promotes contempt for its authority. Illegal law enforcement activities alone may contribute to that attitude, but the failure of the courts to recognize and disallow those activities would make that conclusion by the public inevitable. The courts failure to react would, in effect, condone unlawful law enforcement and render the courts accomplices in the infringement of the constitutional rights they are charged to uphold.[30] Justice Louis Brandeis described this failure: "To declare that in the administration of the criminal law the end justifies the means—to declare that the Government may commit crimes in order to secure the conviction of private criminals—would bring terrible retribution. . . . If so, the government itself would become a lawbreaker."[31] Without constitutional standards and judicial enforcement of those rules, one wonders how far government might go in assuring conformity to the laws of the land.

Given the right conditions, people will forsake individual protections from an oppressive government. If they are sufficiently afraid of the criminal predator, self-preservation will dominate all other human responses. Self-preservation is a basic instinct that can destroy any sense of justice, reason, and compassion for others. As former U.S. Attorney General Ramsey Clark tells us, justice will be denied in order to obtain what is falsely perceived to provide security: "Arm yourself, suppress dissent, invade privacy, urge the police to trick and deceive, force confes-

sions, jail without trial, brutalize in prisons, execute the poor
and the weak. Due process can wait."[32] It appears that fear is
prompting many to hand over willingly the freedoms of due
process to pursue an unrealistic goal of crime control.

These platitudes may sound imposing, but their importance
has increasingly diminished. Professionalization of law enforcement has greatly reduced unlawful practices, thus rendering the
procedural safeguards unnecessary. Yet before you accept this
conclusion a few recent examples should be examined.

Recall that congressional investigations of the nation's most
prestigious law enforcement agency revealed that the FBI conducted unlawful surveillance of civil rights leader Martin Luther
King, Jr., from 1963 until his death in 1968. King was spied on
by agents with high-powered telescopes, his phone was tapped,
and he was constantly photographed. Was this intensive FBI
effort based on the suspicion that King was involved in some
criminal activity? No. Was it instituted to look out for King's
safety? No. King was believed to be the "most effective Negro
leader in the world"[33] and thus considered dangerous. The Bureau attempted to discredit King with national leaders, tried to
break up his marriage, and even encouraged King to commit
suicide.[34] And we ask whether we should be concerned with
tyrannical government intervention in the private lives of citizens? King's persecution is but one of the many well-docu-
mented examples of FBI activity involving illegal surveillance
and harassment of people who are not suspected of criminal
activity but whose political beliefs were unacceptable to the Bureau's leaders.

In 1979 the American Civil Liberties Union filed a class-action
suit in federal court on the behalf of fifty women who had been
strip-searched by the Chicago police department. The incident,
which brought the practices of the Chicago police into the public
eye, involved a young woman stopped for a minor traffic violation who on indicating that she had left her license at home
was taken to the police station. There she was stripped and
brutally—vaginally and rectally—searched by a matron who did
not bother wearing gloves or washing her hands. The entire
search was conducted under the eye of a closed-circuit television
camera. A subsequent lawsuit and investigative report by a local

television station turned up many women who had been treated in a similar manner. Women were customarily searched, while men were merely patted down. In one case, a woman who accompanied a male friend accused of a crime to the station was strip-searched even though she was not charged with a crime; her friend was not searched at all. Though the Chicago police department denies it, it is alleged that the probings of women's breasts, vaginas, and rectums during these searches were watched by officers in other parts of the station.[35] Again, we must consider whether the police abuse their authority. Chicago is not an isolated example; similar lawsuits have been filed in other cities.

If the police engage in such activities against people considered to be innocent of any crime, imagine what some might do if they suspected a person of illegal activity. Perhaps most would not overstep their authority and would abide by the principles of proper procedure, but there is always the potential for justifying the means by the ends. The police have on occasion abused their authority by breaking into homes, arresting people on superficial charges, interrogating suspects under coercive circumstances, cajoling, threatening, and tricking people into pleading guilty. Professionalization has not reached a point where due process is no longer an issue.

Beyond these shocking examples of the misuse of police power is the more usual and real situation involving the question of how to protect a person's rights. Consider the following example. While walking home one night, William Junior Spence, a mentally retarded man with the understanding of a young child, found the frozen naked body of a young black woman lying on the ground. Spence went for help and led neighbors and the police to the body. Upon finding out that the young woman was a "girlfriend" of Spence's, the police became suspicious and arrested him. He was informed of his rights, but the arresting officer "wasn't sure he understood." Spence was interrogated by three white detectives for more than four hours in a five-by-twelve-foot room in the police station. No lawyer was obtained for him because he did not request one, nor was his mother allowed to see him. The detectives told William "he would feel better if he told the truth," and he eventually signed a four-page confession. His court-appointed attorney argued that Spence would have signed anything because, in a childlike fantasy, he believed he was helping the police.

William Spence was tried and convicted on the basis of the statement he signed; no other incriminating evidence had been uncovered. His case was subsequently appealed.[36] The circumstances of this case are typical. The police acted in good faith; they tried to inform Spence of his rights. The interrogation was conducted according to accepted police practices. Despite these efforts, Spence's rights may have been denied and he may have been wrongly convicted. A process intended to find the truth— "Did William Spence murder Jennie Davis?"—may have failed. We do not know.

So far our discussion has focused on pretrial suppression of evidence, but what about the outcomes of posttrial relief? How many people are actually released from prison because their conviction is overturned on appeal? Opponents of the exclusionary rule claim that many criminals escape punishment. Is this really so common?

A large number of cases are appealed—as many as 90 percent in some jurisdictions.[37] To understand this issue fully, one must realize that there are two different appellate systems where a convicted criminal may seek postconviction relief. Within the state judicial system, an individual may appeal a conviction within a specified time period, usually thirty days. Under normal procedures, a case cannot be appealed in the federal system until it has been reviewed by the highest state court, and then only the U.S. Supreme Court can hear it. If a higher state appellate court or the U.S. Supreme Court does not believe a case merits further consideration, the court is not bound to hear it. This side of the appellate system is confounded by the constitutional right to file a writ of habeas corpus, by which a state prisoner may request that a federal district court review the decision of a state court. This right to challenge the legality of one's confinement creates what amounts to a second appellate system.[38]

Most landmark constitutional decisions have come from the second source, and it is here that most of the controversy abounds. Inmates in state prisons recently began to flood federal courts with petitions for writs of habeas corpus. About 1,000 such petitions were filed each year during the mid-1960s; now over ten times that many are submitted. Inmates may file as many petitions as they wish. Some spend their entire incarceration petitioning federal courts to review their cases, filing as many as ten, twenty, and even thirty writs.[39] Allowing federal courts to review constitutional claims against state courts creates considerable intergovernmental conflict, an issue that will be addressed later.

For now, let us consider how many inmates avoid full imposition of their punishment because of successful appeals. American legal scholars Merlin Lewis, Warren Bundy, and James Hague draw this conclusion: "One often hears the comment that the appellate courts are setting guilty persons free, enabling them to commit more crimes against society. Contrary to this popular notion, this is not the usual case."[40] Even though many cases are appealed, few result in a reversal of lower court decisions. In forty-eight states convicted criminals have the right to an initial appeal[41] but the usual decision of the appellate court is to affirm the lower court's decision. With regard to subsequent state appeals or requests that federal courts review a case, a convicted offender has no right to a hearing. Most requests are refused. Rarely are decisions reversed and remanded (sent back) to the lower court.[42] Consequently, few criminals actually end up going free. Of those cases that are overturned, subsequent trials often reestablish guilt. A few well-publicized exceptions distort the public's perception.

The question of whether these few exceptions justify change brings us back to the question faced in evaluating the exclusionary rule. Appellate review is a basic constitutional right designed to ensure procedural reliability in our system of criminal justice. It is the only protection we have from overzealous law enforcement.

Another important issue concerning the exclusionary rule is the argument for replacing its strict standard of suppression with a more relaxed rule, allowing evidence obtained in "good faith" to be used in criminal trials. President Reagan, Chief Justice Warren Burger, and other conservatives endorse this position, asserting that while the intent of the rule is to prevent police brutality, the invasion of privacy, and gross misuse of power, evidence is in reality often disallowed because of some trivial and technical reason. On the other hand, as we have already discussed, few criminals go free because of the exclusionary rule. Evidence is seldom excluded, and when it is the conviction is not always lost. The few cases that do occur create a political issue because they are so widely reported by the press. The question that remains is whether these cases justify a substantial modification of current practices.

The problem with the "good faith" exception is that it lowers the standard of police conduct to that of the most ignorant and least sensitive police officer. As already discussed, some police officers believe that when it comes to catching criminals the ends justify the means. The "good faith" exception would give these individuals one more excuse to justify their enforcement tactics. Any time illegal evidence is collected or such an opportunity presents itself, officers need only claim ignorance.[43]

If this practice is incorporated into the criminal-justice process, we would not simply rely on the officers' word that they acted in good faith; it would be necessary to subject that claim to an objective test, requiring an additional step in the judicial process. And with whom would the burden of proof lie? Must defendants show maliciousness on the part of the police? Or would police officers be required to prove their ignorance? Such a requirement would do little to promote public confidence in the competence of the law enforcement establishment.

Perhaps Professor Frank Zimring was correct in his assertion that exclusion is the "worst system you could imagine, except for all the others."[44] Yes, miscarriages of justice do occur; occasionally a guilty person goes free. But in a nation that values individual privacy and fears governmental interference, protection against coercive intervention must be maintained.

BEYOND EXCLUSION

Two additional procedural issues receiving the attention of politicians and the press are bail and appellate rights. Conservative critics of bail and the right to appeal claim that changes in these areas will reduce criminal behavior.

Bail is a constitutionally provided right which in theory provides that persons accused of criminal acts must be released so that they can prepare their defense but allows courts to require some assurance, monetary or otherwise, that defendants will appear for their trials. The assumption of the American legal system is that no matter how compelling the evidence may be an accused person is innocent until proven guilty and should not be punished until that fact is established by legal procedures. Federal as well as most state laws specify that bail should be set no higher than necessary to require reappearance. Critics of this practice point out that persons on bail are often arrested for new offenses. One study conducted in Washington, D.C., indicated that as many as 15 percent of all persons arrested are on bail. To avoid this problem and to keep known criminals off the streets, critics advocate preventive detention—the incarceration of accused criminals according to their presumed degree of dangerousness. Advocates of this approach argue that it does not make sense to release violent offenders who repeatedly rape, rob, or murder, totally disregarding the chances they will do so again.[45]

There are at least four compelling reasons for not accepting a policy of preventive detention. First, preventive detention is a step toward punishment without conviction. Incarceration of a suspect because one individual—the judge—believes him or her to be dangerous erodes the fundamental principle of the presumption of innocence. It allows judges to jail people suspected of crimes without bothering with judicial process. That practice could easily evolve into a way of harassing suspects for whom sufficient evidence for conviction is unobtainable, or a way of controlling dissidents, radicals, and other rabble-rousers because criminal procedures would not be required for the denial of freedom.[46]

A second and very practical reason that makes the implementation of preventive detention difficult if not impossible is the lack of a reliable method for determining whether someone is dangerous. Medical tests to determine whether someone has leukemia or diabetes exist, methods to determine whether someone is under the influence of alcohol or narcotics are also available, but no test for "dangerousness" has been developed. The implementation of preventive detention would require reliance on the subjective evaluative abilities of judges, who are seldom trained in human behavior. Judges are as susceptible to biases and stereotyping as any of us. For every correct decision made, they are likely to make many mistakes.

Allowing judges to jail suspects who are believed to be dangerous increases the chances of incarcerating innocent defendants. Studies conducted in Philadelphia, Baltimore, Detroit, and Chicago of defendants detained before trial because they could not afford bail found that in some cases over 50 percent were subsequently acquitted.[47] Denial of bail had the effect of punishing innocent people, often in harsh settings.

A third problem is that pretrial incarceration increases a defendant's chances of being convicted, thereby creating a fundamental unfairness in a system supposedly characterized by equal protection and equal justice. Jailed defendants are significantly more likely to plead guilty or be convicted than those who remain free before trial. Incarceration almost forces an individual to plea-bargain. More important, incarcerated defendants are at a decided disadvantage in preparing their defense, compared with those who are freed. The time available to speak with an attorney is limited to specific times and must be spent in less than ideal surroundings, and they must rely on others, who often have much less at stake, to find and contact witnesses and to obtain needed evidence.[48]

A fourth pragmatic factor also precludes the viability of preventive detention. American jails are already overcrowded, and many are poorly ventilated, unsanitary, and dangerous. Preventive detention would only exacerbate these problems. Since cities and counties cannot afford to correct existing conditions, they are unlikely to be able to finance additional cell space for more inmates.

Modifying the appellate system to limit access to the appellate courts is a second suggestion for judicial change. Two review systems are available: state and federal. Because each system has various levels, as many as eleven steps or options may be explored by convicted criminals in trying to get their cases overturned. It is not unusual for a prisoner to try several options. In fact, a collateral attack will often be initiated by filing an appeal in federal court even before the issue is decided in the state system.[49] Many experts believe that the complexity of this system, particularly the number of levels and options available, is carrying judicial review too far. Surely justice could be done in less than eleven steps. But the reader must be wary of the motivations and justifications used by proponents of simplification and unification of the appellate process.

Arguments for changes in the appellate process are often made in the context of proposals for reducing crime, which is not a valid justification. In terms of the total crime rate, the number of new crimes committed by those few individuals released after successful appeals is insignificant. Even if the appellate right were to be totally abolished—a change that would pose a grave threat to individual freedom and human rights—no noticeable decrease in crime would result. If you are tempted to endorse a suggestion by a politician or a criminal-justice official for overhauling the structure of the appellate system, do not expect that it will result in improved crime control. The proposal is simply another attempt to garner public support and to justify the system's activities.

Another argument for modifying the appellate process is that the federal judiciary has no right to interfere with the decisions of state courts. Conflict arises out of the dual review system when a federal district court—a trial court—overrules a decision of a state supreme court. In these situations, one lowly federal judge overturns the decision of five to seven state supreme court justices. The trend of recent U.S. Supreme Court decisions appears to be returning final authority to the state courts.[50] But a trend is one thing; a policy—legislated or judicially decreed—is another. Without federal review, it is likely that half the states would not provide indigent defendants with legal counsel. Federal review of state practices is imperative if some basic and standard level of justice is to prevail throughout the nation, if constitutional safeguards are to be universally applied. On the other hand, some form of appellate reorganization may be justified on grounds of efficiency. It is unreasonable that a case must be reviewed so many times. That simply delays the implementation of justice and is inefficient and costly. The complexity promotes misunderstanding by citizens, as well as defendants.

NOTES

1. As quoted in a compilation from American newspapers, "Crime and (Nonpunishment), USA," *Reader's Digest*, November 1981, pp. 133–134.

2. Steven R. Schlesinger, *Exclusionary Injustice* (New York: Marcel Dekker, 1977), p. 12.

3. Joseph J. Senna and Larry J. Siegel, *Introduction to Criminal Justice*, 2nd ed. (St. Paul: West Publishing Co., 1981), pp. 172–173.

4. 232 U.S. 383, 34 S.Ct. 393, 58 L.Ed. 652 (1914), as quoted in ibid.

5. Ibid., pp. 168–170.

6. Ibid., pp. 169–170.

7. Quoted in Lane V. Sunderland, "Liberals, Conservatives, and the Exclusionary Rule," *Journal of Criminal Law and Criminology* 71 (Winter 1980): 359.

8. As quoted and discussed in "Reagan Urges Law Reform to Fight Crime 'Epidemic,' " Associated Press story in the *Evening Press* (Binghamton, N.Y.), September 28, 1981, pp. 1, 8A.

9. Sunderland, "Liberals, Conservatives," p. 356.

10. Ibid.

11. As quoted in ibid.

12. "Crime in the U.S.—Is It Getting Out of Hand?" *U.S. News & World Report*, August 26, 1963, p. 38.

13. Quoted in Chares E. Silberman, *Criminal Violence, Criminal Justice* (New York: Vintage Books, 1980), p. 354.

14. Ibid.

15. General Accounting Office, *Impact of the Exclusionary Rule on Federal Criminal Prosecutions* (Washington, D.C., 1979).

16. Quoted in Aric Press and Diane Camper, "A Rule the Police Can Live With," *Newsweek*, June 4, 1979, p. 86.

17. Ibid.

18. Alan Carlson and Floyd Feeney, "Handling Robbery Arrestees: Some Issues of Fact and Policy," in Floyd Feeney and Adrianne Weir, eds., *The Prevention and Control of Robbery*, vol. 2 (Davis, Calif.: Center on Administration of Criminal Justice, University of California at Davis, 1973), chap. 8, esp. p. 133; as reviewed by Silberman, *Criminal Violence, Criminal Justice*, p. 355.

19. "PROMIS Research Project: Highlights of Interim Findings and Implications" (Washington, D.C.: Institute for Law and Social Research, 1977, Mimeographed), pp. 59–60; as reviewed by Silberman, *Criminal Violence, Criminal Justice*, p. 355.

20. Silberman, *Criminal Violence, Criminal Justice*, pp. 355–356.

21. Peter W. Greenwood et al., *Prosecution of Adult Felony Defendants in Los Angeles County: A Policy Perspective* (Washington, D.C.: Law Enforcement Assistance Administration, 1973), Table 46; as reviewed by Silberman, *Criminal Violence, Criminal Justice*, p. 356.

22. David W. Neubauer, *Criminal Justice in Middle America* (Morristown, N.J.: General Learning Press, 1976), pp. 166–167; as reviewed by Silberman, *Criminal Violence, Criminal Justice*, p. 356.

23. Press and Camper, "A Rule the Police Can Live With."

24. Quoted in "Reconsidering Suspects Rights," *Time*, March 8, 1976, p. 44.

25. Quoted by Sunderland, "Liberals, Conservatives," p. 351.

26. "Search and Seizure in Illinois: Enforcement of the Constitutional Right of Privacy," 47 *Northwestern University Law Review* 493 (1952): 497–498, as reviewed by Sunderland, "Liberals, Conservatives," p. 366.

27. Jerome A. Skolnick, *Justice Without Trial* (New York: John Wiley & Sons, 1966), pp. 215–219.

28. Neal A. Milner, *The Court and Local Law Enforcement* (Beverly Hills, Calif.: Sage Publications, 1971), esp. pp. 219–220.

29. John Gruhl, "State Supreme Courts and the U.S. Supreme Court's Post Miranda Ruling," *Journal of Criminal Law and Criminology* 72 (Fall 1981): 886–913.

30. Sunderland, "Liberals, Conservatives," pp. 343–347.

31. 277 U.S. at 485 and 471 (1928) (Brandeis, dissenting); as quoted by Sunderland in ibid., pp. 350, 349.

32. Ramsey Clark, *Crime in America* (New York: Pocket Books, 1971), p. 19; quoted in Sunderland in ibid., p. 345.

33. Quoting the Bureau's Domestic Intelligence Division, Senate Select Committee to Study Governmental Operations with Respect to Intelligence Activities (Church Committee), pp. 11–12.

34. Eugene Lewis, *Public Entrepreneurship* (Bloomington: Indiana University Press, 1980), pp. 141–147.

35. Carol Kleiman, "Chicago Police Methods Exposed," *Ms.* (June 1979): 23; and "Outrage in the Station House," *Time*, March 19, 1979, p. 36.

36. Barry Jacobs, " 'He Didn't Know Half . . . ,' " *The Progressive* 41 (November 1977): 42.

37. Harry E. Allen and Clifford E. Simonsen, *Corrections in America*, 3rd ed. (New York: Macmillan, 1981), p. 129.

38. Merlin Lewis, Warren Bundy, and James L. Hague, *An Introduction to the Courts and Judicial Process* (Englewood Cliffs, N.J.: Prentice-Hall, 1978), pp. 33–36, 63–68.

39. "Reconsidering Suspects' Rights," *Time*, March 8, 1976, p. 46.

40. Lewis et al., *Introduction to the Courts*, p. 34.

41. Ibid.

42. David W. Neubauer, *America's Courts and the Criminal Justice System* (North Scituate, Mass.: Duxbury Press, 1979), p. 53.

43. "Just What Is 'Reasonable' in Search and Seizures? A Debate," *New York Times*, February 28, 1982, p. 20E.

44. Quoted in "Reconsidering Suspects' Rights," *Time*, March 8, 1976, p. 44.

45. Stewart Taylor, Jr., "Pretrial Jailing of 'Dangerous' Suspects," *New York Times*, February 25, 1981, p. A28.

46. Ibid.

47. James P. Levine, Michael C. Musheno, and Dennis J. Palumbo, *Criminal Justice* (New York: Harcourt Brace Jovanovich, 1980), p. 277.

48. Ibid.

49. Allen and Simonsen, *Corrections in America*, p. 130.

50. "Reconsidering Suspects Rights."

9

The Prison Situation

For 36 hours, gangs of convicts seized control of the maximum security penitentiary on the outskirts of a city whose name to most of the rest of the nation, had formerly meant sun on stucco, working ranches and Indian art. Now it became the focus of an intense hell: Prisoners, wielding knives, clubs, stolen riot gear and acetylene torches took 12 guards hostage, stripped them and dragged them through the 24–year-old fortress, savagely beating, slashing and in some cases sexually assaulting them. But the worst was reserved for fellow prisoners, especially suspected informers and other outcasts of prison life, such as the mentally disturbed and retarded. Gangs raped them repeatedly, blow-torched their eyes and genitals, lynched them from tiers, decapitated them or fired tear-gas canisters point blank into their faces. When it was over, authorities counted 33 bodies. Physicians treated about 90 more for drug overdoses, stab wounds, fractures and traumatic amputations.[1]

Something horrible had happened in a system that sprang from an idea formulated by a group of religious, humanitarian reformers who on the eve of the nineteenth century attempted to replace the barbaric and nonutilitarian punitive practices of the time with an arrangement to restore "fellow creatures to virtue and happiness." The Quakers were responsible for the establishment of what is perhaps the major contribution by Americans to criminal justice: the prison. Professional law enforcement, procedural protections of individual liberties, and the U.S. court system are legacies from Europe, but the prison system is purely an American institution, and one founded with the optimism that is so characteristic of American innovation.

In 1787 a group of men and women, many of whom were Quakers, formed the Philadelphia Society for Alleviating the Miseries of Public Prisons, an association that shortened its name to the Pennsylvania Prison Society a century later. Prisons did exist at the time, but their primary purpose was detention, the holding of accused but not yet convicted offenders and those awaiting sanction. Punishments, typically meted out in public, were physical and consisted of mutilation, whipping, branding, amputation, castration, and execution. The instruments of these endeavors included the pillory, stocks, ducking stools, whipping posts, and the gallows. Ostracism and banishment were also commonly used. Less severe acts, such as being unable to repay a debt, were punished by hard labor.[2] The members of the Philadelphia Society believed that these practices were both inhumane and ineffective. The Society's resolution to reform the institution of criminal punishment was summarized by Margaret Wilson, who observed the early efforts of the Society: "By the aids of humanity, their undue and illegal sufferings may be prevented; the links which should bind the whole family of mankind together, under all circumstances, be preserved unbroken; and such degrees and modes of punishment may be discovered and suggested, as may, instead of continuing habits of vice, become the means of restoring our fellow creatures to virtue and happiness."[3] Undergirded with this grand charge, the members of the Society worked to establish the first "penitentiary" in 1790, so named because offenders were expected, through "penitence," to reform themselves. The new penal institution stood in sharp contrast to the typical jail of that day, where criminals, debtors, and even witnesses, male and female, the very young and innocent as well as the mature and hardened, were incarcerated together, where food, clothing, and bedding were often inadequate, where jailers were corrupt and violence was commonplace, and where excessive use of alcohol routinely occurred because the keepers operated bars within institutions. The first penitentiaries were by these standards well-run institutions, with little corruption and adequate physical provisions, where inmates were kept in solitary confinement to promote self-discipline.[4] It is from this intent that Crime Myth 9, "American prisons are humane alternatives to barbaric physical punishment, settings for rescuing criminals from a life of social and personal wickedness," has grown.

Today, almost 200 years after the Grand Experiment began, we must ask ourselves what went wrong. Neither the goal of creating a humanitarian punishment nor that of reforming the criminal has been accomplished. The American prison system stands in sharp relief against the ideals on which it was founded, often characterized by severe overcrowding, unsanitary and even dangerous conditions, violence, brutality, and corruption, and a long record of little success in reforming its clients. Neither its administrators nor its reformers have turned prisons into clean, safe, and fair settings in which moral improvement of an individual might take place. Two early visitors to the New World innovation, Gustave Auguste de Beaumont and Alexis de Tocqueville, realized the inherent failure of the system when they wrote in 1831: "While society in the United States gives the example of the most extended liberty, the prisons of the same country offer the spectacle of the most complete despotism."[5] But Americans never saw the tyranny of the prison that their French visitors did.

The situation is so bad today that U.S. prisons closely resemble critical masses of nuclear material teetering at the threshold of explosion. A single incident can set off a chain reaction—like that in Sante Fe—that may take weeks to bring under control. Because of overcrowding and the wretched physical conditions, to say nothing of the volatile emotional environment, a horror akin to that in New Mexico or in Attica, New York, could erupt in institutions across the nation. As Anthony Travisono, executive director of the American Correctional Association, states, "Conditions are ripe for another Santa Fe. . . . All the elements are there."[6] Or as Tennessee correctional commissioner Harold Bradley suggests, "My fear is we'll have an epidemic of riots. When it comes, it's going to be high, wide, and handsome."[7]

Federal courts condemned and ordered the immediate rectification of various problems in several individual prisons as well as in entire prison systems of many states. In Texas a federal district judge cited as typical of Texas prisons the example of an eighteen-year-old man who after being locked in a three-man cell was repeatedly beaten, raped, and burned with cigarettes for three days before guards discovered what was going on, when he ordered substantial changes in that system.[8]

The question facing Americans is not how contemporary prisons have strayed so far from the ideals of the early-nineteenth-century reformers to the conditions today, because early reforms were never fully realized. Riots, violence, brutality, and corruption are found throughout the prison history. Today, the American penal system is a national problem come to a crisis point. If changes are not made it may well explode and crumble.

OVERCROWDING

At the heart of the prison problem in the United States is the pressure and tension created by overcrowding. With the push to "get tough" on crime, prison populations swelled dramatically during the 1970s and continue to increase nationally by more than 170 additional people each day.[9] In 1970 approximately 200,000 Americans were incarcerated in state and federal institutions.[10] Since then the prison population has doubled. The 400,000 people now locked up represent an incarceration rate of 1 out of every 600 Americans. If this rate of growth (fifteen times that of the national population) continues, the prison population will double again by 1988.[11]

Growth in incarceration rates far exceeds (1) increases in crimes committed, which remained stable during the last decade, (2) the growth of reported crime, which rose some 55 percent since 1971, and (3) even the arrest rate, which increased only by about 10 percent during the same period.[12] These differences show that there has been a swing toward a greater use of incarceration and longer sentences. Recent enactment of fixed and mandatory sentence laws, and the restriction of "good time" and parole, have directly contributed to these increases. That arrests increased by 10 percent while prison populations jumped by 100 percent suggests that increases in the number of criminal offenders are far less important in explaining population growth than more punitive decisions within the justice system. Norman Carlson, director of the Federal Bureau of Prisons, explains the problem like this:

While most would agree that our nation's criminal laws are in need of major revision, the "knee-jerk" response of many legislatures in passing harsher sentencing statutes threatens to totally overwhelm our correctional systems. Unfortunately, in considering such legislation, few elected representatives realize the long-run consequences of their actions. They fail to recognize that in many instances they are compounding an already serious problem.[13]

California illustrates this, perhaps better than any other state. After leading the nation in liberal prison reform and innovative rehabilitation during the 1950s, 1960s, and early 1970s, California began to reconsider its approach to crime control in the late 1970s with a series of new laws aimed at reducing inequities and at "getting tough." Before this time it had enthusiastically endorsed the rehabilitation model of corrections, hoping to reduce crime by reforming convicted criminals. Inmates were sentenced to indefinite periods of incarceration where they were exposed to various techniques of reform until the staff was convinced that an inmate was prepared to reenter society. Extensive use of treatment in the community was also part of the approach. To many Californians, who observed steady increases in reported crime, this strategy was no longer acceptable. Rehabilitation was viewed as too lenient and ineffective. Such groups as the Citizens for Law and Order in Oakland fought for change, and in 1976 the range of time that judges could use in sentencing convicts to prison was greatly restricted. Legislation followed, adding an additional element of severity to the new determinate sentencing code by decreasing the minimum prison term for many crimes.[14]

The effect of the legislation was dramatic: inmate counts swelled.[15] Between 1979 and 1981 alone the population grew by 30 percent. Not only did the number of people sent to prison rise, but the average length of sentences increased. For example, sexual assault sentences increased from five to twenty years. The outcome has been a steady increase in the prison population, averaging more than 100 inmates a week. To keep up with the influx of new prisoners, California would have to build a new 500-person prison every month, but instead it crams more people into existing facilities.[16] This may explain why in 1979 a series of gang disturbances throughout the prison system left several dead.[17] In 1980 a full-scale riot was avoided, but 7 among the 2,900 San Quentin inmates were murdered, while 54 others were stabbed, clubbed, or beaten.[18]

California is not alone in its new approach to punishment. At least thirty-seven states have enacted new mandatory sentencing laws with fixed terms for certain offenses, which prevent judges and correctional administrators from shortening or suspending sentences.[19] Several states have also abandoned indeterminate sentencing to for example, two to five years, twenty years to life, for forms of determinate sentencing with specific prison terms for each offense. The purpose of such legislation is to end the ambiguity associated with the imposition of punishment by eliminating inequities and enhancing the certainty of punishment. However, in drafting legislation to assure equal and certain punishment, lawmakers consistently lengthen sentences.[20] Furthermore, fifteen states have restricted parole, and four have eliminated it.[21] As a result, the actual time served in prison more closely resembles the original sentence, but a safety valve that prisons use to ease overcrowding is eliminated. A final trend among states is greater attention to career criminals—individuals known to repeatedly engage in serious criminal acts. New legislation, changes in enforcement patterns, and a willingness to prosecute to the fullest extent of the law has resulted in much longer sentences for hardened criminals. In the end, each of these activities intended to reduce crime actually increased the number of people being sent to prison and the time they spent there. The result: prison populations doubled and are speeding toward redoubling.

Overcrowding has occurred because prison construction has not kept pace with inmate population growth. Some states tried, but all have been unsuccessful. Mississippi, for example, opened a new unit in late 1981 at a cost of $19 million to house almost 1,500 additional inmates,[22] but between January and July 1982, Mississippi's prison population grew by an annual rate of 44 percent.[23] By the end of 1982, Mississippi's penal system once again exceeded its capacity.[24] Under federal court order to reduce overcrowding, Tennessee built four 200–man regional prisons costing almost $40 million, but at its current rate of incarceration it would fill these within three years.[25] Similarly, Illinois' new prison, designed to hold 1,500 additional inmates, is projected for completion in 1985, but the state expects to have 3,500 additional inmates by that time. Florida's penal system, whose inmate population grew by more than 4,000 in 1981, remains overcrowded despite completion of a new prison on the average of every eight months since 1974.[26]

Unable to keep pace with population increases, state after state has surpassed its capacity. A 1979 report indicated that prisons in every state were overcrowded. Nationally, 58 percent of the one-person cells, 90 percent of the multiperson cells, and 20 percent of the dormitories are overcrowded.[27] Overall, over 200,000 more convicts are incarcerated than prisons were designed to hold.[28]

Administrators have been forced to place two inmates in cells designed for one, or three and four people in a space intended for two. To accommodate overflow, some states have resorted to converting recreational areas to large dormitories. In the spring of 1981, Texas bunked about 3,000 inmates on the floor of small cells already holding two other men. Most of these units measured nine-by-five feet, totaling forty-five square feet, less than the recommended sixty square feet of space for a single inmate. Dormitories were packed so tightly with double bunks that one observer commented that it resembled "one gigantic bed." Under court order, Texas phased out triple-celling, but it did so by setting up a tent camp to house 3,000 individuals.[29]

Texas, which has an extreme problem, is not alone. As of December 31, 1979, about 6,500 prisoners were held in local jails because space was not available for them in state prison facilities. In all, fourteen states were so affected, with Alabama and Mississippi leading the pack, each with over 1,300 inmates backed up in local facilities.[30] A national survey conducted in 1978 found that two-thirds of all state inmates are held in cells with less than the minimally accepted space of sixty square feet per person, and since the survey, space problems have worsened.[31]

As of March 31, 1978, twenty-eight court orders and decrees were in effect concerning overcrowding in *fifteen* states. Confinement has been found to be unconstitutional because of the harsh and unsafe conditions created by excessive numbers of inmates, and orders to rectify the situations were in effect and pending.[32]

According to the *Wall Street Journal*, states are currently considering building as many as 169 new prisons at a cost in excess of $5 billion.[33] This represents a total reversal of the calls for a moratorium on all prison construction a decade earlier.[34] It is unlikely that even such an ambitious construction program would do more than make a dent in the problem. The cost of building a prison that meets space and security requirements runs about $75,000 per inmate space. Since more than 200,000 new spaces are currently needed nationally, we face construction costs of more than $15 billion, and that figure represents only what is needed to accommodate present needs, to say nothing of future demands. While such projects ring happily on the ears of a depressed construction industry, they will be less enthusiastically received by fiscally wary American taxpayers. Michigan voters rejected a tax increase proposal for prison construction in 1980, as New York voters did in 1981. President Reagan, while endorsing other recommendations, failed to find funding for what was considered the most important proposal of the attorney general's Task Force on Violent Crime—that $2 billion be made available to states for prison construction. Yet $2 billion would represent little more than seed money, given the tremendous building needs currently faced by the states.

We are in an unresolvable dilemma. The public, compelled by fear, wants to lock more criminals up for longer periods, yet prison construction cannot keep pace with prison population growth. Perhaps the conclusion of a federally financed study by ABT Associates is accurate in its claim that courts will increase sentences to fill whatever prison space is available, making it impossible ever to resolve the crowding problem through prison construction.[35]

THE EFFECTS OF OVERCROWDING

Experimental psychologists were among the first to examine the changes in behavior that are the result of overcrowded living conditions. Studies of rats showed that under normal circumstances they can coexist quite well when caged together but that when the space per animal is reduced there are noticeable negative changes in behavior. The rats become irritable, more prone to violent attacks, and more susceptible to physical and emotional illness. Weight loss and higher mortality are found in crowded cages.[36]

Negative behavioral reactions are also found in human populations confined in crowded and congested settings. Beyond minimal sustenance, shelter, and some degree of security, an undeniable human need is space. It is necessary for privacy and serves as a retreat from the emotional hustle and bustle of social interaction. Our own space provides a familiar setting in which we can relax and feel comfortable and secure, where defenses can be dropped. One can feel in control and experience a sense of familiarity and belonging. Such space separates us from others and allows us to maintain our individuality, autonomy, independence, and personal identity. Without it, the social environment threatens to engulf us.

As the number of people around us increases, we experience anxiety caused by feelings that the world is closing in and that we are losing control. Think about the last time you were in a crowded shopping mall, on a bus, or at a cocktail party. Did the stress produced by the commotion and constant nearness of other people overwhelm you so you could hardly think or concentrate on what was going on? Perhaps you experienced the swelling of emotional anxiety within you: you couldn't breathe, your throat closed, every nerve was on edge, your extremities tingled and you simply could not stand it. After being in a crowded place for several hours, do you feel emotionally spent and physically exhausted upon arriving home?

Space requirements vary from individual to individual according to their backgrounds and socialization. Such needs are not fixed, and people can adapt to more crowded environments and are usually able to cope with the presence of more people and adjust to less space. But there is a point at which the concentration of people creates psychological as well as physiological stress. All people will not be affected or influenced in the same way, but the incidence of problems consistently increases with crowding. Research has shown this to be true in various settings.[37] Residents of crowded college dormitories report increased feelings of loss of control, physiological stress, and complaints of illness.[38]

Crowding in penal institutions may produce the most volatile situation of all. Students living in crowded dormitories can escape by going to the library or visiting home on weekends. But prisoners do not have these options, so the effects of crowding apply steady pressure on them. That pressure is exacerbated by the violence, racism, and sense of hopelessness found in prisons.

Crowding affects prison life in two ways: control of the prison population is more difficult as individual disciplinary problems and major disturbances increase, and individual deterioration is fostered. A recent study, the most comprehensive and authoritative to date, conducted by researchers at the University of Texas at Arlington for the National Institute of Justice, found that population density directly contributed to these problems. Prisoners living in crowded facilities for sustained periods commit suicide, die, are murdered, create disturbances, become ill, and have interpersonal problems more often than inmates not living in crowded surroundings. Both the actual amount of living space available to each inmate and the total number of men or women incarcerated are related to the negative impacts of imprisonment. Large institutions produce more severe physical and psychological effects than smaller facilities. The researchers concluded that the ideal prison setting would not only meet minimal cell-size requirements (fifty to sixty square feet per person) but would also have small populations (less than 1,000 and preferably around 500 inmates).[39]

Dramatic negative effects of crowding were clearly demonstrated in the National Institute of Justice study's comparison of incarceration trends in Texas and Oklahoma. During the period from 1968 to 1978, the Texas Department of Corrections experienced substantial growth in its population without corresponding increases in facilities to accommodate the expanding number of inmates. With the resulting overcrowding, death and suicide rates as well as reports of disciplinary infractions rose more sharply than the population. Conversely, when the inmate population decreased in Oklahoma from 1973 to 1976, an even greater percentage of decrease in violent deaths occurred. This suggests that the physical and emotional risks an inmate faces are directly related to population size and concentration.[40] A penal system may reduce risk by depopulating, but it greatly increases the risks an individual faces as it packs more and more people into limited space.

Based on these findings and current incarceration trends, a dire future for American prisons must be forecast. Evidence of problems to come is already being seen; the number of major disruptions appears to be rising. In the first half of 1981, violence broke out in prisons in Florida, Hawaii, Michigan, Nevada, New Jersey, and New York.[41] Continued concentration of prisoners in already overcrowded facilities will make the situation worse and probably lead to further escalation of prison violence.

The issue of overcrowding was brought before the U.S. Supreme Court in 1981. In *Rhodes v. Chapman* the Court was asked to decide whether doubling up inmates in cells designed for one person constituted cruel and unusual punishment. Kelly Chapman, an inmate in Ohio's maximum security prison in Lucasville, initiated the suit when he discovered that state regulations required at least forty-three square feet of space be provided a five-week-old calf. Chapman's cell space amounted to only thirty-two square feet. It was argued that the incarceration of two men in cells measuring six by ten feet increased the risk of violence and exploitation.[42] The Supreme Court, however, ruled in favor of the state, and double-celling continues.

But we must look beyond the relatively simple relationship of overcrowding and violence. Recent changes in the prison environment and the inmate social structure have altered life in prison. Assaults, drug traffic, and powerful gangs are now common in many prisons. So bad is the situation that one author characterizes the prison as a "tinderbox;"[43] another as "all set for an explosion."[44]

THE PRISON ENVIRONMENT

The image of American prisons held by many people is that portrayed in late-night movies on television. Institutions are old, dimly lit, dingy caverns constructed of stone, mortar, and brick, complemented by gray steel bars, catwalks, beds, toilets, and mesh fencing. Cell blocks are huge with many cells, often in several tiers. Outside, walls with omnipresent guard towers enclose the institution and its small grounds from outside view.

In contrast to the paucity of visual stimulation, noise and smells abound within these massive enclaves. Sound modulates from utter silence to the roar of a thousand footsteps as men move through the institution, to the thundering crash of steel slamming against steel, to the low rumble of a thousand whispers. Smells of food cooking, sweat, garbage, sewer gases, and a thousand human bodies permeate the still, stuffy air of the facility.

Over 40 percent of the 559 state prisons in operation today were built before 1950, and 1 out of every 5 prisons were constructed before 1925.[45] The physical condition of these antiquated facilities is often deplorable and falls far below any standard of humane incarceration. For example, Indiana State Prison in Michigan City has been described as "one of filth. . . . Trash collects in loose heaps. Some as tall as men must have been left for days. . . . The plumbing and ventilation are oppressive."[46]

Still, the physical setting of most prisons is not as wretched as that at Indiana State Prison. Over half were constructed after 1950. Some were modeled after large institutions of earlier years, but most incorporate a variety of new features. Enclosed not by walls but by tall chain-link fences, many modern prisons more closely resemble college campuses than traditional facilities. Living units tend to be smaller, and some complexes consist of a variety of living and special-function units (education, vocational, administration, etc.) spread over the prison grounds resembling a complex of garden apartments.

But whatever the physical facade of these new institutions, total confinement in any facility is much the same. Control is still the dominant theme, and security is tight. Inmates are locked in their cells at night, movement from place to place is restricted and often involves group movement under close supervision, counts of inmates are conducted frequently throughout the day, and an attempt is made to know exactly where each inmate is at every moment. Guards are always watching. *Time* magazine explains: "Some people fear that prisons are now too cushy, so spiffed up that chastisement is nullified. But the 'country club prison' is as unreal as the prison *cum* treatment center. A plain deprivation of freedom is quite severe all by itself."[47]

Beyond the physical features of prisons are the social and organizational aspects of institutional life which have important implications for what incarceration is like. Most prisons are administered by a militaristic regime of personnel hierarchically arranged from guards to warden that exercises tyrannical control over all activities in the institution. In direct opposition to this formal structure is an equally viable informal organization of the inmates, the sole purpose of which is to resist and subvert administrative control.[48] Within the informal structure, inmate leaders exercise a power that has more effect on what happens in the prison than anything the warden does. New prisoners are socialized into the subculture, and each assumes some role within that society.[49]

Until recently the inmate subculture helped control prisons and prevented violence. Widespread endorsement of a code of behavior, which included such rules as "Don't rat on another inmate, Mind your own business, Never exploit another inmate, Never cooperate with correctional officers, Do your own time, and Don't whine,"[50] maintained inmate behavior within certain limits. Inmates refusing to abide by the rules were disciplined by their peers.[51] An inmate who persistently stole from other inmates might eventually be stabbed.

Symbiotic relationships, unacceptable within the formal prison structure but invaluable to institutional control, developed between guards and inmate leaders. In exchange for assurances that no problems (activities that would get the attention of the administration) would occur on the cell block, guards allowed themselves to be corrupted by inmate leaders. They warned of upcoming cell shakedowns and ignored various improprieties and rule infractions (such as the manufacturing of bootleg liquor, possession of contraband, and sexual exploitation of weaker inmates).[52]

In the 1960s, changes in prisons altered this tenuous structure. The social upheaval that changed life in the free world had a devastating impact on prison life. The informal subculture as it existed did not survive, and the stability and control found in prisons in the past was lost. Changing interracial relationships

among inmates served as a major catalyst for many of the modifications in institutional life. Traditionally, black inmates assumed a humble, passive, and subordinate role in prison. They
seldom occupied leadership positions in the inmate subculture
and were for the most part submissive, not only to the predom-
inately white guard force but also to white prisoners. This began
to change in the late 1950s and early 1960s as the proportion of
black prisoners rose and racial awareness increased. As the black
movement gained momentum, tension and divisions among the
races escalated.[53]

With black radicalization, racial hostilities and violence spread.
The resulting racism and polarization of inmate groups led to
the erosion and demise of the inmate social order. No longer
was the rule that inmates should not exploit one another a controlling force. Rigid patterns of informal segregation among black
and white inmates evolved, so that older, influential, and respected inmates could no longer cross racial lines to mediate
disputes. When an incident occurs, violence often escalates because retaliation is more aggressive than the original offense.
Inmate leaders have been unable or unwilling to cooperate with
guards and prison administrators to bring the situation under
control.

Young hoodlums willing to exploit almost anyone, even fellow
inmates, have always found their way into prison. Before the
escalation of racial problems and the demise of the old informal
subculture, these individuals were controlled by widespread re-
sistance to them among the inmates. They were neither liked
nor respected, and while they were occasionally successful in
robbing or raping another inmate, their deviance was in general
not tolerated by the majority of inmates. With the changes in
prison, control of these young criminals was lost and their power
increased substantially.

The violence in prisons today forces the majority of inmates
to withdraw. In its most drastic form, this involves a request for
segregation. An inmate, because he fears for his safety, may ask
the prison administration to place him in protective custody,
away from the main population of the prison. The price for such
a request is virtual isolation in a single cell with few opportunities
for recreation, exercise, or interpersonal contact. The inmate

spends endless hours locked in his cell. Most inmates opt for less drastic forms of withdrawal and remain in the general population. They comply with voluntary lines of racial segregation and avoid prison public life as much as possible by spending much of their time in their cells, alone or with a very few close friends.[54]

According to Gaylor Puckett, a white inmate serving a forty-to-fifty-year sentence in Statesville (Illinois) for murder: "Everyone's afraid." He relates a story of his own trouble with a prison gang when he was ordered killed for supposedly snitching, an accusation he denies. He claims he tried to get word of this to the warden, but the guard in whom he confided failed to pass the message along and instead left Puckett's cell door open for a gang member to execute him. This fate was avoided by a self-inflicted wound that resulted in a hospital transfer. Puckett states, "If the gangs see potential in you, they'll use you."[55]

Once the most respected inmate was the individual adhering to the code, accepting punishment and confinement in a manly fashion and doing his own time. Today the most respected inmate "stands ready to kill to protect himself, maintains strong loyalties to a small group of other convicts (invariably of his own race), and will rob and attack or at least tolerate his friends' robbing and attacking other weak independents or their foes."[56]

The social environments in most prisons today are characterized by violence, hatred, and fear. They have been described as ultimate slums, inhabited by impoverished people hostile to one another, where low commitments to public morality enhance the potential for interpersonal exploitation.[57]

DAILY ROUTINE

Beyond the violence, racism, hatred, and other atrocities of prison, the dominant aspect of incarceration for most inmates is boredom. The unmitigated absence of anything constructive to do, the forced idleness, is what is so distracting, so frustrating, and often so damaging.

What do inmates do with their time? Since in most prisons inmates are responsible for keeping the institution clean, maintained, and operating, prison chores occupy a portion of their

time. Some are assigned to the kitchen to assist in meal prep-
aration; others work in the prison laundry. Skilled inmates are
assigned to maintenance crews to do plumbing, electrical work,
and carpentry. But the most frequent assignment is custodial:
sweeping the unit, taking out the trash, scouring the latrine,
tidying the grounds, and cleaning administrative areas. The work
is menial and monotonous, yet for most inmates it is a welcome
relief from idleness. In many prisons there are not enough jobs
to keep all inmates occupied. In Illinois' Stateville, 15 percent of
the prisoners do not have assignments—not because they do
not want them but because there simply are not enough jobs to
go around.[58]

Why is there not more for prisoners to do? Didn't prisons in
the past operate factories in which inmates produced various
commodities? Surely such practices are better than allowing inmates to sit around with nothing to do but get into trouble. It
is true that prisons once operated their own industries, but free
world entrepreneurs and labor unions objected to the competition so prison industry was curtailed. The few prison industries
that survived (most by limiting their market to state agencies)
are generally inefficient. Plants are run not by professionals but
by inmates and prison officials more concerned about security
than production. Work methods are often outdated, and production activities are poorly organized. Because profit motives
are not strong for either the inmates or the supervisor, there are
few incentives. Equipment and machinery are often obsolete.
Thus, prison-made goods tend to be inferior in design and quality, and consequently the industry is not competitive.[59]

Since the work to do in prison is limited, one of the things
inmates fill their time with is exercise. To the chagrin of many
police officers, who know that most inmates will eventually be
released, the most popular form of exercise is weightlifting (an
activity that produces strong ex-felons who may have to be re-
arrested some day). Within the prison culture, weightlifting is
important for more reasons than occupying time. It is an outward
symbol that a man is strong and can take care of himself, and
it serves as a way for the inmate to protect himself symbolically
and physically in the harsh exploitative and violent prison environment. As a masculine sport with visible signs of improve-

ment, it provides the prisoner one of few opportunities for self-fulfillment and a chance to accomplish something.

Inmates fill some of their time with reading, playing games (chess, backgammon, checkers, and dominoes), and watching soap operas, one of the most popular activities. Ultimately, some time in prison is spent in complete idleness, but perhaps this is as it should be. As one inmate says, "The isolation and idleness are the worst. This is really doing hard time."[60] The lack of anything to do, the forced idleness, may be the punishment criminals deserve. Society may truly get even by denying convicted criminals anything to do.

Few adults are ever in a situation where they have nothing to do. But imagine being confined in a restricted place and further confined by the violence about you, so that you must spend hour after hour, day after day idle, accomplishing nothing. Could you stand it? Would you be able to maintain your sanity? After a few years of this, would you be able to return to a productive life? Or would you slowly become angry with those holding you and those responsible for your confinement? I doubt that many of us would be unscathed. Incarceration, particularly for long periods of time, causes unavoidable individual deterioration.

CONCLUSIONS

The first prisons, which were intended to be humane and to be a means for reforming the worst of society's miscreants, forced idleness through solitary confinement to allow inmates to do penance for their crimes. But the inmates could not take the loneliness, the silence, the nothingness, and they went mad. Abandoning this technique, prisons experimented with new ideas. From penitentiary to reformatory, to the industrial prisons of the North to the plantation prisons of the South, to the rural fortress-like warehouses of the depression to the correctional institution of later, the prison evolved. With a history of such grand design, it is ironic that the poverty of idleness remains as a characteristic of contemporary institutions. People with little to do, much like unnurtured plants, deteriorate, some physically, most emotionally. People with little to do are more likely to resist authority, fight among themselves, and get caught up in the chain reaction of mass disturbance.

Most prison experts have finally come to agree that prisons cannot reform, neither through inflicting pain nor through offering understanding and encouragement. All inmates cannot be returned to the community as respectable members of society. Some can, but it is their own willingness to change that is more important than what the prison does. There are things that can be done in the incarcerative setting that will help, but there are no guarantees, not even that the same effect could have been achieved without imprisonment.

So what are prisons for? They are for incapacitating dangerous and villainous people, and they provide a setting for retribution. But Americans must realize that incarceration is a resource that is limited and can be misused. Because the cost of prison construction is great, the nation cannot afford to create more and more prison space to lock up a larger and larger portion of the population.

The utility of incarceration is analogous to disciplining children. If you over discipline a child, the punishment does more harm than good. At the same time, if you fail to discipline, the child will be uncontrollable and unruly. One simply cannot punish every infraction to the fullest, but must select only those particularly bad or undesirable acts for the most severe sanction. Others, even though bad, must be ignored, and some must be dealt with by reprimand or mild punishment. With increased fear of crime came the desire to punish more criminals more severely. Americans are allowing their fear to push them to a point of overdisciplining and are beginning to see the ill-effects of such actions.

NOTES

1. James Lieber, "The American Prison: A Tinderbox," *New York Times Magazine*, March 8, 1981, p. 26.

2. James P. Levine, Michael C. Musheno, and Dennis J. Palumbo, *Criminal Justice* (New York: Harcourt Brace Jovanovich, 1980), p. 312.

3. Margaret Wilson, *The Crime of Punishment* (New York: Harcourt Brace Jovanovich, 1981), pp. 199–200, as quoted in Harry Elmer Barnes

and Negley K. Teeters, *Criminology* (New York: Prentice-Hall, 1943), p. 487.

4. Barnes and Teeters, *Criminology*, pp. 492–493.

5. Gustave Auguste de Beaumont and Alexis de Tocqueville, *In the Penitentiary System in the United States and Its Application in France* (1833) trans. Francis Lieber; as quoted in Barnes and Teeters, *Criminology*, p. 537.

6. Anthony Travisono, quoted by Lieber, "The American Prison," p. 26.

7. Harold Bradley, quoted by Robert E. Taylor, "Life in Prison: More Riots Are Feared as Overcrowding Fuels Tension Behind Bars," *Wall Street Journal*, August 18, 1981, p. 1.

8. Ibid.

9. Kurt Anderson, "What Are Prisons For?" *Time*, September 13, 1982, p. 38.

10. Timothy J. Flanagan, David J. van Alstyne, and Michael R. Gottfredson, eds., *Sourcebook of Criminal Justice Statistics, 1981*, U.S. Department of Justice, Bureau of Justice Statistics (Washington, D.C.: Government Printing Office, 1982), p. 470.

11. Anderson, "What Are Prisons For?"

12. Federal Bureau of Investigation, *Crime in the United States—Uniform Crime Reports, 1980* (Washington, D.C.: Government Printing Office, 1981), pp. 38, 194.

13. Quoted by Lieber, "The American Prison," pp. 58, 60.

14. Taylor, "Life in Prison," p. 21.

15. Lieber, "The American Prison," p. 60.

16. Taylor, "Life in Prison," p. 21.

17. Lieber, "The American Prison," p. 60.

18. Anderson, "What Are Prisons For?" p. 38.

19. Ibid., p. 21.

20. Ibid., pp. 40–41.

21. Taylor, "Life in Prison," p. 21.

22. Lynnette McIntire, "Prison Gates Open for Officials' Visit," *Commercial Appeal* (Memphis, Tenn.), November 2, 1981, pp. A1, A3.

23. Anderson, "What Are Prisons For?" p. 40.

24. McIntire, "Prison Gates Open."

25. Kevin N. Wright, "An Analysis of the Overcrowding Problem in Tennessee Prisons," (University of Tennessee at Chattanooga, 1979, Mimeographed).

26. Anderson, "What Are Prisons For?" p. 39.

27. U.S. Department of Justice, Bureau of Justice Statistics, *State Correctional Populations and Facilities, 1979—Advance Report* (Washington,

D.C.: Department of Justice, 1981), Table 6, reprinted in Flanagan et al., *Sourcebook*, p. 146.

28. William F. Buckley, "Watergate's Prison Reformer," *Washington Post*, April 20, 1982, p. A25.

29. Taylor, "Life in Prison," p. 1A.

30. U.S. Department of Justice, Bureau of Justice Statistics, *Prisoners in State and Federal Institutions on December 31, 1979*, National Prisoner Statistics Bulletin SD-NPS-PSF-7 (Washington, D.C.: Government Printing Office, 1980), p. 15; reprinted in Flanagan et al., *Sourcebook*, p. 469.

31. Taylor, "Life in Prison," pp. 1A, 3A.

32. Joan Mullen and Bradford Smith, *American Prisons and Jails*, Volume 3: *Conditions and Costs of Confinement*, U.S. Department of Justice, National Institute of Justice (Washington, D.C.: Government Printing Office, 1980), p. 32, reprinted in Flanagan, et al., *Sourcebook*, p. 150.

33. Taylor, "Life in Prison," p. 3A.

34. Gordon Hawkins, *The Prison* (Chicago: University of Chicago Press, 1976), p. 43.

35. Reviewed by Taylor, "Life in Prison," p. 21.

36. J. B. Calhoun, "The Role of Space in Animal Sociology," *Journal of Social Issues* 22 (October 1966): 46–49; and "Population Density and Social Pathology," *Scientific American* 206 (February 1962): 139–148.

37. For a review of literature, see Paul B. Paulus, "Crowding," in Paul B. Paulus, ed., *Psychology of Group Influence* (Hillsdale, N.J.: Lawrence Erlbaum Associates, 1980).

38. Garvin McCain, Verne C. Cox, and Paul B. Paulus, *The Effect of Prison Crowding on Inmate Behavior* (Washington, D.C.: U.S. Department of Justice, National Institute of Justice, December 1980), p. 4.

39. Ibid.

40. Ibid.

41. "U.S. Study Blames Violence on Size, Jamming of Prisons," *Evening Press* (Binghamton, N.Y.), August 24, 1981, p. 1A.

42. Lieber, "The American Prison," pp. 26–28.

43. Ibid., p. 27.

44. Paul A. Gigot, "Life in Prison," part 2, *Wall Street Journal*, August 20, 1981, p. 1.

45. Mullen and Smith, *American Prisons and Jails*, Volume 3, p. 244; reprinted in Flanagan et al., *Sourcebook*, p. 143.

46. Lieber, "The American Prison," pp. 32, 34.

47. Anderson, "What Are Prisons For?" p. 39.

48. See Donald Clemmer, *The Prison Community* (New York: Holt, Rinehart & Winston, 1940).

49. Lee H. Bowker, *Corrections* (New York: Macmillan, 1982), pp. 149–151.

50. Harry E. Allen and Clifford E. Simonsen, *Corrections in America*, 3rd ed. (New York: Macmillan, 1981), p. 283.

51. Clemmer, *The Prison Community*.

52. See Bowker, *Corrections*, p. 192.

53. John Irwin, *Prisons in Turmoil* (Boston: Little, Brown, 1980), pp. 66–72.

54. Ibid., p. 187.

55. Gigot, "Life in Prison," p. 19.

56. Irwin, *Prisons in Turmoil*, pp. 181–182.

57. Ibid.

58. Gigot, "Life in Prison," p. 19.

59. Gordon Hawkins, *The Prison* (Chicago: University of Chicago Press, 1976), p. 120.

60. Gigot, "Life in Prison," p. 19.

PART THREE

Dealing with Crime

10

The Social Context of Crime Control

Most Americans believe that criminals commit their predatory and violent acts for what they get out of them, the advantages they receive. Often those benefits are obvious, as in the case of most property crimes. A person who breaks into a house and steals a television set does so because he wants either the television or the money that can be obtained from selling it. Even in the case of violent personal crimes, the criminal can gain something, whether it is perverse pleasure from inflicting pain, the satisfaction of having control over another human being, or the resolution of a problem by eliminating a person causing that vexation. With practically every crime committed, the offender benefits in some way, typically at the expense of the victim.

The last factor is what irritates us so. It offends our sense of fair play and our belief in honest productivity. From a moralistic perspective, criminal acts are exploitive, and the people who commit them are predatory and parasitic. Criminals live off the labors of hardworking, honest citizens and fail to accept social responsibilities or to make any contribution to the well-being of society.

Because criminals are believed to be motivated by the personal utility of their actions, people also perceive them as having some choice in whether or not to commit crimes. Only in rare cases, such as when one is forced to murder in self-defense or is truly coerced by others, does a person have no alternative. In all other cases, individuals exercise some free will; their criminality is not predestined and their acts are not unavoidable. Of course, the choice an individual makes may be encouraged by social circumstances and past experiences. Various factors are recognized by criminologists as contributing to and prompting the decision to commit a crime. Some suggest that the choice is influenced by the behavior, opinions, and attitudes of people who are important to the individual. If a person's family or friends are criminal, it is more likely that a criminal lifestyle will be chosen, while a person not exposed to such behavioral patterns will be much less likely to choose such a lifestyle. Other experts argue that the lack of legitimate opportunities may increase a person's chances of engaging in criminal behavior. Factors related to the individual's socialization and environmental circumstances are also thought to contribute to the decision. But in each case the offender is perceived as having some choice; alternatives may be limited, and in some cases a decision to commit a crime may be the easier decision to make, but almost never are life's decisions cast for an individual so that no choice can be exercised. We know of people who grew up in criminogenic environments—impoverished settings where family and friends often engage in criminal acts and there are few opportunities to overcome this heritage—yet they became productive and respected members of the community. We also know people raised in good homes by caring parents and offered innumerable opportunities who pursue an immoral and lawless existence. Even within the same family, the presence of one "good" child and one "bad" child is sometimes observed. So Americans conclude that the predator and the parasite are that way to a large extent because they choose to be.

Such thinking is consistent with American ideology in general. The United States is an achievement-oriented nation that expects its citizens to act purposefully and productively. To do otherwise is considered impulsive, irresponsible, and sometimes evidence that the person is no longer in control. In this "land of opportunity," people are supposed to be able to accomplish what they want if they work hard and long enough. According to this ideology, people are the shapers of their own destinies. It follows that the same is true for criminals. Popular beliefs about criminals are thus linked to more general sentiments about human motivations. Crime is a way of fulfilling the American dream, but one that fails to consider the rights of other people. Criminals are people who purposefully set their own needs and desires above those of others and willfully exploit other people to get what they want.

It follows that crime control should be implemented in a manner consistent with beliefs about criminality, which brings us to Crime Myth 10, "The crime control strategy of the criminal-justice system is correct in assuming that personal gain is the primary motivation for crime and that eliminating the profit will reduce crime." Punishments are viewed as a way of imposing some costs on illegal behavior. People assume that if the costs are sufficient, both in terms of likelihood and severity, then potential offenders will refrain from illegal behavior. This philosophy of crime control incorporates a relatively simple idea of cost-benefit. Offenders are assumed to be attracted to criminality by the benefits they may receive and are deterred from such activity by threats of criminal sanctions which pose potential costs that outweigh any benefits to be derived. If the gains fall short of the potential losses, it is assumed that people will refrain from the activity. Yet if the gains from crime exceed any potential losses, then crime makes sense. Rational choice is thus an important factor in criminality as well as in its control.

According to this view, the key to crime control is to make it clear to all that criminal behavior will not be tolerated. People must believe that if they persist in exploiting others they will be punished. If anything interferes with the induction of this threat, potential offenders will think that they can get away with crime. This is one reason people are so disturbed when a criminal escapes punishment because of the exclusionary rule. To make believers out of criminals, justice officials must have the freedom to seach out, catch, and convict offenders, and then to punish them. Severe sanctions will make anyone think twice about offending.

This widely accepted idea of crime control is neither new nor particularly American. It dates back to the eighteenth century, when criminal sanctions were barbaric, cruel, and had little to do with the offense. Cesare Beccaria and Jeremy Bentham argued that the punishment should fit the crime. A utilitarian philosophy, which asserts that people make decisions according to their needs and wants weighed against the cost of those actions, is the basis of this idea. People attempt to maximize their pleasure while minimizing discomfort. A legal system that wants to incorporate these ideas must strike a balance between the criminal act and the sanction to follow. It is interesting to note that the same idea used in the eighteenth century to reduce criminal sanctions is being used today to argue for more severe sanctions.

Most Americans identify with the pleasure/pain principle. Throughout their lives they learn to avoid activities and behaviors that produce an unpleasant sanction and to engage in others because of the pleasure they bring. In learning to resist impulses to do something wrong for fear of what will happen, people are actually being frightened into obedience. Each one of us can relate instances when we refrained from a particular activity for fear of being caught. As children we learned to avoid certain behaviors (taking from others, name-calling, and talking back) in order to escape the sanctions of parents and teachers. As adults, out of fear of reprisal we refrain from telling the boss what we really think of him, from speeding, and from taking items from stores without paying. Given these experiences, it is not surprising that Americans incorporate this technique into their crime control system.

Like beliefs about criminality, this perception of crime control is consistent with broader American ideology. People are expected to be achievement-oriented—to be assertive and ambitious—but blind ambition is condemned. In expecting people to act purposively and to anticipate the outcomes of their actions, we also expect that they will moderate their behavior according to specific and known moral obligations. In believing that the rights of others should be considered, Americans form a strong sense of fair play. Evidence of this is seen in many behaviors and attitudes, but possibly no more clearly than in sporting behavior. Observe the crowd at an athletic event when unfair advantage is taken, as when a boxer delivers a low blow or a football referee fails to call an obvious personal foul. Overlying the strong achievement orientation is an encompassing moral fiber rendering two aspects to the inducement system: achievement with constraint.

THE MISSING LINKS

Efforts to control crime are not as successful as might be hoped. For many people this indicates that changes in the present system of criminal justice are desperately needed. Specifically, the justice system must be shored up to be consistent with the philosophy just set forth. Sanctions must be more certain and more severe. To some people the rights of criminals are protected at the expense of their victims, and criminals, if sanctioned at all, merely have their hands slapped. This imbalance calls out for a reallocation of costs and benefits. In order to protect itself, society must increase the chances of detection, conviction, and punishment, as well as the unpleasantness of the sanction. The threat must be made real and meaningful for those who continue to prey on society. It is from this attitude that Crime Myth 11 arises: "Because crime control efforts have not been effective, additional resources must be allocated to ensure a fuller implementation of the strategy, and the administration of deterrent sanctions must be made more certain and more severe."

Many who argue for "getting tough" claim that the nation can be returned to a time when the streets were safe and criminals were apprehended and treated severely. But we have seen here that this is an image of bygone days that never existed. The United States has always experienced a considerable amount of crime, possibly not as much as today but more than other nations. Crime has always been an issue of public concern. The notion that stiff penalties were once effective is simply inaccurate. In fact, given the conditions of most American prisons today, it is unlikely that sanctions are substantially less severe now than earlier in this century. We lock up a larger proportion of the population than in the past, but the nation realizes no reductions in criminality. Does this not suggest something? Year after year the United States has both a high crime rate and a high punishment rate. Does this not make you skeptical of the practice of criminal punishment itself? Could there not be some problem, some fundamental flaw, in the basic philosophy on which American crime control is based?

I believe there is. Our system of justice relies on fear and coercion to obtain compliance with society's rules. Threats are of limited use. If people generally endorse the principles and behaviors outlined by the rules, then widespread compliance occurs. The formal statement and enforcement of a threat associated with a widely held principle reinforces its importance for the population. People get into the habit of complying with the rules, and the legal threat is accepted and internalized in their behavioral system. When general endorsement is lacking, however, threats will not be effective. Edwin Sutherland, the father of American criminology, stated: "When the mores are adequate, laws are unnecessary; when the mores are inadequate, the laws are ineffective."[1] Unless a fundamental embodiment of well-established morals is present within society, criminality and other forms of deviance will be common. Compliance may be achieved by the threat of sanction so long as the threat is real, but that requires constant surveillance and enforcement. As endorsement declines and deviance becomes more widespread, it becomes more and more difficult, and then impossible, to maintain the effectiveness and meaningfulness of the threat. Then, all efforts to remedy that situation will fail, because the problem lies not with the threat but with acceptance of the principle behind it.

For this reason, having much hope that the justice system will bring criminality under control is a delusion. More effective police forces, more efficient courts, and improved correctional practices will have little effect on public endorsement of law-abiding principles of behavior. And even while the symbolic act of formalizing a rule by making it law may strengthen endorsement by those who already accept it, it will have little meaning for those who do not recognize its value or who choose to disregard it. If you doubt this, recall the success of prohibition.

Social order is not and can never be obtained or maintained by coercion. Law-abiding behavior is acquired primarily through socialization. Think about the last time you were extremely angry with someone, so enraged that you could have struck or even killed that person. What prevented you from going ahead and doing it? Something within you, some unidentified force, kept you from physically injuring your adversary. But you probably never considered that you might be punished for your action. The threat of criminal sanction is simply not a strong or important determinant of behavior. Rather, through a process of learning and socialization you came to know that hurting others is unacceptable.

Assimilation, not coercion, is the important factor in obtaining obedience. We learn what behaviors are acceptable and why, and in the course of these experiences also come to recognize the mutual benefit of restraint. Compliance becomes voluntary and automatic. The acquisition of response patterns while driving is analogous. When one first begins to drive, reaction must be conscious and is often awkward. If an animal runs in front of the car, the beginning driver must consciously think what to do—lift the foot from the accelerator, remember where the brake is, and finally stop the car—but this reaction quickly becomes automatic. An experienced driver will stop the car and not be conscious of the cognitive steps taken. Law-abiding behavior becomes similarly patterned by custom and habit. Compliance generally becomes second nature.

The utility of coercion and socialization is seen in child-rearing. With very young children, coercion is the only effective control. If the child goes into the street, she is disciplined and told that if she does that again she will be punished again. Punishment is used to instill recognition of acceptable and unacceptable behavior. But parents realize that until the child recognizes the dangers and internalizes the rule of not entering the street, no threat, however great, will assure that the child will not reenter the street. Until then, surveillance and reeducation are necessary. Yet as the child grows older, coercion becomes less effective. Parents find it impossible to force the child to do anything; monstrous fights and arrogant rebellion occur. Order in the household seems to be achieved only by voluntary compliance. Threats and punishments continue to be used, but they work only when the child agrees to their use. In extreme situations, it does not matter what is threatened or how severe the punishments are. If the child wants to do something, she will. Eventually every parent must forego coercion. For most this is a gradual process: we stop spanking, then stop limiting freedom, and finally stop telling the child what to do. When that day comes we hope that socialization has been achieved.

Societies find themselves in much the same position as households with teenagers: without voluntary compliance order will not be attained. Threats of sanction tend to be effective only when they are generally accepted; otherwise, people simply seek ways to get around compliance, or they may openly defy prohibitions. Only a strict police state that maintains constant surveillance and rigid discipline can control a society prone to deviance. Even then, the ability of an autocratic government to force conformity is limited for not everyone can be watched at all times. Furthermore, the threat of punishment will influence only certain people. An excellent example is behavior within a military unit. Few organizations embody such strong external controls as those the military uses in disciplining its troops. The troops' performance demonstrates the effectiveness of such measures. Orders and responsibilities are carried out with predictable consistency. Even in the face of great dangers and threats to personal safety, troops will perform as directed. This would seem to suggest that coercion may be effective, yet observance of a unit in which there is dissension in the ranks will dispel this notion. In World War II, when there were strong commitments to the cause, discipline was the norm, but many problems were experienced in Vietnam, where commitments were much weaker. Thus, even in situations when strong formal controls and coercion are used, obedience still rests on acceptance of the legitimacy of authority and the rules.

INFORMAL AND FORMAL CONTROLS

The distinction between formal and informal controls is useful in understanding this problem. The formal controls discussed above are the controls most people think of when they consider crime control. They consist of formally stated rules (i.e., laws), procedures for enforcing those rules, and specific agencies responsible for their enforcement. In the case of criminal sanctions, the substantive and procedural rules are stated in the criminal law and are enforced by the agencies of the criminal-justice system. The ability of the justice system to exercise the threat of sanction is not the only influence in our lives. Informal controls also prevent criminality. They consist of well-established and understood, but seldom written, rules (i.e., norms) that are enforced in face-to-face, intimate relations. For example, stealing is prohibited by both formal and informal rules. Within the formal system, the rule is spelled out in legal detail and enforced by the police, the courts, and the corrections establishment. If caught, one may be fined, incarcerated, or subjected to other suitable penalties. In the informal realm, the proscription is merely understood. We know not to steal from other people, and we recognize that we would shame ourselves and lose the trust of those around us if we did. Informal sanctions tend to be administered within everyday social relations and consist of praise as well as reprimand, criticism, and ridicule. The ultimate punishment is ostracism or banishment from a social group. Gossip is often the technique for enforcement as well as for sanction. Informal controls are administered within groups of known people—family, neighbors, and friends.

In both formal and informal systems, either of the two techniques of control—socialization or external pressures—can be used. Informal systems tend to rely on socialization, while formal systems, particularly the crime control establishment, use external pressures. This is because within groups where informal controls are effective the necessity and the advantage of compliance are universally accepted, but in the context of formal controls greater diversity and differentiation preclude such endorsement. In fact, the absolute interests of some members—often the minority but sometimes the majority—are sacrificed for the interests of others. Consequently, coercion is the only option available.

Informal controls are widely accepted as more effective than formal controls. There are several reasons for this. First, informal controls incorporate more effective techniques of socialization. Within meaningful groups, the learning of acceptable behavior is constantly going on, so that socialization is easier, more appropriate, and effective. This may involve imitation, simple routinization, or informal sanction. But formal controls are further removed and less personal, and their effects tend to be less viable.

Informal controls are also better socializers because they are exercised in settings where surveillance is greater. Friends, neighbors, and family members, in their everyday contact with one another, know what is going on and can enforce group norms and sanction deviance. Children stealing for the first time find it easier to elude the storekeeper and the police than their parents. Formal controls are enforced by a few people who are solely responsible for their administration, rather than by all members of the society.

Informal controls are also more effective because the people involved in norm enforcement are important to the person. I really do not care what some police officer or district attorney or judge thinks about me, but my family, my friends, and my co-workers are a different story. I must face them every day, and I value the respect of these people and want them to think well of me. I am embarrassed when I do something that reflects badly on me. I want these people to believe I am honest and responsible. For this reason, I refrain from acts that would make the people who are important to me think less of me. Consequently, irrespective of any formal sanction, I am more likely to speed or to cheat on my income taxes than to spit in my wine glass during a dinner party or neglect to shovel my sidewalk. The first two infractions would not greatly diminish the respect others have for me, the latter two definitely would.

Informal controls are thus more effective than formal controls, but in certain circumstances informal controls are simply inappropriate. As societies become more complex, social conditions that limit the effectiveness and utility of informal sanctions arise, and gaps in control come to be filled by a system of formal regulations.

Because informal controls work within groups of people we know whose respect is important to us, their efficacy depends on the presence of such personal relationships. As societies become more complex, changes that tend to splinter and break up informal groupings occur. Economies become more complex and people become less dependent on one another. In an agrarian society the survival of the entire community may depend on the services each member performs. In contrast, the lives and survival of few others, with the exception of immediate dependents, are directly tied to our own. If something happens to my grocer or if we have an argument, I simply find a new one, and the loss of my business would not have grave consequences for the grocer. For this reason, economic interdependence is not great, and neither is the ability to control other people. Since survival is no longer contingent on the maintenance of personal relations, motivation to refrain from activities that might harm those relationships is lacking. What the people around us think is of less consequence and less likely to be considered in deciding whether to engage in criminal behavior.

The appropriateness of informal controls is also diminished with the presence of numerous groups within society that each have their own values, needs, and goals. Because such groups desire different things or compete for the same resources, universally agreed-on standards necessary for their peaceful coexistence and a unified effort to socialize everyone in the same way are often lacking. Consequently, individuals cannot be counted on to act in acceptable and predictable ways. Overt and overriding guidance is needed in this situation, and only formal controls uniformly applied by designated agencies can fill this requirement. Disputes among groups also make it necessary to have a formal structure for mediating equitable solutions before conflicts escalate.

The tendency toward formalization has been augmented in the United States by other developmental processes. Extensive social and geographic mobility, the deference for individual autonomy and independece, and strong motivations for material achievement counterpose effective informal controls. Mobility tends to destroy long-standing communities and prevents formation of new neighborhoods with strong informal influence. Many Americans never experience the potent socialization processes and effective controls of an extended social group of meaningful people. Research conducted by Robert Crutchfield, Michael Geerken, and Walter Gove, examining the relationship of levels of residential mobility and crime in sixty-five U.S. cities, supports this argument. The incidence of rape and all property crimes is much higher in cities with high levels of in—and out—migration. Apparently mobility does not allow for integration of individuals "into a meaningful network of social relations." Where relational structures were weak and unstable, informal controls also tend to be absent or weak, thus failing to provide for the development of necessary inhibitors to criminality.[2]

The value placed on automony and individuality in this nation works much like mobility does in reducing social integration and increasing criminality. People are expected to break ties and go out on their own, but because establishing autonomy tends to be such an emotionally painful process, it often must be very complete and requires that friends and family be shut out. Never is this more clear than in the behavior of American adolescents.

The need for autonomy and independence is also seen in Americans striving for privacy. People demand their own space. Members of the family must have their own rooms, and each family must have its own house or apartment. If the dwelling has land around it, there is a fence. But these efforts build barriers that preclude the effective interactions between people that is necessary for informal control.

Throughout our lives, as children, young people, and adults, we feel pressure to demonstrate independence and self-sufficiency, but this may lead one to conclude that others have no right to tell us what to do or to interfere in our lives. To varying degrees we modify this stance, admitting that when people live together some consideration to others must be given. But for people who see themselves as fully independent, threats of sanction may be the only viable source of control. The opinions, beliefs, and rights of others will have no effect.

High regard for material achievement works in much the same way, because it too is a self-oriented value. To the extent that material achievement is stressed more than individual integrity, self-respect and control, and consideration of others, the influence of other people will be diminished and informal controls will not be effective. For people to recognize and respect the needs of others, they must sacrifice some of their own self-interest. A highly materialistic society generates the opposite approach to life.

This is not to imply that informal controls are not used in

American society and that behavior is determined solely by external intervention. It is simply to say that those controls that are so complete in less complex societies are lost in the diversity and complexity of our own. Informal sanctions still play a dominant role in shaping social behavior, but they are now unable to exert the unilateral force sufficient to prevent deviant behavior. We are thus in the position of having to rely more heavily on formal controls, because informal controls are no longer capable of ensuring and maintaining conformity to vital social norms. But formal sanctions are inherently less effective than informal ones, as we have seen. It is a dilemma, given existing social configurations, for which there is no solution. A society like ours experiences greater amounts of deviance and criminality because informal methods of control are inappropriate but formal ones are ineffective.

CRIMINALITY AND INTERPERSONAL EXPLOITATION

The problem with social control within American society is demonstrated not only by criminality but also by widespread exploitive behavior. Not all exploitive acts are considered criminal, but almost all criminal acts are exploitive. Where interpersonal exploitation is common, the distinction between criminal and noncriminal varieties is not important when considering its causes and controls. Criminality and other forms of exploitation occur because they are culturally prescribed and permitted, and because informal prohibitions and sanctions are inadequate within that culture.

Let us begin by considering the vast amount of such behavior in the United States. If exploitation is broadly defined as "taking unfair advantage of another person for personal gain," examples from all aspects of American life become apparent. For example, dishonest students exploit their peers by taking unfair academic advantage. Recent studies indicate that cheating is common to all levels of education. It is widespread in secondary schools[3] and is described as epidemic in universities.[4] Even in military academies, where honor is held in highest esteem, several cheating scandals have recently been exposed.[5] The pressures for academic distinction appear to overpower the inhibitions of probity.

Another example is the widespread occurrence of consumer fraud, where companies market products or services that are not what they are supposed to be. The product may not be genuine or safe or exactly as advertised, or it may break within the first few days after it is purchased. Such practices are exploitive because business is acquired by selling a product that does not exist. Many consider such acts good business and are quick to trot out the old admonition "Let the buyer beware." Whether acceptable or not—a question of value—consumer fraud involves selfish utilization of others.

Even marketing practices that are not so tainted as these often incorporate an element of interpersonal utilization. Take, for example, the hamburger commercial that portrays a father who has no time for his daughter all week but makes up for it on the weekend by taking her for a burger. Or the telephone commercials that suggest that friendship and love can be expressed by a touch of the dial. These advertisements are designed to play on consumers' sentimentality and guilt. They do not appeal to the need for the product or service or provide any indication of quality. To convince the public to consume, they tap into a set of emotions unrelated to the product, which is a form of exploitation not so culpable but still involving taking advantage of someone for profit and gain.

Even the medical profession, which has traditionally been regarded as more altruistically than monetarily motivated, has recently been accused of exploiting patients for economic gain. Doctors order unneeded medical tests or schedule surgeries— particularly appendectomies, tonsillectomies and hysterectomies—when the medical benefits of such measures are not always evident. Investigations of the federal Medicare program revealed this practice, as well as outright fraud involving doctors, hospitals, and other health care providers.[6]

Other subtle forms of exploitation also crept through the practice of health care. Few dentists will fill a cavity without an initial visit and a thorough cleaning of all your teeth. The profession argues that this is preventive dentistry, but the larger fees involved are inescapable. Medical doctors know this trick too and require a complete physical (for preventive health care and mal-practice reasons) before they will become your personal physician.

Interpersonal exploitation is even found throughout the world of charities. Large profits are made by the manufacturers of the candy, ornaments, and other goods sold by charitable organizations. The public feels obligated to support these causes but ends up contributing more to the well-being of the product manufacturers. And if you do not believe that businesses are aware that charities make good sales forces, check the advertisements in any charity's organizational magazine. But utilization does not stop there. Charities, like commercial businesses, have learned to play on the public's emotions. Even if you cannot afford to support their cause or do not want to, you are made to feel obligated, even guilty, for being unwilling. How often do you answer the phone only to be confronted by someone from a worthy cause who through hard-sell tactics denies your free choice and demands your support?

Some forms of American interpersonal exploitation are considerably more seedy than those discussed so far. Pornography, for example, exploits the human body and the act of love by reducing each to an object of lust from the complex beings and human events they actually are. It is demeaning and cheapens life. This is clearest in child pornography, where a young model is taken advantage of for profit and where in the end childhood and children in general suffer degradation from abject portrayal. But look at the popularity of pornography, both soft-core and hard-core. People spend billions of dollars for it—in print, in film and videotape, and for live showings.

And the American news media and the criminal-justice establishment exploit the public by sensationalizing crime. Each profits from the consumption of horrible crime stories either in increased sales or in bigger budgets. It is yet another form of the use of others for one's own ends.

In some cases, the exploited are willing victims, like the newspaper subscriber or the model paid by a pornographic magazine. In others, they are unknowing victims. And in still other cases, as with criminality, the victim is knowingly but involuntarily being used. To an extent, victim participation determines the culpability associated with exploitation, but other factors also enter into the definition. For now, it should be clear that exploitation is part of American life. In fact, in reading these examples you have probably been reminded of other forms of exploitation with which you personally are familiar.

The proposition that exploitation is a common theme in American social life should not surprise anyone. This is a nation that values achievement and prides itself on the ability to overcome obstacles in order to solve major problems and achieve great things. But achievement is a difficult motivation to control and can easily take the form of overachievement when the ends are considered to justify any means and when the act of achieving becomes more important than what one does to reach that outcome. To the degree that this happens within society, achievement will be more highly regarded than honesty, integrity, self-restraint and control, and respect for other people. But is this not the way it is in the United States? People are often evaluated by their possessions—status is determined by wealth—not by the way they live their lives.

As an expedient and effective method of achievement, taking unfair advantage of others is one way, and perhaps a common way, of getting ahead, of gaining the competitive edge, and in the end of acquiring wealth, status, and power in American society. Given the Americanization of exploitation, is it any wonder that criminality is so prevalent? People constantly receive the message that exploitation is acceptable. Examine these common admonitions: "I don't care what it takes to get the job done," "Show them who's boss," "You owe it to yourself," "You deserve it," and "Win at all costs." The motivations, the rationalizations, and even the methods of utilization are all present in American culture. Criminality merely surfaces as one method of expressing this popular theme.

You may object to this assertion. You may argue that criminality is a form of exploitation but that compared with other forms, it is qualitatively more reprehensible and the offender is more culpable. You may not be as frightened or angered by other forms as you are by blatant destruction and theft of property and violent confrontation. But some forms of exploitation are as dangerous as those defined as criminal, and the step from some exploitation to worse exploitation is shorter than from no exploitation to worse. Any number of factors may contribute to the selection of one form of exploitation over another. The fact that exploitation is common makes it more difficult for the inhibitors—self-restraint and control—to be effective. Despite any degree of reprehensibility or culpability, the presence of exploitation and the diminution of important inhibitors creates an environment conducive to crime. Attacking criminality alone is illogical. It is analogous to an attempt to extinguish the flames of a fire fed by an open gas jet: the flames are the major problem, but the cause is the gas.

Two factors are related to the selection of criminality over other forms of exploitation. One is opportunity. A junior executive is more likely to try to make a peer look bad to the company president or accept a kickback from a supplier than to hold up a liquor store. Street crime is not within the junior executive's world. Such individuals seldom associate with other people who rob liquor stores. If they are desperate for money, other opportunities for exploitation exist. And in the end the individual is too sophisticated for such forms of criminality. On the other hand, selection of street crime by those who commit it is consistent with their station in life. Given their age, background, intelligence, and economic and social status, some opportunities for exploitation are precluded, but criminality may not be.

Yet opportunity alone does not explain the occurrence of criminality, because it fails to account for why some people refrain from exploitation even when the opportunity is there. Some people readily engage in such activities, never considering or caring about the harm they cause others, but others never even contemplate doing something that might hurt someone else. Apparently acceptability varies by degrees. Given the right circumstances, you might cheat someone on a business deal, but you could never imagine physically injuring someone for personal gain. Why do these differences exist? Does it have something to do with the calculation of benefits and costs discussed earlier and found to be widely accepted by the public? No, it is unlikely that those who exploit others perceive that there will be greater benefits from such acts and are more willing to take the risks than other people who refrain. It is also unlikely that those who abstain are more conscious of the punishments. Rather, it is a matter of self-control. Each of us, given our own particular background and socialization, has unique images of acceptable and unacceptable patterns of interpersonal interaction. You probably saw nothing wrong with some of the examples of exploitation discussed earlier, you probably had minor reservations about others, but you probably strongly condemned a few forms. The degree of acceptability is directly related to the kinds of exploitation people will consider.

Given this diversity, it is not difficult to see why ideas about acceptability get muddled in the process of socialization. If Daddy can pull one over on his boss and stay home sick when he is not really sick, why can't I cheat on an exam? If a company forces me to work in an unsafe plant, why can't I take tools from it? Other examples could be given, but the point is that in a society where exploitation is common, it becomes difficult to discern what is acceptable and what is not acceptable. Legal definitions are insufficient. Whether people even consider the effects of their activities on others, and whether they care, is determined by how they have been socialized. In a society where one is often reminded that the other guy is likely to take advantage, it is difficult to instill the belief that exploitation is bad. For example, when a mother justifies keeping the extra change from the supermarket, claiming that the store charges too much, what message does this convey to her child? Certainly not one of integrity or of refraining from exploitation even when exploited. The message is that social interaction is inherently self-centered and interpersonal utilization is common, and that if people are to survive and succeed they must fight, achieve, and get the best of the other guy. But this practice fails to instill the inhibitions to exploitation: control, restraint, honor, and integrity.

Crime is determined within the dominant culture of a particular society. As long as people are socialized to accept and practice various forms of exploitation because of the value placed on achievement, particularly material achievement, and not to concern themselves too much with the means of achievement, then crime will be prevalent. This process of acculturation takes place within the informal spectrums of social life to a much greater extent than it involves formal institutions. For this reason, grand threats of sanction will be of limited use in reducing the incidence of criminal behavior.

SELF-CONTROLLED SOCIETIES

This explanation of crime control raises an interesting and important question. Can a modern, achievement-oriented society be well controlled, or are such societies doomed to experience high levels of crime? The answer is that a well-contained, controlled, complex, and modern society is possible. Japan is the best example. It is an achievement-oriented nation that recently outstepped American productivity. Yet the crime rate in Japan is only a fraction of that in the United States. For every crime of any sort in Japan, four *serious* crimes take place in the United States. A person is ten times more likely to be murdered in America, six times more likely to be the victim of theft, and 208 times more likely to be robbed. A woman is thirteen times more likely to be raped.[7] The differences are real, but why?

The key is in effective social discipline resulting from viable informal controls. Most Japanese people live within stable networks of people they know and who know them, so their social environments are more personal than those found in the United States and consist of friends and family with whom long ties and traditions exist. Because such relationships are valued, Japanese people refrain from activities that might jeopardize their acceptance in the social network. A much stronger sense of social responsibility and an appreciation for the dire consequences of deviant behavior results. Social constraints are tied to personal attachments, and people obey the law not because of some external threat from government but because the risks of dishonor within the informal group are too great.[8]

For individuals in Japan, the sense of personal integrity and moral obligation is stronger than that found in the United States. In Japan, just as in this nation, status is associated with achievement and determined by employment and wealth, but people are also judged by their honorableness. An individual without great material achievement can be considered a worthy and respected person. This system works well because known people who are socially important understand what you are like, know whether you are honorable, trustworthy, and considerate. Outward symbols to strangers are less important than meaningful opinions about integrity. Informal social groups serve two important functions: to educate children in proper and respectable behavior through effective socialization, and to reinforce that discipline by their group pressure and importance.

Authority is also regarded differently by the Japanese. In contrast to the assertive, suspicious, and often resentful attitudes Americans have, the typical response in Japan is one of subservience and compliance. The act of pleading guilty by accused criminals provides an illustration of this difference. In the United States somewhere around 90 to 95 percent of all people convicted plead guilty—because they are plea-bargaining, receiving a lesser charge or sentence for cooperating with law enforcement authorities. Approximately the same proportion of Japanese criminals also plead guilty, but in Japan plea-bargaining is illegal. To Americans, who challenge authority and resist intervention, this is inconceivable. But the Japanese offender throws himself on the mercy of the court; to regain his honor, he admits wrongdoing and accepts his punishment. This tells us a great deal about the utility of formal sanctions. As one author suggests, in Japan "rather than official action prompting compliance with social norms, compliant attitudes toward authority enhance the efficiency of official action."[9]

In the United States, suspicion of authority is common. The Bill of Rights fixes limits on government intervention in individual freedoms. Numerous court cases have reinforced these principles over the past two centuries. Distrust is also reflected in public reaction to authority. Intervention is resented and often challenged. For example, speeders confront police officers who stop them by demanding to know why the police are not out investigating "real" crimes. And crime suspects immediately want the protection of an attorney.

Crime control in the United States is delegated specifically to criminal-justice agencies and carefully defined by legal code. Police authority is limited to criminal acts, and with the exception of a few victimless crimes, more general control of unruly and immoral behavior is prohibited. In Japan, informal and formal authority are not distinct, and the policing function extends beyond law enforcement to community control. This is possible because the Japanese believe that government is not an entity created as an extension of society but is intrinsic to it. In the United States, formal standards and institutions emerged as state and society were differentiated; in Japan, that distinction was never made, and formal controls remained integrally tied to both.[10]

Switzerland is a modern Western nation with Western customs, but it too has little crime. According to sociologist Marshall Clinard, "Switzerland represents an exception to the general rule that a high crime rate accompanies a high degree of affluence, industrialization, and urbanization. Even in the largest Swiss cities crime is not a major problem."[11]

Several characteristics of Swiss society contribute to this distinction, not the least of which is an extremely high standard of living, the absence of slums and a persistent, impoverished class of people within the nation. Yet after a year of close study, Clinard concluded that effective articulation of expected and acceptable behavior through informal socialization was the most important contributor to the lack of crime.[12] Just as in Japan, social atomization has been avoided, and there are informal groups that are capable of applying pressure to assure conformity. Familial stability and strength has remained largely intact in Switzerland, and this allows families to exercise significant influence on their members. Until recently a distinctive youth culture was not present in Swiss society and greater intergenerational integration occurred, allowing for closer supervision and more complete socialization of young people.

Strong identification with the commitments to the localities in which they grew up are maintained by the Swiss. If possible, they continue to live in these areas, but if not, close ties are sustained. In this way the Swiss, like the Japanese, are encapsulated in stable networks of people who know them and have meaning to them. These groups exert informal pressures that assure conformity. Since group-to-group consensus on acceptable patterns of behavior is high, there is consistency throughout the nation.[13]

The different ways the Japanese and the Swiss avoided atomization as state and society were differentiated are intriguing. The Japanese successfully kept state and society integrated, while the Swiss, for the most part, avoided formation of the state, at least on a national level. Compared with the United States, the federal Swiss government is extremely weak. Legislative decisions are made by consensus rather than by majority rule, and as a result national legislation that conflicts with local customs is seldom enacted. Consequently, most authority and responsibility for governing the citizenry is retained within localities (cantons). Society and governments are integrated at the local level.[14] The Japanese also have local governments that exert considerable influence over local residents, informal associations known as *chokai*. A primary responsibility of these institutions is neighborhood control and the protection of the citizenry.[15]

It could be argued that the low level of crime in Japan is attributable to the high social homogeneity within the population. To a degree this is true and irrefutable. But social heterogeneity and a low incidence of crime are found in Switzerland. This would suggest that social homogeneity, while helpful, is not necessary for the maintenance of a restrained society. It might also be suggested that the absence of poverty in Switzerland accounts for its lower crime rate, but in Japan there is considerable poverty yet little crime. The feature the two nations hold in common is clearly the effective informal controls.

Americans should note that in neither Japan nor Switzerland are criminal punishments severe or used extensively. When criminals are arrested and convicted in either nation, they are much more unlikely to go to prison than in the United States. The sentence may be suspended, or the individual may be placed on probation. If a jail term is administered, it is usually short. In contrast to the United States, an offender rarely spends more than one year in prison in either nation.[16] So we must avoid the mistaken notion that strong formal sanctions are the key to crime control in either nation. Deviance is rare because of effective social discipline, but when it does occur, harsh sanctions are unnecessary because informal sanctions work. It is as Sutherland stated: "When the mores are adequate, laws are unnecessary."

Control of the citizenry in the Soviet Union provides an interesting contrast to that found in Japan and Switzerland. Since the revolution in 1917, the Soviet government has tried to produce "good" Soviets: sober, conscientious, industrious people eager to work for the common good. It has been their philosophy that the behavior and personality of Soviet citizens should reflect inculcation of the principles of the workers' revolution and the communist view. To assure proper acculturation of the Soviet identity, the government employed various methods of socialization and coercion, most notably including education, propagandization, prohibition of dissent, and close surveillance and sanction of deviants.

This attempt to mold the citizenry has not been a success. The Soviet Union experiences substantial problems with alcoholism and its accompanying problems. Crime, while not as great as in the United States, has not been eliminated, despite predictions of early communists who believed it would die away as socialism replaced capitalism, the alleged ultimate cause of crime. Juvenile delinquency and adult criminality involving violent personal crimes, theft of state property as well as private property, and various other crimes remain. The failure to establish a well-controlled society is best reflected in the high incidence of "hooliganism," a broad offense category encompassing a variety of minor public order offenses including everything from violations of state-dictated rules of dress to public disturbances by the intoxicated, to failure to show proper respect to Soviet officials and institutions. Because they involve an obvious rejection of the proper Soviet identity, these crimes, though minor, exemplify the failure of formal institutions to establish control.[17]

More than any other contemporary nation, the Soviet Union tried to mold its citizens into a conscientious and hardworking collective. Extremely strong (indoctrinating, by American standards) techniques of socialization were used. To manipulate compliance coercively, police employ close and secretive surveillance to supervise the population. When deviance occurs, the Soviets rely on severe punishment involving hard labor, which incorporates an underlying strategy of resocialization to return the offender as a productive member of society. The failure of these methods in over sixty years speaks to the ultimate failure of state-imposed formal controls.

The life of the "good" Soviet is, for the most part, boring and

monotonous, with few personal luxuries (since such self-in-
dulgence has been sacrificed for rapid development of the mil-
itary-industrial complex). This way of life in a society that has
a strong drinking culture creates the potential for significant
problems of social control—people drink too much, and some
subsequently become involved in public-order violations and
criminal acts.[18] Without the commitment and informal and internal controls like those found in Japan and Switzerland, no
amount of formal intervention will succeed. Norms will not be
internalized by individuals or reinforced by meaningful groups.
Instead, they are formulated, dictated, and enforced by external
agencies that do not have the legitimacy and significance for
individuals that informal groups do.

CONCLUSIONS

The recently rekindled belief in punitive techniques in the
United States is uncomfortably similar to the Soviet control strategy. We too hope to create good citizens, good Americans,
through the use of coercive methods. Like the Soviets, Americans view criminals as parasites of society, predators who exploit
others for personal gain and satisfaction. It is interesting that
the powerful totalitarian Soviet government and the democratic
U.S. government both assume responsibility for the problem.
Formal, state imposed methods of control are considered the
key to bringing criminality under control.

The similar approaches of these so different nations should
not be surprising. Each strongly endorses the achievement ethic
and espouses citizens' moral obligation to be productive. Individuals are expected to be hardworking and achievement-oriented, for their own personal gain in the United States and for
the good of the collective in the Soviet Union. This achievement
orientation extends into government responsibilities, where there
is a belief like that found in the private world that proper application of appropriate technologies will produce success. If
crime is a problem, it should be solvable. The state must do what
it can to control it.

This assumption has been proven invalid in this chapter. If
people subscribe to the norms outlined by legal standards, com-

pliance will follow. If high levels of noncompliance are present, a problem with subscription to the underlying norm is indicated, not inadequate enforcement of the law. Improved criminal-justice practices among the police, courts, and correctional institutions are directed at improving law enforcement rather than at getting people to subscribe to the desired norms. For this reason, none of the changes or improvements in the criminal-justice system have been or ever will be very effective in reducing crime. Criminality is culturally prescribed by the acceptance and practice of exploitive behavior within American society. The distinction between criminality and other forms of exploitation, while perhaps qualitatively different, is predominantly one of legal definition which often becomes muddled.

Low incidence of criminality is attributable to the inculcation of self-control within a population. If there is a strong sense of interpersonal responsibility, and if individual worth is defined by honor and integrity as well by as by achievement, criminality is unlikely to be a significant problem. Cultural assimilation of these values occurs not because of formal dictates by the state but within small, informal groups of known people who can effectively socialize and supervise one another. This is possible within a society only when cellular, tribelike groups survive the social atomization that occurs as society and state are differentiated.

Such cellular configurations are not found in American society. In fact, specific characteristics of the United States work directly against the development of such stable networks. Americans prize individualism, social and geographic mobility, privacy, and autonomy. They are suspicious of authority and believe in the separation of public and private responsibilities. These attributes work directly to preclude effective use of informal controls.

So the United States finds itself in an unfortunate situation. It experiences high levels of criminality, and many citizens are injured and robbed each year. People wish the problem could be reduced, if not resolved, and as a nation accustomed to accomplishing its goals, this objective does not appear to be unreasonable. But punitive formal controls will simply not work. And given the social characteristics of American society, neither will informal constraints. Criminality is an unfortunate by-product of the American way of life.

NOTES

1. Edwin H. Sutherland and Donald Cressey, *Principles of Criminology*, 7th ed. (Philadelphia: J. B. Lippincott, 1966), p. 11.
2. Robert D. Crutchfield, Michael R. Geerken, and Walter R. Gove, "Crime Rate and Social Integration," *Criminology* 20 (November 1982): 467.
3. "Symposium on Cheating," *Today's Education* 69 (November/December 1980): 42GS–54GS.
4. Stanley N. Wellborn, "Cheating in College Becomes Epidemic," *U.S. News & World Report*, October 20, 1980, pp. 39–42.
5. "What Price Honor?" *Time*, June 7, 1976, pp. 18–29.
6. See Jeffrey H. Reiman, *The Rich Get Richer and the Poor Get Prison*, 2nd ed. (New York: John Wiley & Sons, 1984), pp. 61–62; and Harold E. Pepinsky and Paul Jeslow, *Myths That Cause Crime* (Cabin John, Md.: Seven Locks Press, 1984), pp. 48–51.
7. David H. Bayley, "Learning About Crime—The Japanese Experience," *The Public Interest* 44 (1976): 55–57.
8. Ibid., pp. 61–63.
9. Ibid., pp. 63–65.
10. Ibid., pp. 65–68.
11. Marshall B. Clinard, *Cities with Little Crime* (New York: Cambridge University Press, 1978), p. 1.
12. Ibid., pp. 150–155.
13. Ibid., p. 106.
14. Ibid., pp. 107–110.
15. Bayley, "Learning About Crime," pp. 63, 66–77.
16. Ibid., pp. 59–60; Clinard, *Cities with Little Crime*, pp. 115–121.
17. Walter D. Connor, *Deviance in Soviet Society* (New York: Columbia University Press, 1972).
18. Ibid., chap. 4.

11

Concluding Thoughts

American children learn that "all the king's horses and all the king's men cannot put Humpty Dumpty together again," but as adults contemplating crime control, they either forget or never understood that admonition. Even with a lengthy record of unsuccessful changes, few authorities have been willing to admit that the criminal-justice system is doing about as well as it can. Instead, there is a determination to make it succeed. Idea after idea is tried, and dollar after dollar is spent—but always with few objective indications of increased crime control. Blame is laid on unfulfilled expectations. Noting that crime is epidemic, this politician or that writer will lash out at the system, claiming that it has been unfaithful to its objectives, that not enough effort has been devoted to offender reform, or that sanctions have not been sufficiently severe to deter the miscreants among us.

Historically, criminal-justice policy has varied considerably. It has been harsh, as well as lenient. It has been legalistic and benevolent. Policing methods have become more sophisticated, the courts are more efficient, and numerous ideas for changing, threatening, and reshaping criminals have been tried. But above all else, the crime control establishment has grown. New agencies have been created and more personnel have been employed. Research into the causes and cures of crime has been under way continually. But none of these efforts has made a great deal of difference. Crime remains a significant problem in the minds of most Americans.

Is it not time to stop believing that something more can be done? Apparently, none of the "wars on crime" that appear regularly as policy priorities in American politics will be won. No new commission, no project or program, no change in the justice system is going to produce the results desired.

This conclusion is not satisfactory. Some will even consider it un-American. Because the United States is an achievement-oriented society, criminal-justice professionals are motivated to control crime in order to win the war on crime. It is painful to recognize that you are doing as well as you can, particularly when that is not very good. So the crime control establishment continues to search for new ways to succeed. These efforts are supported by a fearful public, who want someone to solve the problem for them, and by politicians, who play on public sentiment to gain votes. The failure of the system becomes self-promoting. Each failure becomes a reason for trying something new and for further expansion of the system.

But each new innovation produces few changes in the incidence of crime because the burden of social control cannot be carried by the criminal-justice system single-handedly. Order cannot be achieved by coercion alone; it must be obtained through voluntary and automatic compliance.[1] Improvements in criminal justice cannot produce voluntary compliance and consequently will always fail.

INTERPRETING CRIME IN MODERN SOCIETY

If people begin to understand and internalize the proposition that government cannot resolve the crime problem, the potential for reducing criminality may improve. As long as people believe that the institutions of government can handle the problem for them, they will be tempted to abdicate their own responsibility for it. With crime, it is easy to say that it does not involve me, that it's not my problem, that it only threatens me, and then to demand that local agencies do something about it. In this way, responsibility for both the causes and the cures of crime is shifted to others. As individuals, we avoid the obligation of self-constraint as well as that of social constraint. This position is more comfortable than recognizing one's own contributions to the social ills of society, but it is not realistic.

The myths we have examined in this book allow people to assume such a position. Acceptance of the official interpretation of crime statistics indicating a new wave of criminal activity (Crime Myth 1) allows the public to focus on a common enemy: a group of predators toward whom anger and hate can be directed. In doing so, one's own transgressions, those forms of exploitation not defined as criminal or considered culpable, may be vindicated, and criminals become the scapegoats for everything that is wrong. In this way, society maintains a clear distinction between right and wrong. Criminals are other people— not ourselves or anyone we know. They are worthy of moral condemnation, and it is society's duty to avenge the pain they have caused.

If crime is perceived to be increasing, it follows that the quality of life in the community must be deteriorating (Crime Myth 2). Fear causes people to sequester themselves in their homes and to avoid social contact with other people, particularly strangers. By directly limiting social variety, withdrawal impoverishes lives. Furthermore, it eats away at the fabric of society, increasing distrust and destroying the ties that bind the society together.

In response, the public clings to a simple interpretation of the causes of crime and its control. Human behavior and criminality, in particular, are considered to be motivated by utilitarian drives. For society to respond, the threat of punishment must be sufficient to diminish the utility of criminality. To do this, criminal sanctions must be made more certain and more severe (Crime Myths 7 and 10).

The public consistently places its faith in the criminal-justice system, apparently never questioning its potential for success (Crime Myth 11). Even when crime is perceived to be worsening, people turn to the system without considering any other alternative. As long as the crime control establishment reinforces beliefs about criminals by arresting and vigorously prosecuting only individuals whose characteristics are consistent with those commonly perceived by the public—willful wrongdoers who threaten public safety—people are happy that someone else is taking responsibility for the problem. But the image of crime and its control fostered by these myths is unrealistic and fails to help Americans deal with the problem.

To understand crime in the United States, changes in the community that occurred during the 1970s must be considered. Think about how your neighborhood has changed over the past ten, twenty, or even thirty years. It is no longer a significant point of reference for many of life's activities. Because of modern transportation, socializing often occurs outside the neighborhood. The same is true for employment and leisure activities. The growth of municipal, state, and national governments and the expansion of the services they provide has lessened the significance of community politics and voluntary service. Neighborhood schools have been replaced by larger, consolidated institutions. The activities of the neighborhood police precinct are now less important than decisions made by the city police commissioner.

As significant as any change has been the expansion of geographic boundaries through technological advances in communications. Because of the relatively low costs of long-distance telephoning, business and social relations can be maintained with people all over the nation, and there is a tendency to keep up with what is going on in other areas, whether it is the weather, sporting events, or violent crime. These changes have increased the number of people with whom individuals interact and have expanded the events of which they are aware. Before rapid communications, syndicated news services, and television, ties to the outside world were more restricted and word of significant events often took several days to penetrate the local news. Today we hear of them immediately. The effect is the expansion of our world beyond the neighborhood.

Increased social and geographic mobility has removed many people from the old neighborhood and replaced them with new families. Children who once remained in the area no longer do so. Of particular significance is the recent breakdown of ethnic and racial barriers in housing. Fewer urban neighborhoods, whose residents are predominantly of one ethnic or racial group, now exist. Continued escalation of housing costs and growing dissatisfaction with commuting and suburbia has brought whites into "coming back" neighborhoods in many cities. These changes have modified the environment of residential neighborhoods, rendering them different from the neighborhoods of the past.

Other significant social changes have also altered the community. As growing numbers of women joined the work force, fewer people were in the neighborhood during the day. And the women, who in the past maintained the social ties within the community, giving it solidarity and influence, are no longer there. Social relations are now more often configured by business associations. People who work for IBM socialize with "IBMers," and university people associate with other academics rather than with their neighbors. Divorce has also changed neighborhoods. When families break up, their patterns of association and the people with whom they socialize almost always change. Responsibility for child-rearing is shared by people living in different neighborhoods.

These changes have caused the neighborhood to become less meaningful as a social unit. To a much greater extent today than in the past, people live in a society of strangers. Neighbors are less likely to know one another, and the frequency and intimacy of their social interaction is diminished. This is a matter of degree, not one of total elimination, but on an aggregate level, significant social changes have occurred in American communities. People within the neighborhood are now socially less significant to one another. Membership in a particular community, other than the status inferred and its relationship to property values, is less important to people today. These changes have contributed to further atomization of American people. Rather than moving toward more tribelike organizations within particular areas, social networks became more diffuse.

One should not infer that these changes indicate deterioration of the social fabric of this nation. They do not necessarily signify any reduction in social integration that is leading to further interpersonal exploitation and criminality. American communities have never been well-integrated tribelike social units with universally ascribed-to norms. In the past, some neighborhoods were more socially meaningful and more tribelike than today. They may have been more ethnically homogeneous, and social relations within them may have been more important. But across neighborhoods considerable normative diversity has always existed.

There remain the people who are socially important to each of us: family, friends, and fellow workers. Informal norms and sanctions that influence the choice of behaviors endure. We refrain from certain acts for fear we will embarrass ourselves. Young people still undergo strong and important socialization processes as they grow and mature socially. That informal controls have become geographically more diffuse suggests that these controls may be weakened. This could explain some of the increase in crime during the 1960s. Sociologist John Conklin argues that "if neighbors do not know each other and if no web of social relationship exists, people will not be able to guard each other from harm." In this situation, residents will be unable to distinguish the intruder from fellow inhabitants, and effective surveillance of the community will be diminished. Furthermore, as people become more fearful, they withdraw from social contact. Because fewer people are on the streets, informal social controls are weakened, and public places become the domain of criminals. Conklin suggests that in this way fear of crime becomes a self-fulfilling prophecy.[2]

Since victimization rates stabilized in the early 1970s, however, these changes are more significant for their effect on the way people perceive crime. With any unknown, fear and misunderstanding are greater. In a society of strangers, you never know if the person you meet on the street is a friendly neighbor or a mugger. Someone who offers to help you with a load of packages may be a helpful stranger or a bold thief. As you jog through the park, you worry that a fellow jogger might be an assailant. Irrespective of whether crime is actually increasing, the outcome is that fear grows and the quality of life is diminished.

Signs of incivility exacerbate this trend. Urban decline, demonstrated by burned-out buildings, graffiti, litter, and derelicts, leave people uneasy. Boisterous, assertive, cocky teenagers, instead of the respectful young people we thought we were or knew in the past, worry us. Rude and aggressive people contribute to our distrust and fear of what someone might do to us. Both the people around us and the physical environment are not as familiar as they once were. They appear to be more harsh, more impoverished, and more violent than ever. We feel less in control of our environments and our fates. With such negative stimuli, is it any wonder that fear has risen steadily?

Because the people around us—neighbors and the individuals in our expanded environments—are strangers, patterns of social interaction have become more formalized. Informal processes work only within groups of known and meaningful people. Outside these groups, one must rely on formal processes and pressures to resolve conflicts and ensure some level of conformity. As neighborhoods lost their familiarity, incidents that in the past would have been handled informally—interpersonal conflicts, vandalism, petty theft—are now resolved officially and often are defined as crimes. When people do not know the individuals involved and are afraid, they tend to be less tolerant of offenders. So as neighborhoods changed, the method of problem resolution shifted from informal to formal, and the interpretation of what is criminal changed.

The present crime problem in the United States is therefore as much a product of faulty interpretation as anything. Contemporary lifestyles are changing. One must look at the context of those changes in order to understand crime and to consider the potential for doing something about it.

HOW TO LIVE WITH CRIME

The inability of official control agencies to decrease the incidence of crime and violence does not necessarily mean that nothing can be done. As people recognize the limitations of the criminal-justice system, they may assume greater responsibility for social control.

A reduction in crime could be produced by the diminution of social atomization in the United States. Building stronger networks capable of effective informal control would help bring about this change. After six years of study, Charles Silberman makes a similar suggestion, claiming that reduced crime is possible through development of self-control processes in poor neighborhoods rather than through improving the coercive threat of criminal justice. Silberman argues that impoverished communities require massive amounts of outside help to overcome the inertia of years of economic malaise, but the help given in the past in the form of federal welfare programs has only fostered dependence and a sense of individual impotence and powerlessness. As a result, poor people are less able to control their own lives. In contrast to unsuccessful traditional and official approaches, Silberman describes several self-help programs implemented in poor neighborhoods that built on the idea of community. Leadership developed from within, and self-direction and independence followed. With these programs, greater community control evolved and crime was often reduced.[3]

Reorienting antipoverty programs to develop self-reliance rather than dependence may be a step in the right direction, but it alone will not solve the crime problem in the United States. Crime is not just a problem of the poor; it is but one manifestation of the exploitive behavior prevalent in our achievement-oriented but weakly constrained society. Street crime is the form of exploitation available to the poor, but crime is tied to other forms of exploitation, and it alone cannot be eliminated.

There are also problems of how to induce the formation of meaningful groups and then get them to accept a common set of norms. It would require formal institutions of government to undertake such a program of socialization and indoctrination. The failure of the Soviet government to instill the "good" Soviet identity in its workers speaks to the futility of such practices. If informal controls were sufficient to maintain conformity in the first place, the formal controls would not exist. Since they do, it is unlikely that they will render themselves useless.

Another activity with the potential for strengthening community solidarity for control are the neighborhood groups formed to prevent crime. People band together to patrol their community, watching for suspicious behavior while maintaining surveillance of property and possessions. But because these programs are designed to catch intruders and deter outsiders, rather than control the behavior of community residents, they are limited in what they can accomplish. They may prevent some crimes, but they do not attend to the fundamental issue of informal controls, which will ultimately reduce the likelihood of offenses being committed. On the other hand, one favorable aspect of these programs is that people get to know one another. As residents begin to interact and care about each other, social atomization may be reduced. In the long run the benefits to crime control may be greater because of improved social integration in the community than because of surveillance and prevention.

Other social trends could also contribute to the reduction of social atomization. Some parents are realizing that frequent job relocation has negative consequences for children and are now considering that in making employment decisions. The result may be a strengthening of ties in certain communities. Recent national economic problems could also affect social interaction and integration. With employment opportunities scarce and fewer possibilities for mobility, people may have no choice but to remain where they reside. Economic adversity may also heighten interdependence so that people must interact more and so that neighbors end up being more important and meaningful to one another. To the extent that adversity pulls people together for their own survival, informal controls will be strengthened.[4] Renewed interest and participation in formal religion may increase the attention given to individual honor, integrity, self-restraint, and greater concern for others. As people also come to consider how their actions affect others, exploitation might decline. But these possibilities are speculative at best, and at this time it would be unwise to pin great hopes for crime control on them.

If people can come to the conclusion that crime cannot be eliminated, or even reduced, they may be willing to explore how they might live with the problem. We have already noted that one way to do this would be to reduce the physical signs of incivility within communities. Reducing deteriorated conditions, burned-out and abandoned buildings, graffiti, litter, and other signs of disorder may lessen the impression that control is getting out of hand and increase perceptions of personal safety. Since the harm caused by fear alone appears to be substantial, community improvement, while not affecting the incidence of crime at all, might contribute significantly to reducing the effects of crime.

Incivility is also conveyed by the open practice of vice—for example, prostitution, pornography, drug use—which leaves the impression of disorder and a feeling of insecurity. Increasing recognition that these activities are victimless crimes that may be morally offensive but are not serious threats to public safety has led to a reduction in enforcement activities. Most police departments believe that their resources are better spent on protection from criminal behavior. But this perception fails to recognize the symbolic damage that vice can cause, that it makes people feel less safe. To help Americans regain some of the lost sense of security, perhaps vice as an enforcement priority should be reconsidered. If it can be removed from residential neighborhoods and hidden from public view in other areas through more intensive enforcement and rezoning efforts (given the expanding demand for such activities and services, it is unlikely that it can be eliminated), residents of many communities may feel safer.

The way individuals interact is also important in their perceptions about personal safety. As people build emotional barriers around themselves, not even looking at strangers they pass on the street, the message they convey is one of unfriendliness and callousness, which fosters the perception that the community is becoming cold and less caring. These attitudes are heightened when people are rude and impatient. In the end, perceptions of security are diminished, as compared with times when people lived in neighborhoods composed of people they knew. Government can do little about this. People cannot be forced or cajoled to interact differently. Only their recognition of the pathology of such behavioral patterns will change this aspect of contemporary urban life and reduce its effects. Citizens must realize that barricading themselves, both physically and emotionally, from their environments only heightens their fears.

Minimizing the effects of victimization—the hurt, the pain, the suffering, and the damages—may be another way to cope with crime. Historian David Rothman notes that other adversities of life—fires and industrial accidents, for example—are generally accepted as unavoidable and inevitable. Rather than investing all our resources and efforts in determining whose fault such things are, attention is directed more toward preventing their occurrence and coping with their effects. Various methods of aiding victims and survivors have been devised. Insurance money rebuilds burned-out buildings, and worker's compensation aids people out of work because of an injury. Yet little attention, either in the form of economic compensation or emotional support, is given to victims of crime.[5] In over 80 percent of all property crimes, losses are not recovered by insurance or any other method of compensation.[6] Victims of crimes are seldom counseled to help them deal with their fears and feelings of being violated. Programs for rape victims have appeared only recently. Americans prefer to chase crooks; they want to find the perpetrator, to fix blame, to get even. They want to right the wrong. But since so few criminals are caught and punished and the victim's plight is virtually ignored, we must ask whether many wrongs are being righted. Perhaps some of the money spent on law enforcement should be diverted to helping victims cope with their losses.

These ideas will not eliminate crime or even substantially reduce it. Crime and other forms of exploitation have been around for a long time, and it is unlikely that they will suddenly disappear. But it should be clear that coercion is of limited usefulness in controlling crime. The time has come for people to consider other alternatives, to reassess their own activities and what they can realistically expect their government to do for them. The answer to crime lies in improving informal controls, but that cannot be legislated and it involves slow cultural changes. It is not even clear that Americans would prefer a well-controlled society. That would require giving up some of their individualism, autonomy, mobility, and the separation of public and private functions. But these suggestions could reduce some of the effects, some of the pain, associated with crime. And if nothing else, they provide an alternative to spending more money on retooling punitive sanctions.

THE VILE AND VICIOUS

But we cannot ignore the nagging and emotional issue of what to do with depraved and heartless thugs who injure or kill innocent human beings. Twice recently I faced such tragedy. My cousin was shot and killed by a robber in the liquor store where he worked, and in my own small community two storekeepers were murdered by armed robbers for no reason at all. In each instance, a human life was taken by a person who apparently had no feeling or regard for the sanctity and dignity of life. There is no explanation for such acts. They are not fair. And I cannot rid myself of the hatred I feel for the criminals in each of these cases. They should suffer and pay with their own pain for the anguish they have caused.

So how do we achieve retribution and protect ourselves from such people? Despite its lack of appeal, the answer is to continue doing just what we are doing. This nation cannot afford to base its entire criminal-justice process on reaction to such vicious incidents. They are the exception, rather than the rule. Most crime involves property loss, not physical injury, and when violence occurs it more often than not ensues from conflict between people who know one another. Statistics show that violent crimes committed by strangers are not common, but media reporting and changes in society have left us with a different impression. The threat of violence is a painful reality of life in contemporary America, but not one that is as threatening as often believed.

In considering what should be done with violent criminals, we should realize that the criminal-justice system has been relatively successful in catching these offenders. Nationally, only 20 percent of the crimes reported to the police are cleared by arrest, but the clearance rate for violent crimes is much higher. An arrest is made in over 70 percent of the reported murders, 60 percent of the aggravated assaults, and 50 percent of the forcible rapes. The only violent crime with a low clearance rate is robbery, in which only 25 percent of the reported crimes result in an arrest (and with robbery the violence is often only threatened, not actually executed). Property crimes are the difficult incidents to solve, with only about 17 percent of the reported burglaries, larcenies, and motor vehicle thefts culminating in an arrest.[7] These figures indicate that the people we truly fear and from whom we want retribution—the violent offenders—are usually caught.

The notion that criminals are literally getting away with murder is also not accurate. In 3 out of every 4 murders, someone is arrested, and most are successfully processed through the justice system and eventually removed from society.[8] The period of incarceration for violent criminals is generally quite long—twenty years, thirty years, and even longer. What criminals are getting away with is property crime, but in this case fewer opportunities for detection arise, because property crime is more likely to be committed by strangers and the volume is overwhelming. Consequently, there is little hope for ever improving the system's ability to control these offenses.

The occasional slipup, where a truly violent criminal is not severely sanctioned, is paroled too early, or through a procedural loophole escapes punishment altogether, is rare. Think about it—how often do you read about such cases? It really isn't very often: a few such cases each year. But you can be sure that when some mistake happens anywhere in the United States it will be reported in every newspaper. Since there are more than 10 million arrests for serious crimes and over 50,000 prisoners are paroled each year, that so few procedural slipups and incorrect parole decisions occur speaks well of the system. Given that most violent criminals are caught, convicted, and punished, we must ask whether it is worth modifying the system to get rid of these few problems. The exclusionary rule is one of the few protections citizens have against police intervention. Parole keeps correctional costs down and helps control incarcerated inmates. The United States already has the longest sentences of any modern nation.

If nothing else, Americans need to curtail their preoccupation with crime. Realistically, it is but one of the many evils in our society. People are also injured by fires, accidents, tornadoes, and automobiles. Yet these events do not receive the attention crime gets from the media, in political campaigns, or even from the entertainment industry. The hold crime has on people is unhealthy. It has become a basis for interpreting everything from bumps in the night to the missing car keys. Americans need to come to terms with their fear.

To regain a sense of security, Americans should not look to the criminal-justice system. Plans to be more vigorous, more punitive, and even more innovative will only be more costly. Citizens should resist the temptation to believe the politician, the police chief, and the prosecutor who claim they can do something about crime. They cannot. The system is doing as well as it can. The answer to crime lies not in coercion but in self-restraint and informal controls. Some day the norms may be sufficient and laws will be unnecessary. Until then, Americans should ask how they might cope with those unfortunate events that will continue to occur.

NOTES

1. Charles E. Silberman, *Criminal Violence, Criminal Justice* (New York: Vintage Books, 1980), p. 581.

2. John Conklin, *The Impact of Crime* (New York: Macmillan, 1975), p. 145.

3. Ibid., pp. 580–606.

4. See Kevin N. Wright, "Economic Adversity, Reindustrialization, and Criminality," in Kevin N. Wright, ed., *Crime and Criminal Justice in a Declining Economy* (Cambridge, Mass.: Oelgeschlager, Gunn & Hain, 1981), pp. 51–68.

5. David Rothman, "Prisons: The Failure Model," *The Nation*, December 21, 1974, pp. 656–569.

6. J. Frederick Shenk, *Criminal Victimization in the United States, 1979*, U.S. Department of Justice, 1981, p. 71.

7. Timothy J. Flanagan, David J. van Alstyne, and Michael R. Gottfredson, eds., *Sourcebook of Criminal Justice Statistics—1981*, U.S. Department of Justice, Bureau of Justice Statistics (Washington, D.C.: Government Printing Office, 1982), pp. 370–371.

8. Federal Bureau of Investigation, *Crime in the United States—Uniform Crime Reports, 1980* (Washington, D.C.: Government Printing Office, 1981), p. 181.

Bibliographical Essay

This book deals with a broad array of criminal-justice issues. Included in this essay are some of the major contributions to those topics. I begin with several books that outline major policy orientations for the criminal-justice system and appear to have influenced trends in the system. Next, several readily available sources of information about crime statistics are included. Then major contributions concerning the fear of crime, the motivations of criminal-justice personnel and agencies, due-process protections, prison conditions, and crime control in other cultures will be presented.

Among the contemporary books that propose strategies for criminal justice to control crime, Norval Morris and Gordon Hawkins' *Honest Politician's Guide to Crime Control* (Chicago: University of Chicago Press, 1970), is now a classic. After making a strong case for having the system move away from enforcement of moral standards, Morris and Hawkins outline a legislative and administrative plan to reduce crime and the fear of crime. Their intent is to present pragmatic suggestions that will lead to real reductions in the problem.

In the same year that Morris and Hawkins' work was published, another significant but very different book about the crime problem appeared. In *Crime in America* (New York: Simon and Schuster, 1970), former U.S. Attorney General Ramsey Clark makes a passionate plea for reforming society to reduce crime. Clark argues that healthy people in a just and humane society will not commit crimes. He uses this argument to justify attacking the problems of poverty and discrimination rather than focusing on changes in the criminal-justice system as a primary method of reducing crime. Within the system, Clark highlights the need for rehabilitation of criminals and protection of individual liberties.

In what appears to be a response to Clark, James Q. Wilson points out in *Thinking About Crime* (New York: Basic Books, 1975), that the welfare and social programs of the previous decade had not reduced crime. Wilson argues that "wicked people exist" and that a punitive orientation is the only realistic strategy for reducing crime. A system of justice that stresses incapacitation and deterence is advocated.

After a six-year study, Charles Silberman, in *Criminal Violence, Criminal Justice* (New York: Random House, 1978; reprint, New York: Vintage, 1980), concludes that violence is strongly rooted in lower-class and black ghetto culture. To reduce it, we must overcome the strong traditions of that culture. According to Silberman, the solutions do not lie solely in modifying the criminal-justice system but require self-initiated strategy implemented within the cultures where violence is most prevalent.

The most recent addition to this list of notable works is Harold Pepinsky and Paul Jeslow's *Myths That Cause Crime* (Cabin John, Md.: Seven Locks Press, 1984). In contrast to earlier editions, Pepinsky and Jeslow suggest that the form of crime most Americans fear, street crime, is not as bad as most people believe it to be nor is it becoming worse. They argue that upper-world white-collar and corporate crimes are the truly serious problems that Americans face. Unlike earlier writers, who propose changes in the criminal-justice system to reduce crime, Pepinsky and Jeslow reach conclusions about the inability of the system to do something about crime that are similar to those of this book.

Readers interested in more detailed information about crime statistics and the characteristics of the criminal-justice system can go to original sources. Each year the Federal Bureau of Investigation publishes its report of Uniform Crime Report statistics in *Crime in the United States*, and the Bureau of Justice Statistics releases its National Crime Survey Report, *Criminal Victimization in the United States*. These statistics, as well as other relevant information, are also contained in the *Sourcebook of Criminal Justice Statistics*, compiled for the U.S. Department of Justice by researchers at the Criminal Justice Research Center at the State University of New York at Albany. An informative and useful analysis of crime trends, victims, and criminals has recently been produced by the Bureau of Justice Statistics. The title of the document is *Report to the Nation on Crime and Justice*.

One of the most informative studies of criminal victimization and fear of crime is Michael Hindelang, Michael Gottfredson, and James Garofalo's volume entitled *Victims of Personal Crime: An Empirical Foundation for a Theory of Personal Victimization* (Cambridge, Mass.: Ballinger Publishing Co., 1978). Using the results of a national survey of victimization and personal attitudes, these researchers tell us much about how people react to crime.

A detailed analysis of the underlying goals of criminal-justice agencies and their personnel is contained in William Chambliss and Robert Seidman's textbook, *Law, Order, and Power* (Reading, Mass.: Addison-Wesley Publishing Company, 1971). While not written for the lay reader, this volume thoroughly outlines how personal and organizational interests influence the formation of the law and criminal-justice policy.

Three recent books provide specific analyses of criminal-justice policy formation. Thomas and Tania Cronin and Michael Milakovich, in recounting the history of the Law Enforcement Assistance Administration in their volume *U.S. v. Crime in the Streets* (Bloomington: Indiana University Press, 1981), conclude that the massive effort often served nothing but the political exploitation of crime. Stuart Scheingold, in *The Politics of Law and Order* (New York: Longman, 1984), analyzes the impact of law and order on street crime and concludes that crime control is often an objective secondary to that of political gain. Herbert Jacob, in *The Frustration of Policy—Responses to Crime by American Cities* (Boston: Little, Brown and Company, 1984), focuses on policy formation at the local level to find that political interest often confounds sound program implementation.

An important and thorough analysis of different methods to reduce crime is found in Harold Pepinsky's *Crime Control Strategies* (New York: Oxford University Press, 1980). This book examines different ways of reducing crime and their potential for success.

One of the most thorough and lucid reviews of the issues surrounding due-process provisions and the exclusionary rule is contained in Lane Sunderland's 1980 article in the *Journal of Criminal Law and Criminology*, "Liberals, Conservatives, and the Exclusionary Rule." Sunderland considers not only the legal issues but also the practical issues of each side's arguments concerning the necessity and effectiveness of the rule.

To learn more about contemporary American prisons and the problems they have, one can turn to John Irwin's readable description in *Prisons in Turmoil* (Boston: Little, Brown and Company, 1980). Irwin traces the social changes in the prison culture that have led to increased prison violence and exploitation. For a more graphic view inside the prison, one should examine Ethan Hoffman and John McCoy's *Concrete Mama* (Columbia: University of Missouri Press, 1981). McCoy provides detailed descriptions of the lives of ten inmates, a visitor, and a guard to accompany Hoffman's excellent photographic essay of life in Washington State Penitentiary at Walla Walla.

For those who are interested in crime and justice in other cultural settings, there are several works that one can turn to. Marshall Clinard concludes in *Cities with Little Crime* (New York: Cambridge University Press, 1978), that Switzerland is an exception to the rule that high crime accompanies affluence, industrialization, and urbanization. William Clifford, in *Crime Control in Japan* (Lexington, Mass.: Lexington Press, 1976), reaches a similar conclusion about crime in Japan. Both volumes conclude that informal control is of greater importance in determining how great the crime problem is than anything the criminal-justice system does. In her assessment of crime in ten nations, reported in *Nations Not Obsessed with Crime* (Littleton, Colo.: Rothman, 1984), Freda Adler finds that social solidarity is an important variable in determining how much crime a nation will experience.

Index

About the Author

KEVIN N. WRIGHT is Assistant Professor in the Criminal Justice Program and Department of Political Science and a Research Associate in the Center for Social Analysis at the State University of New York at Binghamton. He is the author of *An Organization Approach to Correctional Effectiveness* and the editor of *Crime and Criminal Justice in a Declining Economy* and articles that have been published in *Criminology, Journal of Research in Crime and Delinquency, Journal of Criminal Justice,* and other scholarly and professional publications.